CRACKED

OPEN

Discovering the Unseen

World

Cracked Open: Discovering the Unseen World

First printing August 2024

Library of Congress Cataloging-in-Publication Data

White, Kelly
Cracked Open: Discovering the Unseen World

Paperback ISBN: 979-8-9914468-0-8
Ebook ISBN: 979-8-9914468-1-5

Interior design by Eva Myrick, MSCP

Printed in the U.S.A.

CRACKED OPEN

Discovering the Unseen World

by

Kellee White

.

To Mom,

You told me I could do anything, and I did!

CONTENTS

Foreword by James Van Praagh, Evidential Psychic Medium & Master Teacher

For I know the plans I have for you," declares the LORD, "plans to prosper you and not to harm you, plans to give you hope and a future.

- Jeremiah 29:11

We must let go of the life we have planned so as to accept the one that is waiting for us.

- Joseph Campbell

FOREWORD

Right now, in this space we call "Earth," it seems as if we are living in a perpetual state of hustle and bustle just to survive. The constant "fight or flight" urge has been cemented into the psyche of society. Whether it is a result of the Covid pandemic, social media, ongoing wars, political extremes, or a combination of everything all at once, we have forgotten our true and divine natures. Instead of nurturing ourselves gently, unfolding the mysteries of our inner light and spirit gradually and naturally, we insist on immediate gratification. By making feeble attempts at controlling and possessing the world around us, this "wanting to know" forces us to discard the fullness of appreciation for the present moment. As sacred and miraculous beings, we are here to uncover our divine selves gradually, step-by-step, without a sense of urgency and distress.

There is a great spiritual hunger in the world today. When we, as souls, attempt to search for fulfillment outside in the world, we cannot fill the empty void within ourselves, and so that hunger is never satiated. There is so much pressure to be "relevant" or "to be seen." Often, we resort to creating a "shock" persona or contorting our bodies and faces merely to make a unique "selfie" in order to gain more followers on our social media platforms.

People have become experts on everything from bikini wear to vegan desserts, from tech to travel. It suddenly became the way to understand the latest and most popular trends. Who knew that being an influencer would become a "thing" to aspire to? We became obsessed with a desire to share our opinions with everyone. In fact, the more eyeballs, the better. Social media platforms were and are the perfect stages for people to have their fifteen minutes of fame. We have become our own "reality show."

With the Covid pandemic, exploitation exploded. We began an entirely different relationship with our computers and devices, becoming more isolated and insular, limiting our perspective of ourselves and the world. All we could do was look at our screens. We were glued to our phones for hours at a time, checking global and local events via online news and social media platforms. With all this information came a glut of misinformation. The global community became the proverbial fodder for the proliferation of deception. We assumed and even trusted that there would be honest and genuine assessments of world events, people, places, and products. However, we were naive in thinking that everything online would be genuine and reliable. We became either distressed or complacent, looking for all our answers out there in the ethers of the digital world.

In truth, all souls come to this school called "Earth" to learn various lessons for growth and understanding—to honor and love ourselves and to understand that our thoughts are the building blocks of our physical reality. These lessons vary enormously from soul to soul with a curriculum fashioned for optimum learning opportunities. When there is little expansion of the self, our consciousness becomes somewhat stagnant. Most people are either "sleepwalking" or in an anxious and agitated struggle to find themselves. It can become an exasperating race with little gain as we throw away any sense of the important and commonly shared virtues of kindness and compassion. Instead, we replace these ideals with a distorted sense of entitlement and aggression.

Earth school is actually an illusion, and in true reality, time does not exist. Our soul knows that life on Earth is merely a speck in time; our true home is in the "Spirit Lands." Think of Earth like a movie theater that is continuously playing the feature film over and over again. There are souls here experiencing this Earth theater for the very first time and may believe that war, power, and wealth are the primary goals. And there are many souls that migrate from a variety of elevated worlds or realms, galaxies, and beyond. These evolved souls and honored minds recognize the illusive nature of this physical vibration. They come as experts willing to teach us in the hope of uplifting the consciousness of the human mind. Their focus is to remind us of our loving natures while imparting spiritual insights, healing, and a sense of connectedness. In the middle of new and old souls are the rest of us attempting to understand the different layers of who we are and where we fit in. Eventually, through trial and error, a soul will understand that the fastest way to evolve is to utilize their own soul's limitless supply of love, for love is the essence of life—our life force as it were. Souls eventually discover that the carnal satisfactions of the physical earth—fame, notoriety, control, sex, drugs, wealth, power, certain relationships—are limiting by their very nature, needing to be constantly sustained.

At this moment in "time," being higher-minded is becoming increasingly difficult, and it seems we are being forced to indulge in the pettiness of the physical world. It is a struggle to stay positive amidst so much negativity. Unfortunately, we have created a space where there is a lack of true connection to the empathetic nature of who we are and who others are. Instant physical gratification has claimed us, and we live to have more and more strangers follow us, thinking in some way it will validate our existence! We are searching outside ourselves for success. But this way of being, this pretense, is merely a quick fix. When we don't take the necessary time to reassess our lives and truly begin a journey of self-discovery, we get lost in the cavernous dwellings of the mind. We become mentally and emotionally paralyzed and trapped in a sort of wormhole we cannot find our way out of. Instead of dealing with the emotional, physical, mental, and spiritual selves, we escape from them. Escapism takes many forms; there are many of us spending much of our earthly time as victims—of childhood trauma, mental, physical, or sexual abuse, bullying, name-calling, or loss, aging, and so on.

It is only when we begin to have a relationship with the great power within can we truly begin to fully live! With this insight, souls begin to witness the truest of realities and can then utilize their unique "soul-self" essence. This essence is individualistic to each soul much like a fingerprint. The special facets of spiritual insight, solution, and strength needed to successfully fulfill our specific lessons on earth are incorporated into the soul essence through every lifetime and every experience we have ever had. We never come here ill-prepared. For example, a mother who loses a child, or someone who appears to have one tragedy follow another, must have in their soul the essence of a spiritual "superpower" completely individualized to accomplish those specific lessons. It has been scientifically proven that those who have had a moderate or severe level of hardship report greater mental health and well-being. Overall, these souls have a sense of empathy for others and can deal better with tough situations.

Remember, you are what you think, and action follows thought. If we use our mental creative energy negatively, the result will be a life of repeated negativity. By going within to understand the lesson behind an experience, we uncover our eternal wisdom. We are divine beings filled with a limitless capacity to love. When we do not love ourselves or refuse to bring love to others, we do not evolve as quickly as we are capable of. Every day in life, the Universe offers us choices to move forward utilizing the power of love or stay stagnant in the grip of fear.

As I have noted earlier, when a person feels that their reality is only validated by the directives of society or attempts to live a life forced by parents or teachers who are endeavoring to make them something they are not, these souls are not truly living, but merely existing. I have found through my work with souls on the other side that in the long run, many souls become trapped in a "people-pleasing" existence. Over time, this behavior turns into an unhappy, unsatisfied, and joyless life. Many souls will spend lifetimes in this mundane existence. Then there are others opened by an experience in life that shifts their perspective to greater awareness. These souls are ready to wake up. For the first time in their lives, they experience a glimpse of who they truly are, not who they thought they were. They begin the journey of self-discovery. When this awakening occurs, the soul is in a prime position to unfold its spiritual superpowers. It seems a bit of a dichotomy that horrendous and unthinkable experiences are the most pivotal in awakening us to a greater understanding of the human condition. The more difficult the lesson, the greater the advancement. Sometimes it seems as if we are forced into situations that we think are too demanding to handle. But these are the very opportunities that will unfold our spiritual abilities of infinite possibilities. The mind and body come into perfect harmony.

The story you are about to read is a perfect depiction of one soul's life journey filled to the brim with adversities of every kind imaginable. You will find yourself asking, "Did this really happen?" The answer is "Yes!" Kellee's experiences have added to her intuitive empathetic nature. As you read the following pages, you will see how a soul who was lost in the darkness of her own world had the innate sense to follow her "inner soul light" or intuitive guidance to lead her to a greater sense of self and ultimately to the person she is today. A common theme you will notice throughout the story is Kellee's utmost determination, no matter if she is attempting a new corporate job, shouldering the responsibilities of her family drama, or witnessing glimpses of the unknown. She is steadfast in doing the best she possibly can, and at the same time striving to understand the significance of her circumstances and the greater purpose of her life.

Her awakening is reflected in her work as a therapist and spiritual medium. As she has unfolded her inner abilities, she has developed an expansion of self that has afforded her a greater understanding, tolerance, and love for all beings. With a quiet attitude and calmness of spirit, Kellee has learned to handle any experience thrown at her, no matter how strange or painful. Through heartbreak and misfortune, she has come to have a better acceptance of human evolution and the various levels of human perception.

As a medium with years of experience, I know that any time one speaks about unfolding their natural spiritual abilities, one fears that they will become "oversensitive," and dead people will not leave them alone! This could not be further from the truth. When one begins to utilize their soul light and strengthen the various spiritual, mental, physical, and emotional bodies, there is an inner strength that comes forth, giving one inward poise and balance. They begin to know who they truly are.

Utilize this manuscript wisely and let all the experiences you will read about sit with you. Meditate on them to see how you would have handled the same situation. You may be very surprised. And as you do, always remember surrounding you is your soul light, always present to bring your mind to new places and experiences. Use it as you do your breath, bringing an awareness of this luminosity to your inner being. In turn, the broken and neglected parts of yourself can begin to heal. Remember always, that to live in this space and time is a privilege, and you can bring the Universal truths into the heart of all those with whom you interact. Let Kellee's living example remind you that anything in life is possible because God always says "Yes." Only the human part of us says "No." Strive to be your higher self at one with God. Only then can you make a difference.

-James Van Praagh, #1 NY Times bestselling author, spiritual teacher, internationally renowned psychic medium, television producer and successful radio host. **www.vanpraagh.com**

PREFACE

There comes that time when the soul must once again leave the sanctuary of the spirit world for another trip to Earth. This decision is not an easy one. Souls must prepare to leave a world of total wisdom, where they exist in a blissful state of freedom for the physical and mental demands of a human body.

- Michael Newton, Ph.D.,
  Journey of Souls

Looking out from my spiritual home on this magnificent plane called Heaven, the embodiment of peace and love, I see my upcoming adventure on planet Earth. Although it has beautiful qualities, Earth is a tough place to incarnate. To be in a physical, dense environment with souls at various stages of growth makes Earth a challenging "school." The Universe has many schools in many dimensions, but Earth is more complex and specifically designed for spiritual growth. In spite of this, it is one of the more popular schools to attend. Believe it or not, souls line up for an experience on Earth.

Although I have lived many lives on Earth, far too many to

count, there is excitement for this particular journey because it will be a completion of several spiritual lessons for me. I will do my best to finish everything I began in previous lifetimes. Along with my spirit guides' help, I plan to utilize all of my spiritual gifts this time around. How exciting!

All the meetings with my soul group in Heaven have been arranged, and I am looking forward to sharing life with each of them on Earth once again. As a soul group, we have shared many lifetimes together, and we resonate energetically on mental, emotional, physical, and spiritual levels. Each of us has a purpose and plan to help one another fulfill our destinies. On Earth, we will be drawn to each other—when we meet, we will have the feeling that we know one another. As soul groups, we connect to learn lessons, grow, and transform for a higher purpose. Sometimes, our lessons will be difficult, but all have agreed to take part.

On a larger scale, there are many soul groups today that are helping to raise the consciousness of the planet. Some work in war-torn areas and poverty situations, with abused children and women, for animal rights and rescues, and in schools, hospitals, and even governments. What is extraordinary are the groups that decide to survive a disaster together or those who plan to leave the Earth plane together.

Between each incarnation, we create a soul plan designed specifically for each incarnation. The plan includes the choices, tests, and experiences that will expand our consciousness while in a physical body. Mostly, we have to balance the karma created from previous lives so that we can advance on our soul's journey. Karma is another word for consequences. Every thought and action has an influence on a future result. Karma can be corrected in the same life or in another life. A soul's journey on earth is decidedly a learning experience. The sooner souls remember who they are and develop a greater perspective of life and their roles in it, the quicker they can advance to higher levels on the spiritual spectrum. We are here to expand our awareness and to bring it to others.

For this particular incarnation, I've chosen, or been elected, by my soul family to be the firstborn. This position will help with my life theme of "responsibility," and I will have plenty of experiences based on this theme. Trauma, drama, abuse, healing, and forgiveness are in store for me. From my perch in Heaven, I am aware of these challenges, but I am confident that I will overcome them. The Universe has some surprises planned along the way specifically designed to ignite my soul's memory of living a gentler life. Kindness, compassion, and empathy will be highlighted.

Right now, Earth is also very special because souls lucky enough to incarnate will have the opportunity to advance quickly. Earth's energy has been set with a higher vibration to help souls spiritually awaken and remember who they are—souls having a physical experience, not merely bodies. Because the vibration is higher, more souls will wake up. When one person spiritually awakens, others awaken as well. Of course, this all depends on how we use our free will. After all, free will has gotten many a soul into trouble. Souls may have had the best of intentions in Heaven, but on Earth, a plan can be interrupted by a change in choice, thus creating karma.

I spend a lot of time with my spirit guides planning the trip back. Spirit guides are energetic beings that help us navigate our journey while on Earth. They love us unconditionally and are always with us. We are never alone. Most spirit guides have had at least one life on Earth and know how difficult the journey can be. I have two spirit guides that will remain with me this lifetime. They know my plan and will help me navigate my journey.

When we are born into a physical body, we enter a very dense dimension. It's as if we have plunged into quicksand because Earth is a heavy, dull, and dim atmosphere. Upon arrival, we immediately forget that we are souls with a divine plan. The material world of Earth is filled with distractions, distortions, confusion, and instability. It is the home of egos—our personal identities—and our egos are predominantly interested in the survival of self. Egos prefer to look outwardly at all the commotion and interpret it in relationship to self. Our souls—our spiritual identities—focus inwardly into our minds and hearts and see the unity we share with others. Believe it or not, when we come to Earth, we are fully prepared, and it is important to understand that we are all in this master plan together.

At present, there is so much chaos on Earth. I am needed at this particular period to generate a shift in consciousness. I have set my intentions and prearranged as much as I could for this specific lifetime. But, as often is the case, there is a dreaded anticipation of returning. Earth is changing at such a rapid pace, and the majority of souls incarnating are quite young. And they are causing pain and distress because they are just beginning to learn who they really are. I know how difficult this time period will be for all souls visiting Earth.

However, I have a mission. I understand this Earth dimension very well. I have been teaching souls in Heaven about the Earth plane for eons. I know that I will meet the people along my journey who will assist in my spiritual development and will help me with my mission. That is why I am being sent this time—to help others remember who they are.

Most importantly, I know I will have help from the "other side," as it is called on Earth. Ironically, as physical beings, we think of Earth as our home, when actually, Heaven, or the other side, is our true home because it is where our souls reside. We may be in physical forms, but our souls partially stay in Heaven to help direct us on Earth. My hope is that as you read this book, you will see your life and your place in it through the vision of your soul and have more compassion for the rest of us soul travelers.

My story is pretty incredible. *You are never going to believe it!* I use this phrase a lot when describing some of my experiences. So, reader, fasten your seatbelts, keep your legs and arms inside the car, and welcome to my bumpy ride on Earth.

PART 1

MY JOURNEY BEGINS

Chapter 1

⁓

THE UNIVERSE HAS A PLAN

We are not human beings having a spiritual experience;
we are spiritual beings having a human experience.

- Pierre Teilhard de Chardin

Let me begin by saying that my mother was alive when we started to write this book. We wanted to share our experiences from diverse points of view—from my spiritual perspective as a psychic and medium and my mother from her psychological perspective as a practicing psychologist for 45 years.

Very sadly, my beloved mother became sick with cancer and passed away in April 2018 before we could complete it. But Spirit definitely had a plan. And immediately, Mom decided one of her first missions from Heaven was to guide me in the completion of this book. That was Mom—always making sure things got done! My mother literally became my "ghostwriter." And she continues to influence me every day with her new perspective from the other side. Together, from her perch in Heaven to my seat on Earth, we have created this wondrous work.

Responsibility Theme

It all began when I was in my mother's womb. I clearly remember myself as a soul traveling between Heaven and Earth, in and out of my mother's belly, preparing for this lifetime to come. While in her womb, I had an innate sense of Mom's anxiousness about becoming a new mother while having to deal with my self-absorbed father. He was a handful, to say the least. I so badly wanted to telepathically send her a thought—to let her know that it would all work out. At the same time, I became keenly aware that one of my major life lessons would be to learn "responsibility." I was the firstborn in a very challenging family, so my position was at the front of the class, so to speak, to understand the full aspects of being responsible. How lucky could a girl get?

Psychologist Alfred Adler developed a theory of birth order in the 20th century. The theory claims that the order in which a child is born shapes their development and personality. Firstborn children act like mini-adults. They're diligent and want to excel at everything they do. As the leader of the pack, firstborns often tend to be reliable, conscientious, structured, cautious, controlling, achievers, and responsible.

Birth order does not explain everything about a personality—family, community, and other social aspects shape a child—but it does begin to shed some light on the process that defines us as individuals. Using the birth order theory, I can see the reasons why my parents thought and behaved in a particular way. Here's why.

My mother was the youngest of her siblings, and incidentally, so was my father, both by 12 years. That alone is really peculiar—a difference of 12 years to the nearest sibling. Taking the idea of birth order theory into account, because both my parents were the youngest children, and because the closest sibling was 12 years older, they were considered "only" children. Why is this important? Let me tell you.

Normally, one would think of an only child as being more responsible. But because both my parents were the youngest of their siblings, that trait seemed the strongest. Dr. Kevin Leman, in his book, *The Birth Order Book: Why You Are the Way You Are,* states: "Youngest children shoulder less responsibility, so the youngest child tends to be carefree, easygoing, fun-loving, affectionate, and sociable, and they like to make people laugh."

That fits my parents to a tee. The result was that neither of them knew or had any inkling about being a responsible adult. When I came along as the oldest child, born to two "only" and "youngest" children, I became the responsible adult in the house. Responsibility for others has been an ever-present and dominating theme throughout my life, and it has clearly defined who I am today.

I'm Not Normal

I am often asked, "Kellee, what was it like growing up? Were you always able to read people's minds?" Or, "Have you always been able to talk to dead people?"

Here's what I remember. My mother repeated over and over to anyone and everyone, "Kellee is normal. Very normal. She's so cute. Long blonde curly hair. Laughs all of the time. She's very sweet. Very normal." It was so hysterical how often Mom said the word "normal."

All along, I knew, and she knew, too, I wasn't "normal." I was a walking "sensory machine." I was always able to feel the swirling energy in a room and was constantly bombarded by people's thoughts. As a child, I thought, *Isn't everybody like me?* So, I could never understand why some people would hurt other people. It just didn't compute. Why would anyone hurt an animal? Again, it didn't make sense to me. I was overwhelmed by empathy for all living things. At the time, I didn't know the word "empath," but it was my soul's "language," and it spoke to me loud and clear.

As an empath, I could feel another person's sadness, excitement, or dread, as if perceiving life from their perspective. It was like living in another person's body, and it was a heavy load to bear. Most people hid their true feelings and, more often than not, didn't understand their feelings. Even my own family never discussed how they felt, but I knew. Being a child, all I wanted was to "fit in" like the rest of the kids my age. So, I pretended to be that child my mother always referred to as "normal." Mom was good at keeping her secret, and maybe by repeating over and over that "Kellee is normal," she was trying to convince herself. But Mom knew that I was a grown-up with a small body and anything but normal.

We Choose Our Families

Yes, it is true. Aargh! We choose our mothers, fathers, siblings, and relatives while we're on the other side. I can hear a lot of you say: *No way!* I'm sure you're all asking yourselves, *Why on earth would I choose this particular mother or father, and why this family?* Going back to what I said at the beginning—we are all a part of a soul group, and we all agreed to come to Earth to be together and help one another learn our lessons. Yes—you have been with the people in your household before, in fact, many times before. If you can think about this idea for a bit, you may discover some answers about what you are here to learn.

Our families challenge us, and here is the hand that I was dealt this time around. Mom, born LaWanda, or Lu, as my father nicknamed her, and her older brother Charles were Indiana Merit Scholars and could have been accepted to any university in the country. They were pretty darn smart. My sharp-witted uncle chose Notre Dame and stayed to earn a master's degree in trigonometry. On the other hand, my mom wanted to stay closer to home, so she chose Indiana University.

My father, Lee Katzman, had a music scholarship to Brown University and attended for one year. At the end of the year, he was offered a chance of a lifetime—to go on the road with jazz great bandleader Stan Kenton, and he took it.

My father, the hip Jewish trumpet player—yes, there is such a thing—had been on the road playing jazz when he was introduced to my mother through a mutual friend. Mom was a WASP and a popular senior and sorority coed. She became the "Sweetheart" of Sigma Chi fraternity, which was a big deal back in her day. My parents were young and emotionally immature when they met. One would be hard-pressed to find two more culturally divergent people in the early 1950s. "Ozzie and Harriet" they were not! (If you're too young to remember, Google them.)

As a child, I was loved by both of my parents, but my mother and I had a strong affinity; we not only shared a special bond but also a soul contract to be of service to others. We all make soul contracts with others before incarnating. We create these contracts with a specific purpose, and they can vary with each person in our lives. Some last a lifetime or part of a lifetime, while others may last a season or a moment. The soul contract I had with my father was very different from the one I had with my mother. Often, our soul contracts revolve around various shared themes and experiences. As you will read, mine pretty much ran all over the place—from responsibility, abuse, and hardship to the supernatural, healing, and self-awareness.

Overall, I felt an overwhelming responsibility to take care of my parents and siblings, but especially my father, who was an alcoholic and a drug addict. Even as a child, I knew my dad marched to a different drummer, or in his case—a trumpet. He hung out with other famous jazz musicians, playing with the likes of trumpeter Miles Davis, tenor saxophonist and composer Pepper Adams (my godfather), bassist and bandleader Charles Mingus, pianist and singer Bobbie Dorough (a composer and performer in the acclaimed children's TV series, *Schoolhouse Rock!* among his many accomplishments), and provocative comedians Lenny Bruce and Mort Saul.

In that era, many jazz musicians were heroin addicts, and a few had died of overdoses. Unfortunately, Dad began using heroin, too. He once told me that he got hooked at a party when he had too much to drink, and someone had shared a needle with him.

When I was three years old, while my mother, who was pregnant with my baby sister Carol, was teaching in high school, Dad was home supposedly watching over me. Instead, he overdosed on heroin. I found him lying on the ground in the front yard. At first, I thought he was asleep, but then my soul instinct kicked in, and I ran to the neighbors' house, and they called an ambulance. Thank goodness he was saved.

Imagine a young toddler, who was an empath, having such a traumatic experience? I felt so responsible for my father that, to this day, I cannot be around anyone who uses drugs. I literally have a visceral reaction.

It was difficult for my mom to have two young children and a drug-addicted husband, but Dad eventually recovered and got clean. At that point, my family thought it would be better for all of us to leave California and move in with my mom's family on their farm in Indiana. I remember that period as being pleasant and peaceful. Farms also seem to be a theme in my life experiences. As I share my life story on these pages, I'm writing from my home—a beautiful and restful farm in Wisconsin.

Growing up on the family farm in Indiana, I had the great opportunity to spend time with my grandparents and, in particular, my grandfather. He was one of 13 brothers and sisters. People had big families back then, that's for sure. His brother, my Uncle Curly, was one of my favorites because he was always full of life. He brought a perspective of fun, joy, laughter, and happiness everywhere he went, and he made sure the skies were always sunny and rainbows appeared after every rain.

However, I appreciated Grandpa Charlie the most. He and I

had a special kinship. I was fascinated by his ability to simply "know" things. Little did I understand back then that he was psychic. For instance, he had an uncanny ability to find wells on the farm. I remember his walking around with a big stick and then stopping and pointing to a spot. Lo and behold, water! Grandpa Charlie was an especially good dowser. I also remember the house being filled with people, many of whom would travel from all over the state to seek his advice. In his own way, Grandpa Charlie always helped people.

After nearly three years on the farm, we returned to California. My father had an offer to join Doc Severinsen's Band on *The Tonight Show, Starring Johnny Carson.* I was particularly sad to leave my grandparents, but it was an incredible opportunity for Dad. I think my parents were secretly eager to leave the all-too-quiet farm and begin city life again.

My brother Danny was born in 1963 when I was 6 years old. With him came added responsibility, and I felt overwhelmed. We did have a housekeeper, but in my mind, the responsibility for my family fell on me. For anyone with responsibility as a life theme, you have my sympathy, support, and compassion.

With Dad's new-found success, our family moved from a small home in the rustic North Valley of LA to the idyllic area of Toluca Lake, home of NBC Studios. It was a town full of celebrities; even our mayor was Bob Hope. It was a time of security and hope for the future. Our beautiful home was my sanctuary. There was always jazz playing on the record player and wonderful aromas emanating from the kitchen.

Mom was teaching but started to attend graduate school at

night and on weekends. She received her first master's degree in education from UCLA. Two years later, she went back to graduate school and received another master's degree in psychology. She was one busy gal. But her workaholic tendency put an extreme amount of pressure on me to make sure everyone was taken care of—again, another layer of—what else— responsibility!

Self-Reliance

Because I felt always "in charge" of my family, one of the fringe benefits was learning to rely on my intuition. I grew to become very self-reliant. I trusted my instincts and sensory data, so to speak, and learned to utilize these characteristics to assist me with any problems that came up.

As a little girl, I remember watching spellbound as both of my grandmothers cooked and baked, measuring and mixing, in their respective kitchens. My southern grandmother on the farm made the most luscious biscuits and pies. My Jewish grandmother in the city made the most delicious cakes and soups. One day, I had the school day off due to a teacher's meeting. Mom was in graduate school, and I thought it would be great if I could surprise her by baking a cake.

I asked Dad, "Can I have a quarter to go to the store and buy a cake mix?"

To my surprise, he said, "No."

I protested, "But Dad, it's only a quarter. I'm not asking you to drive me to the store. I'll ride my bike. You don't need to do anything."

"No!" He said again. "I won't give you a quarter. If you want to bake a cake, go into the kitchen, put together the ingredients, and create your own cake. I know you can do it."

What? I was shocked. I had never been left alone in the kitchen to cook or bake. After all, I was only 10. I didn't even have an *Easy Bake Oven*. *Was my father crazy?*

I searched around the house for a cookbook but came up empty. I wasn't even sure I could decipher a recipe if I found one. The only thing I had going for me was the memories of my grandmother's cooking and baking. I was glad that I had paid attention to all those many hours spent with them in the kitchen. That my father was actually giving me permission to go into the kitchen and create a cake was even more surprising, if not downright mind-blowing.

I got up on a chair and reached for the flour and sugar. I remember adding eggs, butter, and milk and mixing it all up. Somehow, I managed to turn on the electric oven, place the cake pan on the wire rack, sit down at the kitchen table, and wait. I had absolutely no idea what to expect. After thirty minutes, I took the cake out of the oven and let it cool down.

Then I announced, "It's ready!" I anxiously awaited my father's critique. He came into the kitchen, looked at the cake, took a big whiff of it, then cut himself a piece. He put his hand over his heart and exclaimed, "Honey, this is the best cake I have ever had. It's absolutely delicious."

That proud moment lit the spark of creativity in me. I felt on top of the world—that I could do anything if I put my mind to it. The most important thing was my dad's belief that, indeed, I could do it. As I reflect on how perfect that moment was, I know exactly why I chose my father. He was my creative inspiration. It was his inspiration that lit the creative spark of my soul to carry on, no matter what life threw my way.

Chapter 2

DESTINY CALLS

Everything we experience, every encounter, and every exchange in our lives talk to us. To the individual who perceives life with feeling and sensitivity, everything has a specific meaning. Whatever you encounter in your life (even an animal on the street) pertains to you and directly involves you. You must make this connection.

- Grace Speare, *Everything Talks To Me*

The reason I'm sharing my story is so others can understand the meaning of a *"spiritual awakening"* and how it affects our view of ourselves and others. According to Deepak Chopra: "Awakening happens when you are no longer living your life in a dream world, where you filter every experience through your ego, focusing on the future and the past."

Instead of thinking about what was and what will be, being awake means, we are living in the present moment. To rephrase Eckhart Tolle, "Your power is in the now." We've heard the saying,

"Once we know, we cannot go back to not knowing." Once we have a spiritual awakening, we cannot go back to "sleep" no matter how much we try, although I have to admit, our egos never stop trying to deceive us. But once you truly know who you are and honor your true self, that flame within your soul is lit forever, and you can never go back.

So, what exactly do I mean by "spiritual awakening?" It's a shift in the way we see ourselves and one another. We have an almost simultaneous awareness of our individual selves and a connection between ourselves and everything else in the world and even the worlds beyond. We perceive an oneness with all of existence.

A Spiritual Awakening

I have often said that a spiritual awakening is a "calling" from your soul to wake up to a higher consciousness, a deeper mental awareness, and a sense of inner well-being. The process of a spiritual awakening brings tremendous personal transformation. Simply put, we begin to look at ourselves and the world from the "inside out" instead of the "outside in."

There are dozens of situations, circumstances, and life experiences that will awaken a soul. Right now, you may be wondering, "Kellee, what are the most common catalysts for a spiritual awakening?" I can tell you right now most of them can be very difficult and some heart-wrenching, like the lamentable loss of a child. It could be a life-threatening illness, a traumatic incident, a divorce, a Near Death Experience, or an existential crisis, sometimes referred to as "the dark night of the soul." You begin to ask introspective questions like, "What is the meaning of life?" "Why am I here?" Or "Do we exist after physical death?"

We never really know what will prompt our awakening. Believe it or not, just by reading this book, you may be having some sort of spiritual awakening right now. The words you are absorbing may resonate with a deeper understanding within you. On a certain level, it is "mana," or your soul's required nourishment.

Because each of us is unique, we will awaken in our own distinct time. For some, it may take only one major life-altering experience, but for others, like myself, it can take a great part of living life until we actually realize our spiritual legacy. Remember, you are here in "divine time," not "human time."

As you follow my life journey and my particular spiritual awakening, you will understand the extraordinary importance and significance that each life experience had in weaving my destiny. I had many hints from Spirit along the way, but it took me quite a while to recognize them. So be on the lookout because all of your life experiences bear significance in understanding the soul, its wisdom, and the incredible power of unconditional love.

I find it interesting that over the years of counseling, especially working with empaths, how often individuals would describe various indications of a spiritual awakening without ever realizing what was happening to them. Some of these "signs" include feeling hypersensitive and hyper-alert to their surroundings, increased intuitive awareness, synchronistic events, and déjà vu, or the feeling of having already "been there before." One may also experience feelings of greater love of self and compassion for others, as well as a deep respect for nature, animals, and all living things.

At the same time, one may also experience a sense of loneliness because once awake, you may find it difficult to relate to relatives, friends, and peers. You might have nothing in common anymore and little to talk about with them. Even though I could sense things others couldn't, no one else I knew could. I felt alone on my own island. It can be especially distressing if you don't have someone by your side who loves you no matter what you're experiencing. Like Kermit the Frog often sings, "It's not easy being green." It's not easy to be aware when others around you are still asleep.

We all need someone who is supportive. Thankfully, I had my mother. She was my support system, and I turned to her throughout my spiritual awakening. Allow others to share in your journey, but never force or push your new insights on anyone, for everyone awakens at a time specific to their soul's own evolution. If they do not understand what you're going through, let it be.

As you begin to explore all the possibilities of life and the deeper worlds within and around you, you will become quite conscious that your journey is uniquely your own. You understand that you should never compare yourself to others or let others place their expectations on you. Think of yourself as a sparkling diamond, and you are beginning to uncover your beauty and luster.

Perhaps you, or someone you know and love, are currently going through some sort of spiritual breakthrough. There are tools to comprehend this big change. Later in the book, I share several ways I used to strengthen my resolve. It can be quite daunting to face things you can't explain or understand. For me, it seemed as if no one understood what I was going through. As you read on, you will see that I was well into my adulthood before I finally understood this idea of "spiritual awakening." It was a long and winding road littered with a few traumas along the way. Only when I was able to honor my destiny as a spiritual medium, connecting between the physical world and the other side, bringing messages from Heaven to Earth, did I allow my inner diamond to glitter and gleam.

My friend, world-renowned medium James Van Praagh, taught me that to be a good medium, you first need to go within and know your truth. Secondly, you need to use your own life experiences to assist grieving souls in need of help. Every one of my life experiences has shaped my spiritual and psychological perceptions and awareness, and I am honored to be able to pass these insights on to you, the reader, and all my clients.

The best advice I can possibly give you is to begin to think with your heart, NOT your head, and gently begin to open to your inner awareness. There are incredible possibilities and opportunities that surround each and every one of you. When we are aware, we are more open to these life-changing experiences that awaken our souls to their magnificent heritage and enrichment.

Every day, people are waking up in ways they never thought possible. Personally speaking, I have found five distinct ways that sparked my awakening. These five are just the tip of the iceberg.

1. Near Death Experience

Dr. Raymond Moody coined the term "Near Death

Experience" in his book *Life After Life.* In his extensive research, patients were declared either clinically dead or close to death and "came back" to life with memories of a spiritual experience, such as meeting dead friends and family members, seeing a white light, and feeling supreme love and joy during the time when death was near.

Talk about strange yet wonderful!

My first spiritual awakening occurred when I was very young. I became very sick with encephalitis, which is an inflammation of the brain, commonly referred to as *sleeping sickness.* Apparently, it was caused by a mosquito bite. My parents and grandparents watched me around the clock, worried by the thought that they could lose me at any moment.

I remember that I was asleep all the time and had been given baths with vinegar and cold water to bring down my high temperature. At some point, my fever rose so high I was rushed to the hospital and suddenly slipped into a coma. I vividly recall leaving my body and wandering through a dark tunnel. At the end of the tunnel, I could see a bright white light. The light was very familiar to me—like being back at home. In the midst of this incredible light, two familiar hands were waving to me. They were those of my two favorite aunts, Josephine and Ulia. I cannot express the amount of unconditional love and the incredible sense of peace I felt when I saw them, as well as the strong desire to push myself through the light to the other side so I could be with them. But some sort of membrane restrained me and kept me from completely going into this blissful, luminous light.

My two great aunts telepathically communicated, "It is not

your time, Kellee. You will have to go back to Earth; otherwise, you will change the course of your mother's destiny." They continued, "You have a special job to do, and you need to complete your journey."

Immediately, I felt a sort of thud, and instantly, I found myself back in my body, covered by a blanket of sadness that enveloped my entire being. I remained in a coma for nearly a week, and although I wasn't able to consciously communicate with others, I became keenly aware of all of their thoughts and emotions. The feelings that stood out the most were those of fear and apprehension, which my loved ones held on to because of their constant worry about my possible demise.

Innately, I knew my mother could **never** lose me; she simply would not be able to recover from such a loss. Besides, my leaving would prevent her from doing the work she came to Earth to do. Together, we had important spiritual contracts to fulfill.

This early experience was definitely a "destiny point" in my life. It was a treasured experience that shaped my understanding that there is indeed no death! I knew that Heaven actually existed and it was Home. I had no doubt that everyone had a destiny to fulfill and a soul plan in place, and each of us came to Earth to carry it out.

My destiny was to help others. But at what price? With this newly-discovered awareness came an added stress of... what else? RESPONSIBILITY!

2. Heredity

Back on the farm, when I was growing up, I had no

understanding that Grandpa Charlie was not only a dowser but also a very respected physical medium.

Physical mediumship is different from spiritual mediumship and is very rare. It was an important part of the Spiritualist movement of the late eighteenth and early nineteenth centuries, where table tapping or tipping, physical materializations in the form of human shapes and voices, and object manipulation were common occurrences during séances.

In Grandpa Charlie's case, every Sunday, he would gather his twelve brothers and sisters together for a séance. We've all seen séances in movies and TV where everyone sits around a table holding hands, waiting for spirits to appear. During Grandpa Charlie's séance, everyone sat around the family table, but instead of holding hands, they placed their fingers on the table in anticipation of something to happen. Mom described Grandpa as "rubbing his hands together and saying **table dance**!" And the table would begin hopping around. Family members would then ask their questions, and the table would thump once for **"Yes"** or twice for "No." Sometimes, the table would rock back and forth. Grandpa was known all around the countryside as the "Table Tipper."

From my mother's point of view, this Sunday's family activity was quite normal. "Didn't everyone's family do it?" Really, Mom? Apparently, my grandfather and his forefathers were psychics and mediums, but no one put what he did and his abilities in that context in rural Indiana. A dowser was an important person back then when farmers needed water to save their crops. Although I knew my grandfather was special, I had a very limited grasp of the powers that psychics and mediums retained, let alone know that one day I would inherit some of these same paranormal abilities.

3. Spontaneous Clairvoyance

My next important spiritual experience happened quite unexpectedly. I was eight at the time. Sometime in the middle of the night, I was awakened by a bright light over my bed, and through this brilliant light, I saw a man radiating so much love. I recognized the man—it was my beloved Uncle Curly.

"Kellee Jo," he said, "Go tell your momma Uncle Curly passed." I felt as though I was in some kind of trance, yet I wasn't a bit afraid. All I sensed was an incredible amount of love in the room. Despite not wanting to leave the profound love I felt, I knew I had to deliver this important message. I ran to my parents' room and shook my mother awake.

"Mommy, mommy, wake up. I have to tell you something."

She bolted upright. "What? Are you okay?"

"Uncle Curly came to me and told me to tell you that he passed."

"WHAT?"

"Uncle Curly told me he passed."

My mother immediately jumped out of bed, took my hand, and walked as fast as she could back to my bedroom.

In a very gentle voice, she asked, "Where did you see Uncle Curly?"

I pointed over my bed to the side. "He was glowing."

Although she was quite shaken, I knew she had taken me seriously.

"Thank you, honey. I'll let Daddy know in the morning."

Mom didn't sleep the rest of the night. She waited until daybreak to call her cousin and tell her to go to the "holler," the farm where my grandparents lived, and let them know about Uncle Curly. When I was young, I didn't realize just how remote their farm was, nor the fact that they didn't have a phone. They had to rely on friends and neighbors to bring them messages. It was the 1960s, but it could have been 1930 in that part of the country. This explained why people would just stop by—it was the only way to find out the news. Apparently, not being able to contact her parents was a source of frustration for my mother. After this incident, my grandparents immediately installed a phone.

When my grandfather Charlie found out that I was the one who saw Uncle Curly and delivered the message to my mother, he shouted, "She's got the gift!"

I was relieved that my father—a very light sleeper—NEVER woke up. Spirit clearly was involved. It was at this moment my mother knew that, yes, I was indeed different.

4. Head Injury

The fourth way of having a spiritual awakening, which has been experienced by many well-known psychics, is a result of a devasting and traumatic head injury.

One of the most famous psychics was Peter Hurkos, a Dutchman who manifested his psychic ability and mediumship after suffering head trauma and coma caused by a fall from a ladder. He came to the United States in 1956 and became the first celebrity psychic. He often appeared on television and traveled the country doing psychic exhibitions. He was involved in the investigation and identification of Albert DeSalvo, known as *The Boston Strangler*, and Charles Manson, the demonic schemer behind multiple murders.

Another psychic, Shawn Lerwill, suffered a shattering brain injury while on a skiing trip in Central Utah. He was standing behind his car unloading his skis when his vehicle was struck by a mining truck. The lid of the trunk smashed Shawn so forcefully that it was torn off the vehicle. He doesn't remember losing consciousness but remembers being outside of his body. Besides a traumatic brain injury, he, too, went through a Near Death Experience. This occurrence opened his mind to new vistas of healing and clairvoyance. Today, he teaches workshops on mindfulness and inner wisdom.

Another well-known medium, George Anderson, began his spiritual journey after a near-fatal illness when he was six. Although he did not have a head injury, his illness caused high fevers that, in turn, caused changes in his brain chemistry.

Derek Amato was 40 when he dove into the shallow end of a swimming pool and hit his head on the bottom. Along with concussion-related side effects, including amnesia, Amato discovered a previously unknown musical gift. He described being drawn to a keyboard one night and visualizing "a fluid and continuous stream of musical notation" in his mind. He played until 2 AM, engrossed in an instrument he had never before touched. He was diagnosed as one of the few "acquired" savants in the world. Amato described the hearing loss and headaches that followed his accident as a "price tag" for his musical gift.

25

According to Professor Rachel Derrington, in her article, *The Gift of a Head Injury*, "a brain injury can be a precious gift. The existential crisis that more than likely occurs after a brain injury is a catalyst that can change one's life positively forever."

In Chapter 7, I will cover my own personal experience with a head injury.

5. Emotional Trauma

The fifth way of awakening to the Spirit is through experiencing an emotionally traumatic event/s. When a person experiences such trauma, often certain areas of the brain turn on, and other areas turn off. Suddenly, the person may feel lightheaded or tingly as if not wholly in the body. This may lead to an opening of psychic/spiritual sight. Experiencing an unforeseen emotional trauma can drastically change someone's life in a matter of moments.

In an article by best-selling author Dr. Daniel Amen, entitled *The Neuroscience of Psychic Experience*, he asserts, "It (psychic experience) generally is associated with a decrease in frontal lobe function (disinhibition) and increases or decreases in right temporal lobe function (similar to seizure phenomena)."

After such an experience, a person may spend weeks, months, or years coming to terms with the trauma, as in PTSD (Post-Traumatic Stress Disorder). The brain must continually rewire itself in order to heal. Often, memories of a traumatic event are repressed. If a person was abused as a child, or someone was in a war or had been personally and violently attacked, the mind compensates by expanding the survival instincts. Most people don't need to be in survival mode every day, but people with trauma often feel like they are constantly in a "fight or flight" crisis.

In an article, *Can Trauma Induce Psychic Awareness*, Mary Trettenero states*:* "Because of this constant battle inside your head, whether from grief, fear or displacement, it can open your mind to a variety of different perceptions and new skills, some being psychic abilities. If you have a genetic predisposition to being highly psychic, a traumatic event like a car accident, divorce, death, and even getting fired from your job can increase your sensitivity, causing those abilities to come forward more."

This description fits me to a tee because such a traumatic event happened to me, as you will read in Chapter 4.

Having experienced all five ways of a spiritual awakening, I am convinced that the Spirit was at work with my guides to make sure I opened my mind and heart to my gifts. After all, I came with a purpose, and if I went through this lifetime as a sleep-walker, I would then have to return and do it again. No thanks!

Fear of the Unknown

As a medium, I'm often asked if I have or had any fear of seeing spirits. Since I have become educated in the spirit world and the various methods of communication, my answer is definitely NO! Every time I pierce the veil and communicate with spirits, I experience the same overwhelming love I felt so many years ago during that visit from Uncle Curly.

But when I was twelve, I had an experience of a different sort, and fear crept into my psyche. This experience taught me a lot about spirits that I will call "earthbound," or ones who I feel have "unfinished business" on Earth. Such spirits are sort of "stuck" in their minds and need whatever is stuck to get resolved. The word "ghost" comes to mind. In his book *Ghosts Among Us*, James Van Praagh explains, "Only those of us who are afraid choose to stay behind and cling to this earthly atmosphere." Unfortunately, this next experience with the spirit world left an indelible impression on my young self and was a defining moment of who I was and how I would handle it.

Let me set the stage. At the time, we lived in our Toluca Lake house. It was 1969, and Toluca Lake was primarily a Catholic neighborhood. When most people were heading to church on Sundays, we stayed home listening to jazz and eating pancakes. My father was culturally Jewish, and my mother was raised Southern Baptist. Neither practiced their faith, so, therefore, none of us kids had any religious education. By then, Dad decided to switch jobs from *The Tonight Show* Band to join the *Baja Marimba Band*. At the same time, Mom was finishing her doctoral thesis in Clinical Psychology at the University of Southern California. Let's just say we didn't fit in with the rest of our neighbors.

I had just turned 13 and wanted to" fit in" and be like everyone else. But how could I fit in if I could feel and sense spirits moving around the rooms of our house? Unlike my encounter with Uncle Curly, where I felt nothing but love, the spirits in our house seemed to have scared me. Instead of love, the energy I felt was really heavy, almost a haunted feeling, as if the spirit was somehow lost on its journey home.

One afternoon after school, I had an encounter with one of the apparitions floating around. I was doing my homework in front of the fireplace on a table in the living room. I looked out the window to keep an eye on my brother and sister playing outside in the backyard, and when I turned back, I saw a beautiful woman in her 20s dressed like a flapper walking toward me. I felt a cold shiver go through my body, and instead of feeling love, I felt terrified and wondered if the spirit could hurt me. In the blink of an eye, she drifted up to the ceiling and disappeared. I stopped doing my homework, curled up on the couch, and waited for my mother to come home.

As soon as Mom walked in the door, I told her about the flapper. She could sense my fear and anxiety and was able to calm me down by validating what I had experienced. She explained, "This old house had been used as a speakeasy during prohibition. There are probably spirits here who never wanted the party to end."

Mom had an incredible presence, and as she held me in her arms, she whispered, "Kellee, you're safe. Ghosts cannot hurt you. Believe me. They are phantoms merely looking for the light and just haven't found it yet." She really rallied my inner warrior!

About this time, Los Angeles was at the beginning stages of New Age cults and practices. The Ouija Board gained popularity as an accepted tool of the occult. Mom began to show interest in these New Age ideas and thought an Ouija Board might help me. Why she thought an Ouija Board would accomplish anything, I don't know. Maybe she thought it would give me a better understanding of my psychic abilities or soothe my fears about seeing ghosts. But I can tell you it didn't help at all. In fact, it did quite the opposite.

An Ouija Board is a flat board with the alphabet arranged in two semi-circles. Above the letters are numbers 0 to 9. "Yes" and "No" are in the corners, and "Goodbye" is at the bottom. To access answers to questions, you place your fingers on a device called a planchette, which moves around the board, spelling a response.

Back then and even now, people used the Ouija Board as a game and didn't take it seriously. But when Mom came home with an Ouija Board for my friends and me to "play with," I was totally surprised. *Wasn't it enough that I could see spirits roaming around our house? Did I really need the help of an Ouija Board?* Needless to say, none of my Catholic friends would play with the "tool of the devil." Anything to do with "spirits" was considered unholy to Catholics.

One day, I decided to test the board myself to see if it really worked or if it was indeed the devil's tool, as everyone said. Alone in the living room, I sat at the table and put my fingers on the planchette. That was a big mistake. The board flew straight out of my hands and crashed into the wall. I freaked out! From that moment on, I never wanted to touch an Ouija Board or see another apparition again. I was beginning to think I was some kind of weirdo. I wondered why this was happening and what was going to happen next.

What Happens When We Die?

Mom's effort to allay my fear of the unknown failed. Apparently, my fear and anxiety were sealed deep inside my being. Perhaps the fear of death was the real cause of my concern. Since I had no religious training, I had no idea what others thought about death.

My father's parents were from the old country. My great-grandfather Noam was a Rabbi, and I had many great-uncles who were Cantors. Although my father was secular, we would take part in some of the Jewish traditions. I always enjoyed holidays with Dad's family, but I knew it was particularly difficult for my mother, who had never met a Jewish person in her life until my father.

My parents married in 1954 at a time when mixed religious marriages were not well tolerated. My mom's sorority sisters were very concerned that her children would be raised Jewish and go straight to hell when they died. That always made her laugh; she could not have cared less about rules or religion, and she certainly didn't believe in "hell."

I was very close to my dad's mother, Grandma Clara. I adored her, and she loved me so much. I would sit in the kitchen and watch her cook. She would make me the perfect cup of tea with sugar and milk. I was always intrigued by her talent to bake and cook such delicious meals, especially her homemade coffee cake and matzo ball soup, two of my favorite comfort foods. I always felt safe and comfortable being near Grandma Clara.

It was around the time of the incident with the Ouija Board that the topic of death came up—this time upon hearing the news of a cousin who had died.

I asked Grandma Clara, "What do you think happens when we die?

She replied quickly and decisively, "Nothing! It's over. You're dead."

31

My grandparents had no belief in an afterlife and thought the concept absurd. Well, this was too much for my fragile psyche to hear—*You died, and that was it?*

Fear of death gripped me. I seemed to have forgotten any of my earlier experiences as a small child—seeing my Uncle Curly or having a near-death experience when I was sick. Somewhere in my mind, I knew the other side did exist, and there was no such thing as death, and yet, the fear of death caused acute anxiety.

From my psychology background, I learned that according to Sigmund Freud, people express a fear of death as a disguise for a deeper source of concern. He asserted the unconscious mind does not deal with the passage of time or the void. Under this assumption, it was not death people feared because one has never died. Freud suspected death-related fears stem from unresolved childhood conflict. In my case, it must have been the overwhelming responsibility I felt for my loved ones. The thought of them dying and the fact that I could do nothing to save them was a source of real fear for me.

So, despite my otherworldly experiences, I believed my grandmother. After all, she was a reliable, strong-willed individual, and I trusted her judgment. But her emphatic announcement provoked the first of my many panic attacks. I couldn't come to grips with the thought that there was nothing after you died. *Why did I see all those spirits? Was there something wrong with me? Did I have some mental defect?*

My mother became very concerned with my fears. Although she was a psychologist and had helped people with their fears, she was unable to alleviate my anxiety. Mom had studied

Humanistic Psychology, the holistic study of persons as bio-psycho-social beings. Abraham Maslow first coined the term "positive psychology." Mom thought I would benefit from Maslow's theory of "positive thinking." If I were able to change my fearful thoughts into positive ones, then I would feel less fearful. I was a people-pleaser and wanted it to work, but no matter how hard I tried, it didn't. I couldn't reframe my fearful thoughts, and the fear of death was all-consuming.

Fortunately, Mom had learned from a friend in grad school about a New Age spiritual group called Eckankar. Again, I'm quite sure my spirit guides interfered with this one. Thank God. Mom and I attended only one meeting of Eckankar, but this one meeting was all I needed.

One of the basic tenets of this group was that the Soul, or true self, travels to other planes of existence in full consciousness. Dreams are highly regarded as teaching tools, and dream travel is the "gateway to Soul Travel." Eckankar regarded "spiritual experiences as the most natural way back to God." The leader of the group explained that there was no such thing as death and that we are souls that come to this dimension to learn lessons, like in a school. He went on to say that we reincarnate in many lifetimes, and each time, we have the opportunity to spiritually evolve. As he spoke, I identified with everything he said, and it resonated within my heart. For the first time in months, I felt I could breathe easily, and in a flash, my anxiety went away. Finally, I thought that people who were able to see, or at least believe in, the other side, like me, weren't crazy.

From that one Eckankar meeting, I never again feared death.

I had anxiety about other things—such as, you guessed it, too much responsibility, and later, public speaking. But death? Never again!

What A Surprise!

In my third year of college, I learned that my beloved Grandma Clara suddenly died of a heart attack. The pain and grief of losing her were overwhelming, especially compounded by the thought that she believed death was so final. Completely unexpectedly, on the very first night of her passing, while I was asleep, Grandma Clara came to me in a dream.

"Take care of your grandfather," she said rather emphatically.

Imagine my shock at seeing her in my dream. Even with no understanding whatsoever of the afterlife, she was very much alive and exactly like she was in life—pushy!

For several nights, Grandma Clara came into my dreams and communicated her concern for my grandfather. "You need to make sure he's okay. I'm worried about him."

I described my nightly visits to Mom and told her I was exhausted from lack of sleep.

She said, "Tell Clara to stop bothering you and let you sleep."

So that night, I told my grandmother in the nicest way possible, "I got your message. I will take care of grandpa. Don't worry. Please let me sleep."

It worked. Grandma Clara stopped bothering me. Being true to my word, I took care of my grandfather, and one month after my grandmother's death, he passed away. That very night, they both came to me, and I could tell that they were so happy to be together again.

After that, my grandparents would periodically make appearances in my dreams. About fifteen years after she had passed, Grandma Clara came to me once again.

"Tell your father that Uncle Abe passed." My father and his half-brother Abe had not spoken in years. Whatever the issue was, there would have been no way that Dad would have known Abe died.

She also mentioned that a certain cousin had been having an affair. "She has to stop. She is creating a lot of problems for herself. She will have to repay them in another life." Imagine that! Grandma Clara learned about the concept of "karma" on the other side.

I told my mother about Clara coming to me and the message about Abe.

"You need to call your dad and tell him."

So that morning, I called Dad and told him about his brother. I wasn't sure if he would believe me as this kind of info was a little too airy-fairy for him. If the subject wasn't music, specifically bebop, he was flat-out not interested. The afterlife or any kind of spiritual mumbo jumbo was not his bag. But to my amazement, he listened as I explained my dream and his mother's communication.

"Okay, I'll check it out," he answered.

It's a funny thing. Over the years, when I try to explain seeing spirits to people, some, like my Dad, think, "there's no such thing." But if I tell them spirits appear in a dream, it's a whole different story. Everyone can relate because everyone dreams. And we all know that anything is possible in our dreams.

Because my dad and his brother didn't get along, I didn't really believe he would check it out, but he did. And he called me back. He had called his mother's youngest brother, my great-uncle Fred, who was nearly 100 years old. Uncle Fred didn't know about Abe either, but he had called another cousin back east who indeed confirmed the news. Uncle Abe had died the day before my dream.

I was so glad that I got over the fear of death. Fear is a paralyzing emotion, and like most people, I've had to deal with it plenty of times throughout my life. But as my friend James Van Praagh often says, "Your soul knows that fear is merely a wasted human emotion. The soul is pure love, and it might take many human experiences to remember that. Life is a series of choices; we choose either love or fear in every situation. Only love is real. Fear is an illusion."

It would take many more years to awaken to my full spiritual abilities. There were a lot of spiritual tests to come that had me questioning my judgment and reason. I needed all the faith and hope I could muster to ultimately triumph over fear.

Chapter 3

SPIRIT INTERVENTION

Both the Old and New Testaments are replete with examples of purported communication between the living and "beings" from other realms through experiences that we would today categorize as paranormal or extrasensory. Messages delivered by angels were almost commonplace, dreams and visions provided guidance, prophecy was a highly prized gift, and conversations with the Lord—in which voices were heard, and physical phenomena occurred— were frequent. Such experiences were not distrusted but rather were received as being from God.

- James A. Pike, *The Other Side*

Around the time, I had visitations from my grandmother, and just before turning 21, my parents got divorced. They had been separated for years, and Dad had moved to Europe and continued working as a musician. Mom thrived as a psychologist in her private practice in Beverly Hills.

Believe it or not, years later, both of my parents remarried.

Mom married Marc, a prominent Beverly Hills attorney who was the opposite of my father—stable, home at night, and attentive to my mother and me. Dad married Judy, an accomplished artist in the field of advertising and creative design. They had a son, Theo, a multi-instrumentalist and lead singer and guitarist in the funk band Vulfpeck.

In that same third year of college, 1979, my mother was diagnosed with breast cancer. Mom was only in her mid-forties and had a tumor the size of a grapefruit. In those days, this was considered a death sentence. Fortunately, her dear friends, Ann-Margret and Roger Smith kept her informed about cutting-edge medical advances in cancer treatment. Roger suggested that Mom check out an experimental treatment at a Houston hospital. When I look back at this period, I believe the spirit world was once again working on my mother's behalf because she had a destiny to fulfill and was not ready to leave Earth. I didn't realize the importance of Mom's illness, but I definitely signed up for this class; it was another destiny point for me.

The experimental program was at the Stehlin Foundation for Cancer in partnership with the Sisters of Charity of the Incarnate Word and Houston's St. Joseph Hospital. Dr. John Stehlin's approach was unconventional yet well-regarded in the treatment of cancer. His care focused on a patient's psychological, emotional, and spiritual well-being to boost physical health and, thereby, increase a person's chance of survival. Dr. Stehlin was the first surgeon to publish an article concerning the psychological aspects of cancer therapy. It was an unusual, even radical, method back then.

In early June, Mom and I left Los Angeles and flew to Houston. We felt confident that we were going to beat this illness together. I spent every day in the hospital, never leaving Mom's side, encouraging and supporting her throughout the treatments. Dr. Stehlin and his staff were wonderful to me and to all the families in his care. To say the least, it was an extraordinary experience to be a part of this new experimental therapy.

The treatment involved raising the body temperature to 105 degrees Fahrenheit and then infusing it with enormous amounts of vitamin C. The idea was to mobilize the immune system so that the body could fight off cancer. This went on every day for eight weeks, and it was tough to watch my fearless mother, always strong for everyone else, endure such pain and suffering.

Most of the time, Mom was too weak to do anything, let alone eat. Often, I would leave the hospital to find some food that might stimulate her appetite, but I was never gone more than an hour. Every single time on my return, she would say," Did you see that wonderful nurse who was here? She just left. I was hoping you would meet her. She always tells me I will be all right. She says that Jesus is here with me, and so are lots of angels."

"Describe her for me, Mom?"

Mom replied, "She's about 50, black, a bit on the heavy side, and speaks with a southern accent. She says she's a special nurse on this floor."

I wanted to meet the special nurse who was so kind and supportive, and I thought she couldn't be too hard to find. I asked the floor nurse on duty and explained Mom's description of this special nurse.

The nurse behind the desk responded, "I have no idea who you're talking about, but let me ask the other nurses—maybe she's one of the visiting nurses."

Regrettably, nobody seemed to recognize this mysterious nurse. I asked every nurse myself, but no one seemed to know who I was talking about. I was terribly disappointed and wondered if my mother was hallucinating from the treatment. When I joined Mom in her room the next day, there was a priest sitting by her bed talking to her. He spoke with a South African accent, and I could tell he was kind and compassionate.

"I'm Father John," he introduced himself. "Can you come and join me in the chapel."

Immediately, I thought that he was going to give me bad news. Surely, a priest was elected to give patient's families the "bad" news, and since I had never met a priest and didn't know what to expect, I began to worry. But I agreed to meet him.

As soon as Mom began her treatment, I headed down to the small chapel in the hospital, where Father John was waiting for me. I was pretty nervous and told him how I was feeling. He began by saying, "Your mother is a remarkable woman, and I enjoy her company. You do not have to worry about her."

Apparently, when she detected his South African accent, she had asked him to speak with me about going on *Semester at Sea,* a college program aboard a ship that went around the world. Before Mom's cancer, I had planned on attending *Semester at Sea* after summer vacation. But because Mom was so sick, the idea went completely out of my head. She knew I would never leave her side, so she asked Father John to talk me into going on this life-changing trip. Of course, one of the stops was Cape Town, South Africa, where he was from.

He continued, "I have it on good authority that your mother will beat this cancer and live many years. Every week, I meet with a nurse, and she tells me your mother will live a long life. The cancer is a lesson for your mother. She must learn to slow down and take care of herself and not solely her patients. Go on this trip. You will learn many things about yourself. God will look after your mother."

For the first time in a long time, I could feel the tension leave my body. At last, there was a glimmer of good news, and it sent chills through my body. I was hopeful that Mom was going to be okay. This was my first encounter with faith; Father John's words brought me an indescribable sensation of inner peace.

I was curious about the nurse he mentioned. "I've been asking about the nurse at the hospital, but nobody seems to know who she is. What's her name?"

"Her name is Angel."

"I never met Nurse Angel, but she seems to visit Mom every time I leave the room. No one but you and Mom have ever seen her. I'm grateful to her because she's given Mom the will to live and the hope that she'll survive."

Mom did indeed survive—she lived another forty years. During her life, she became an ardent supporter of breast cancer research and raised over one million dollars in one night for The Dr. John Stehlin Foundation in Houston, Texas.

Was Nurse Angel an angelic being who visited the sick and dying in the hospital? I never saw her, but I believed Mom, and I know now that her spirit guides, and certainly angels, were by her side. She had to survive. She had to finish the work she came to do.

The Illusion of Fear

After a summer of experimental cancer treatment, Mom continued with traditional chemo and radiation, and with blessings from Dr. Stehlin and his staff, the two of us headed to Los Angeles. I can't tell you how happy we were to be back home.

Mom immediately insisted that I attend *Semester at Sea*, but the thought of leaving her really upset me. We were deeply attached to one another, and I felt responsible for her well-being. But to make Mom happy, I finally agreed to go on the trip. When the day arrived for me to leave, I couldn't control my extreme nervousness and apprehension. We traveled north from LA to San Francisco, where the ship was docked. As we entered the parking area, my anxiety went through the roof.

Quite unexpectedly, feelings of numbness and tingling, chills, and hot flashes flowed from the tips of my toes to the top of my head. My heart began racing, and I was sweating. I couldn't breathe; I couldn't move; I couldn't speak because my mouth was like cotton, dry and numb. I was paralyzed with fear, and it was the worse-possible feeling I had ever experienced. I thought to myself, *I'm going to die!*

I heard my mom say, "Kellee, you're not dying! You're having a panic attack."

Panic Attack

A panic attack is a psychological diagnosis that is described in the DSM-5 or The Diagnostic and Statistical Manual of Mental Disorders. The DSM-5 is the handbook used by health care professionals in much of the world as the authoritative guide to the diagnosis of mental disorders. It also provides a common language for researchers to study the criteria for potential future revisions and to aid in the development of medications and other interventions. The DSM-5 classifies panic attacks by providing two very clear categories: expected and unexpected panic attacks. Panic attacks are characterized by four or more of the following symptoms. Fewer than four symptoms may be considered a limited-symptom panic attack.

- Palpitations, pounding heart, or accelerated heart rate
- Sweating
- Trembling or shaking
- Sensations of shortness of breath or smothering
- A feeling of choking
- Chest pain or discomfort
- Nausea or abdominal distress
- Feeling dizzy, unsteady, lightheaded, or faint
- Feelings of unreality (derealization) or being detached from oneself (depersonalization)
- Fear of losing control or going crazy
- Fear of dying
- Numbness or tingling sensations (paresthesia)
- Chills or hot flushes

Expected panic attacks are those associated with a specific fear, like the fear of flying. In my case, it was the fear of leaving my mother and possibly losing her. Unexpected panic attacks have no apparent trigger or cue and may appear to occur out of the blue.

As I sat immobilized, Mom got out of the car, took a paper grocery bag from the trunk, and gently placed the paper bag over my head to slow my hyperventilation.

"Kellee, listen to me. Breathe slowly and calmly. You're going to be fine. You are not dying—you're having a panic attack."

Fortunately for me, this odd technique worked, and I recovered in about 30 minutes, thanks to my mother's coolheaded reaction. I was able to calm down and get out of that incapacitated, fear-based state. It's astonishing how the mind can quickly move into fear and literally paralyze a person. This intense experience opened my awareness to the idea that fear is an illusion of the mind. It also gave me a complete understanding of how to help future clients who suffer from panic attacks.

The Book of Life

With Mom's blessing, combined with the heartfelt meeting I had with Father John, I was able to keep faith that Mom would be all right without me and that I would survive without her. I was able to turn my anxiety into excitement. Fueled with thoughts of new explorations ahead, I hugged Mom goodbye and headed to the ship for a once-in-a-lifetime experience.

Semester at Sea set sail in September 1979. I had just turned 21 and was one of 500 students on this thrilling adventure, traveling from North America eastward. We stopped in China, India, North Africa, South Africa, and many other countries.

When we arrived in New Delhi, I had a feeling that wouldn't leave me; I knew I had been there before. In fact, it felt like home to me. I was so comfortable in India, with its ancient ways and exotic aromas, that I made the decision to go off by myself. I wanted to experience an existential moment—that I could survive anywhere alone.

We were always told to leave our passports with the purser on the ship. For whatever reason, I didn't even bring a driver's license with me, just a small over-the-shoulder purse, along with some rupees I had exchanged at the purser's desk before disembarking the ship. It was a sweltering hot day, and I remember wearing army pants and a tee shirt, a popular look at the time.

I figured the best place to begin my adventure was at a temple in Old Delhi. I got into a taxi, and off we went. Back in those days, taxis were not air-conditioned, so all the windows were wide open. As we drove by, I noticed people staring at me. I assumed they were intrigued by my long, blonde curly hair. As I entered the sacred temple, an Indian man, probably in his late 50s, approached me.

In a lyrical English accent, he asked, "Have you noticed that people are staring at you." Although I had indeed noticed that people were looking at me, I thought, *How would this stranger know this?*

I asked, "Do you know why?"

"May I read your thumb," he asked, extending his hand.

45

I was taken aback. "What? My thumb?"

He explained that he could read the Akashic Records and he could tell me everything I needed to know about my life. I had never heard of the term Akashic Records, but I was intrigued. Years later, I learned that the Akashic Records was a storehouse of every thought, word, and deed, good, bad, pleasant, unpleasant, and everything in between, of every living being for all eternity. That must be the biggest house in the Universe! Those familiar with the Akashic Records report that there is no judgment or implied penalty for any word, action, or thought—it is simply a record of each soul's journey through the infinite.

Psychic and clairvoyant Edgar Cayce, known as the "Sleeping Prophet," was known to access the Akashic Records in a trance state. Sometimes, he would suggest a mere selection of the available material because the individual "was being given that which would be most helpful and hopeful." I also learned that Spirit gives us only what we need to know at the time we need to know it, as long as the info doesn't interfere with our future if there are lessons yet to be learned.

So, I held out my left thumb, and the Indian looked it over and over, seemingly receiving some information. He took a pencil and a small piece of yellow paper out of his pocket and began writing. Then he folded this tiny paper and held it in his hand. He stared at me with very intense eyes. Finally, he spoke.

"I am going to give this to you. I am not asking anything from you. I only want you to have this knowledge, and someday, this information will become important to you."

He handed me the paper. I had no idea what to think, but I

carefully opened it and began reading it out loud. Please remember, I had no identification with me—no driver's license and no passport that he could have somehow seen.

He listed my first, middle, and last names, as well as my mother's first, middle, maiden, and married names. Next was my current boyfriend's name.

Then he added with a smile, "You will never marry him. You will marry a few years from now and have one daughter."

But what he said next was even more incredible.

"You are wondering why everyone is staring at you. It is not because of the way you look. It is because of soul recognition. You had been a revered psychic during a previous lifetime right here in this area. You lost your life near those stairs. You were so fatigued because you were tirelessly working all of the time. When you could not help someone due to exhaustion, that person became very angry and stabbed you to death."

Okay! This bit of news left me speechless, and I felt chills of another sort coursing through my body. *Were some of these people reincarnated in the same place? Was reincarnation even a real thing? Was I really a psychic in a past life? Was it possible that I had traveled throughout India and these people shared some recognition?* These were all questions I kept in the back of my mind until I found answers. As far as reincarnation, Eastern religions have always claimed that the soul leaves the body at death and continues to live on the other side for a period of time until the soul is ready to continue life on Earth and is reborn again.

The Indian psychic continued, "In this lifetime, you will need to make a decision about whether you will use your second sight as you once did. It is a gift that you have had for many, many lifetimes. For some reason, in your Akashic Records, you left that part open to choose from. I believe you will choose to use it again in this lifetime and help others as you had previously. But this time, you will learn to have self-restraint and the need for boundaries."

Although dazed by such detailed information, I profusely thanked the Indian and headed into the temple. I sat down, and for the second time in my life, I prayed. The first time was after my mother's cancer diagnosis. Subsequently, I turned to prayer many times in my life and found that answers came in ways I didn't expect. Again, thoughts flooded my mind. *A psychic? I always knew I was not normal but a psychic? How would that even be possible?* I had no idea where my life was headed, and although at this time it didn't make sense, I somehow knew it would mean much more later on.

Looking back, I see the importance of meeting Father John in Houston, who truly encouraged me to take this particular voyage and explained why I felt I had to be alone in India. At the very least, I became aware that there was a deeper, more transcendent meaning to life and that I would be able to tap into a very mysterious and mystical source in the future. I was filled with enthusiasm, wondering how and when my "psychic self" would be fully revealed to me!

Chapter 4

SHOCK AND TRAUMA

Each one of us has lived through some devastation, some loneliness, some weather superstorm or spiritual superstorm. When we look at each other, we must say, I understand. I understand how you feel because I have been there myself. We must support each other and empathize with each other because each of us is more alike than we are.

- *Maya Angelou*

When I returned home, I finished college and graduated with a bachelor's degree in Child Development. I had no plans for future work, but I knew I didn't want to be a teacher. My curious mind led me to graduate from a clinical psychology program at USC, where my mother was a professor in the psychology department. Although my courses were incredibly fascinating, I felt I was too young and didn't have enough life experience to become a psychologist. Seeing patients all day long seemed overwhelmingly stressful, and I just knew deep down that I couldn't cope with any more responsibility. So what could I do?

The first thing that popped into my mind was my deep passion for cooking. I learned the art of food preparation from my grandmothers. Each time I stepped into their kitchens, I would smell such fragrant aromas from the incredible feasts they were creating. It made me love being in the kitchen. It was so creative, and the feeling took hold inside me. I knew if I lived my passion for cooking, it would take me to many places where I would meet all types of interesting people—an experience of a lifetime.

While attending grad school, I became a cocktail waitress at a popular local restaurant to offset my expenses. I remember some very incredible moments, but one in particular that I will never forget. One fateful evening, just as my shift began, I heard a loud scream in the kitchen. We all ran to see what had happened. The chef had accidentally slashed his hand with a knife. As he was rushed to the hospital, the manager panicked. He needed someone to take over the kitchen, but no one volunteered, not even the sous-chef. A bit surprising, I must say. I have no idea why, but the next thing I knew was me saying, "I'll do it."

Maybe it was all those times in high school when my boyfriend's father owned a successful restaurant, and I was allowed to watch the kitchen staff at work. All I know is that my inner chef took over, and I went into the kitchen and took control. I felt my soul spring alive. I had an overwhelming sense that I had done this before, likely in several past lifetimes. Cooking seemed so second nature to me because I thoroughly enjoyed creating and plating fabulous meals. In fact, I had done such a good job that night that I was asked to stay in that position, and a few months later, the owner of a restaurant across the street asked me to run his kitchen. *What?* Obviously, it was an offer I couldn't refuse, but, more importantly, a chance to prove myself. I immediately dropped out of graduate school to pursue my heart's desire. In the back of my mind, I had hoped that one day, I would own my own restaurant.

Believe it or not, I was given free rein to do exactly what I wanted. I went from working as a line cook to the executive chef of a trendy LA restaurant. Every day, I had to pinch myself because I thought, *Am I dreaming?* I was elated to be able to create a menu and design a working kitchen. But, as they say, "be careful what you ask for." Although I was where I wanted to be, I was running myself into the ground, working 18 to 20 hours a day, 7 days per week. I knew at this rate, I would burn out.

To stay in the culinary world and make something of myself as a chef, I desired a deeper understanding of technique and time constraints. I would have to learn the ins and outs and shortcuts from the professionals. It was this realization that prompted me to apply to culinary school. And if I was going to do it right, I might as well go all the way. Instead of going to any old culinary school, I applied to the École de Cuisine La Varenne in Paris. After two long years as a working chef, I was accepted. The next stop is Paris! The city of my dreams. It was the beginning of one of the happiest chapters of my life.

It's Now Or Later

As the psychic in India had predicted, I didn't marry the

boyfriend I was dating. Rick was a good guy, and although we had dated on and off for two years, it was not meant to be. Eventually, I wanted to get married and have a family, and he wanted to wait. However, Rick played a pivotal part in my life because he did something amazing—he introduced my mother to his cousin, Marc, who became her future husband. At the time, it seemed very strange how everything came together so effortlessly, but little did I know that the spirit world had a plan all along.

Once Rick was out of the picture, I was free, and it was around this time I met my future husband, Craig, in one of my psychology classes. It was the end of the semester, and everyone in Psychology was ready to party. I was too busy at the restaurant to think about going to a party, but my girlfriend, who had a crush on Craig, begged me to go with her. Reluctantly, I said, "Okay." At the time, I thought I'd *stay a while and leave when she and Craig got together. No one's going to miss me, and I can get back to work.* But once again, Spirit had a different plan. That evening was another one of my soul's destiny points written in the stars.

At the party, as I socialized with classmates, I walked over to the hot tub and said hello to some of the people I knew. Craig was sitting there, and he smiled at me. At that moment, I heard a voice in my head say: *You can do this now, or you can do this later.* A message I will never forget. I thought, *What?* The voice repeated. *You can do this now, or you can do it later.* The really odd thing was that I actually knew the voice meant "this lifetime or another lifetime."

There was a battle going on inside my mind as I wrestled with the message, especially the messenger. *But I have so many plans, and I'm not sure he's the one for me.* The voice was insistent, but so was I. It was a tug of war, but I sensed I had to choose, and I had to choose NOW. I literally felt like being shoved into the hot tub next to Craig. I swear that it must have been my daughter on the other side pushing her parents together.

Craig and I soon moved in together, and I became pregnant. We decided to get married before I left for culinary school. It was a big shindig of a wedding at the California Yacht Club in Marina del Rey. After a very quick honeymoon, I flew to Paris to start class. To say I was elated to be pregnant in Paris and learning to cook French cuisine all at the same time would be an understatement. I was giddy with glee. *Could it get any better than this?* I wondered.

Although the program lasted almost eight months, Craig never came for a visit. It never occurred to me that we would be apart the whole time I was pregnant. But he was terrified of flying, and he convinced me that it was better if he stayed at home to work. After all, he argued, "I have a family to support." He got a full-time job selling insurance while working part-time as a drummer in a band.

Mom and Marc (who married a few years later) came to visit me, and some of my other friends came as well. Thank God. Without my visitors' moral support, I would have felt very lonely. Even though culinary school was a full-time commitment, whatever time I had left over was time spent bonding with my beautiful baby-to-be.

After graduating from culinary school, I flew home, and not a moment too soon. In October 1984, I gave birth to our beautiful daughter, Holiday. A new baby is a lot of work, and I soon discovered that it was almost impossible to be both an executive chef and a new mother at the same time. The long working hours took a toll on me, and sadly, I had to give up my passion for cooking and start heading in a different direction. *Was it going to be motherhood or a career?* It was a hard choice. I was young, full of energy, and wanted to have it all. *Wasn't that what life was all about?*

Although I dreamed and planned about being a chef and owning my own restaurant, Spirit had another road for me to take—my new life with my baby and Craig. I was forced to put on the brakes, go inside myself, and nurture my faith that everything was as it should be. But I couldn't fathom what was next.

It was this faith and trust that all will work out for the good that was the impetus for my study of Vedic Astrology. Based on the Hindu Vedas, and quite different from Western Astrology, Vedic astrology instantly spoke to me. It gave me an understanding of my destiny and the direction I was headed. I fell in love with all the cosmic patterns and celestial undertones of the planets and their influence on our lives. It was a map and a guide to my new journey—a journey for my soul. To this day, I use Vedic astrology as a tool in my practice. It offers a blueprint to understanding ourselves at a deeper level of awareness, to make sense of our lives, and to learn our purpose for living in this world.

Planning For the Future

My baby Holiday was growing up fast and was a year-and-a-half old when I was still feeling a bit adrift with no plan for the future. As a chef, I had purpose and direction, but as a young mother, I needed to do more. Like many young mothers of my generation, I struggled internally between staying at home and finding my next big adventure. Besides, I was completely responsible for the Holiday. I had no help. My workaholic mom lived an hour away, and Craig worked full-time, so he was gone all day. And when Craig was at home, he allowed Holiday to do whatever she wanted. On the other hand, I was the opposite—the authoritative and responsible one. What a surprise!

Again, I was at a crossroads. I felt an inner urgency to take flight, but how could I leave Holiday? I was faced with a tough choice. I wasn't cut out to be a stay-at-home mom, and I knew that I had to work at something or lose my mind. Craig and I discussed the possibility of my working and getting someone to watch over the Holiday. I felt that in my heart of hearts, I was supposed to do something important with my life. Big words, I know, but I had to honor what I felt inside. There was much I needed to accomplish. Besides, my mom certainly followed her heart. She went to work and earned post-graduate degrees as a mother. She managed to accomplish her goals even with three children in tow. And I was my mother's daughter, and if she did it, I could do it.

And so I began my search for the next chapter in my life. It was the 1980s, long before the Internet and cell phones. One of the most common ways to find a job was by looking through the want ads. Yes, my friends, "the want ads." My eyes darted down the page of the *Los Angeles Times Classified* section and stopped at *Wanted: The director of purchasing at Japan Airlines*. I thought, *Ok. This sounds like something I can do.* The ad was for someone with strong food purchasing experience. *Oh my God, that's me!* I have a lot of experience dealing with food vendors in restaurants.

But I hesitated. *Japan Airlines. They wouldn't hire a young, female, non-Japanese, new mother.* I was certain that my background certainly would work against me. And then there was that voice inside my mind asking, *Are you really ready to leave Holiday and get a job?* But I heard that quiet inner voice say, *Go for it.* To my amazement, I pushed aside my doubts and fears and applied for the job.

All in all, I had five interviews for the position. My competition was well-qualified, older Japanese men. I thought, *Five interviews! Holy cow! Are these people playing a game, or are they just being polite?* It was hard for me to imagine they were actually considering me for the job.

Right after the last interview, Wendy, an old friend from culinary school, called to invite Craig and me to an art opening. The gallery was down the street from where my mother and Marc lived. I thought it would *be great to get out of the house.* Craig and I hadn't socialized much since Holiday was born, and besides, Craig went back to graduate school for a Master's in psychology, so we had little time to have fun.

Mom insisted that Holiday stay with her. I trusted my mother to take good care of my tiny baby girl, but I also felt uncomfortable leaving her for the first time, even if it was only for a couple of hours. It was a curse to always feel so responsible. But I would have to get used to the idea if I really wanted to go back to work. Since Craig had a class that night, I invited my friend Eve to join me. She, too, had a one-year-old, and she left her baby with her mother. We were two nervous moms finally going to have a night out.

My Worse Nightmare

Mom and Marc had recently moved into a beautiful and spacious newly-built home above Sunset Boulevard in Beverly Hills. I had only been there once during construction. When we arrived to drop off the babies, Marc began to show Eve around the house while I was on the third floor in Mom's master bedroom, talking to her about my fears about working and leaving Holiday with a babysitter.

"I'm wrestling with myself about giving Holiday some autonomy," I said to Mom.

"She has to have some freedom, Kellee. You can't hover over her all the time."

Wanting to let go of my clinging attachment to my daughter, reluctantly, I released Holiday from my grip so she could look out the large picture windows. As she gazed out, I felt an uncontrollable panic surge through me. I had always had a fear of heights, and I had a bad feeling as Holiday stood close to the tall windows.

It happened so fast. Holiday touched the windowpane with her tiny hand, and the window swung open. I watched in complete horror as Holiday flew out the window and fell three floors to the ground below. She landed face down on the lower balcony, literally at the feet of Marc and Eve. In one split second, my life turned into a nightmare.

I let out a blood-curdling scream. "CALL 911!"

(As I relive this scene in my mind, my body is shaking.)

Mom and I raced down the stairs. Holiday was motionless, lying on the cement. Before I knew it, Marc had swooped underneath her limp and seemingly lifeless body, and instead of waiting for the paramedics, we climbed into Marc's car and rushed down the street to Cedars Sinai Medical Center. We arrived in barely five minutes. Holding Holiday, I was in complete and utter shock and trauma, thinking, *This is the hospital where she was born, not, please God, where she may die.*

The Emergency Room doctors took my baby's limp body from my arms, and immediately she started to howl. *A good sign*, I thought. She was moved to pediatric intensive care, where she underwent every possible test. A fall from such a height can cause a ruptured spleen in a toddler, never mind broken ribs, collapsed lungs, and so on. She had to be watched around the clock. My precious baby remained in pediatric intensive care for 48 hours, and I was by her side the entire time.

In the meantime, Mom was able to locate Craig at school, and he was rushed to the hospital. When he arrived, he began shouting at me, blaming me for the accident. The doctors quickly removed Craig from the intensive care unit until he calmed down. After two days, Holiday was discharged. She had no broken bones, no ruptured spleen, not even a scratch. *How in the world could that be?* The doctors claimed: "It's a miracle!"

Mom, Marc, Craig, and I left the hospital bleary-eyed, exhausted, and traumatized. We never spoke about this incident again. I understood Craig's anger, and I forgave him for blaming me. I would have blamed him if the roles had been reversed.

Besides, I had plenty of blame, shame, and guilt to last a lifetime, and I had no idea how I would ever possibly recover.

In hindsight, I believe experiencing such trauma was part of my soul contract. It was something I had to experience and a lesson in responsibility I needed to learn. Going through such an ordeal became invaluable for the future treatment of clients who had suffered the loss of a child or had some traumatic situation involving a child. I know that Holiday and I had a soul contract that included this difficult learning experience. I also know that we had been together for many lifetimes, taking on different roles—as mother, sister, aunt, cousin, father, etc.

As a result of this accident, both our lives changed in profound ways. Of course, at the time, we were completely unaware of the changes and that it would take years for both of us to process the trauma. When I think back, I am amazed at how souls undergo the most horrendous experiences life throws at them, and not only do they survive, but they are able to thrive.

God Calling

Craig and I drove home in silence, with Holiday sleeping in her car seat. We walked into our condo, and I immediately put Holiday to bed. Then, slowly and deliberately, I said to Craig loud enough for even the neighbors to hear, "I'm going upstairs. Do not disturb me. I don't want to speak to anyone. Do you understand? I don't care if my dad calls or friends call. I don't care if God himself calls me."

Craig didn't say a word. He had never seen me in such a state. I must admit, I'm sure I had the look of a deranged woman.

I was completely unhinged at the time. That and lack of sleep will do it. Craig was smart enough to say nothing but a soft "Okay."

I headed up the stairs to our third-floor bedroom. Clearly, I was in a state of shock. I didn't feel attached to my body, and my mind was filled with disturbing thoughts. I blamed myself for the accident. I felt I was a horrible mother. I was totally irresponsible for letting this happen. I could never be trusted to take care of my daughter again. The pain was unbearable, and I wanted it to end. It was the first time I thought about killing myself.

As I got to the top of the stairs, I heard the phone ring. I continued to head into the bedroom with the intent of throwing myself off the balcony when Craig yelled, "Kellee, Japan Airlines is on the phone. You got the job. Please come downstairs and take this call!"

My mother always said to me, "You never know where your angels will come from." At that moment, my angel came in the form of Mr. Kuwano. He hired me to be the Director of Purchasing for Japan Airlines. In that instance, my traumatic trance was broken, and thoughts of suicide ended.

The Voice of a Theosophist

Although everyone in my family knew I was traumatized, no one spoke about it. Months after the accident, I was still tormented by thoughts of blame and guilt. By then, Mom had heard of a medium named Sally Vickers in Malibu who helped people with trauma, so she set up an appointment. I had never worked with anyone who channeled spirits, and even though I had my own personal experience with the spirit world, I had no idea what to expect.

Sally channeled a woman named Annie Besant, a well-known British theosophist and activist in the early 1900s who wrote many books on spirituality and socialism. When Sally began the reading, her voice dramatically changed—she spoke with an English accent. She began by saying, "They were aware of an accident with the daughter. All the angels were present when she fell, and they carried her gently down. There was no pain and nothing physically broken. We are sorry for your suffering, but this lesson will help you later in your life."

Startled by this information, I began to cry and was too upset to continue listening. "Thank you," I said as I stood up from the chair. I quickly headed out the door to my car and sat sobbing, trying to process the medium's words. *The angels carried her down? Is this for real? Did my mother tell Sally that my daughter was in an accident? What kind of lesson was this, and how would this help me later on?* There were too many unanswered questions, and I was far too emotionally shut down to understand her message at a deeper level.

Because of my experience with Sally, I learned why some people cannot process the messages I receive from the spirit world until sometime later, or possibly not at all. Although I was still in shock, on a soul level, Sally's message gave me a bit of relief, and I was "seemingly" able to forgive myself.

Many years later (I'm sure due to Spirit), I learned from my psychologist, of all people, that the window manufacturer was at fault for Holiday's accident. The construction of the windows in my mother's new house looked like they were properly installed, but they weren't. When Holiday pushed on the glass, the window was not entirely attached, and it gave way.

The Aftermath of Trauma

I was fortunate in that I did not lose my child, but the strain of the event remained deeply imbedded in my psyche. I didn't receive the help I needed until much later. Over and over, I had the irrational thought that I couldn't take care of my daughter. When trauma is not addressed and treated either spiritually or psychologically, as in my case, the trauma will remain hidden and rear its ugly head at the least expected moment. Trauma does not disappear on its own.

According to the American Psychological Association, "trauma is an emotional response to a terrible event. Immediately after the event, shock, and denial are typical. Longer-term reactions include unpredictable emotions, flashbacks, strained relationships, and even physical symptoms like headaches or nausea. While these feelings are normal, some people have difficulty moving on with their lives."

It was obvious—I was in denial. I couldn't bear to think that I failed in my responsibility to care for Holiday. I knew I had to submerge my volatile thoughts; otherwise, I would become erratic and unstable. This one traumatizing event had long-term effects. Instead of getting the help I needed, I kept running from place to place, job to job, and eventually, man to man as fast as I could.

The first of the many changes that occurred because of the "accident" was the end of my marriage. Craig and I couldn't sustain any relationship. He blamed me for the accident, and I agreed with him. We were divorced a few months afterward. It's not unusual for a couple to divorce after a traumatic event involving a child or the death of a child. Grief is complex, especially when shame and blame are involved.

There are some couples who actually grow closer through trauma and are able to forgive and heal. I'm always in awe of such relationships because the healing that takes place makes each person stronger and more compassionate. Ironically, it was my new job that saved my sanity and made me stronger, but the marriage couldn't be fixed.

I redirected my passion for cooking and running a restaurant to a corporate life of purchasing food for Japan Airlines. I was proud to be the only female and only non-Japanese member of the team. I loved my job and believed it would provide a comfortable future for Holiday and me.

I learned so much about Japanese culture. It was steeped in traditional values: the importance of interacting with others, having respect for others, and working hard to reap rewards. All of these concepts are invaluable in my present work as a psychotherapist and medium. The job provided a sense of security, and although I felt secure, I never felt safe. Trauma followed me like a lost puppy dog. I couldn't shake off the fear that more terrible things were in store for me.

When I was hired, I was told that I had the position for life. In Japanese culture, it is assumed that once you have a job, you stay in that job for the rest of your life. It was a stunning realization, but I couldn't imagine staying there longer than five years—there was so much I wanted to do.

When I approached my manager and respectively asked for a raise in salary, I was flatly turned down. It was company policy. Raises were hard to come by. Instead, I was offered a bigger title—Vice President of Western Relations. And as flattering as the title sounded, I felt that if I stayed, there would be little opportunity for advancement. After five years, I needed to explore other possibilities, and it was time to leave my comfort zone.

Besides, Holiday was growing up, and I was responsible as a single mother for her welfare. And to do that, I wanted to make our lives as comfortable as possible with all the advantages that money could buy. Sayonara, Japan Airlines. Domo arigatou.

Moving On

When I left Japan Airlines, I instinctively knew it was time to go. There were other times in my life when I knew it was time to leave. I remember when I was 16, I fell in love with a young man, and we had a sporadic relationship that lasted until I was 24. Although we lived in different parts of the country, I knew I could never move to the South where he lived. I knew we were heading in two different directions, and although we loved each other, I knew I had to break it off. I had learned what I was supposed to from the relationship, and my self-esteem had greatly benefitted from it. Understanding that the lesson was completed was significant because once I got the message, I was able to move on without regret.

Leaving Japan Airlines was similar in that I felt I had fulfilled a karmic obligation and completed another lesson. I left Japan Airlines with gratitude for the unique and positive experience I had at a time in my life when it was needed. I also gained confidence in bridging Western and Eastern cultures, learning from my co-workers and vice versa. I had done what I came to do, and it was over. I was ready for the next chapter.

Since my divorce from Craig, I have begun dating on and off. I was definitely looking for a knight in shining armor. Unfortunately, I was still running from grief and trauma and never took the time to process all the changes in my innermost self, especially in regard to relationships with men.

For a brief time, I was involved with somebody who was gay and deeply in the closet. That was a tough one. We were compatible on so many levels, except one, and that one was very important. After all, I was still young and toyed with the idea of having more children. *What was I thinking?*

During the hunt for my next perfect job, I met Peter. He had the kind of attributes I was looking for—tall, dark, and handsome. Just kidding. He was kind and attentive. He showered me with love, affection, and gifts. We seemed like a perfect fit. Because I was like an open wound that couldn't heal, I didn't have the ability to see that I needed to get better myself before jumping into a new relationship. Let me tell you, it took me far too many years to figure that one out.

As far as a new job, I was offered a position at the new food division of Anheuser-Busch Corporation. My culinary and purchasing skills were exactly what they were looking for in a new startup branch of the company. But talk about culture shock! Although I had been in a unique position in a completely different culture at Japan Airlines, I entered a rarefied atmosphere at

Busch—playing with the big boys. I quickly advanced to National Accounts Manager, and my salary doubled.

A new job, a new boyfriend—I was on an emotional whirlwind—and before I understood all the ramifications, I experienced what is called "love bombing."

Love Bombing

"Love Bombing" is an attempt to influence a person through demonstrations of attention and affection. It happens when someone overwhelms the victim with loving words, physical actions, and manipulative behaviors used in a variety of ways—for either positive or negative purposes. Psychologists have identified love bombing as a possible part of a cycle of abuse and have warned patients against it.

Recently, I saw an episode of *Sex and the City* about "love bombing." Who would have thought it could happen to me?

Although we had just begun to date, I never told Peter where I lived. So, when he turned up at my door with a bouquet of roses, a red flag popped into my mind. WARNING!

Peter was so solicitous. "I heard you were sick, and I was worried about you." Unfortunately, I chose to ignore my gut feeling and invited his attentiveness into my life, hook, line, and sinker. His demonstrations of affection and care were something I needed at that very moment. *Perhaps he is the knight in shining armor I've been looking for. Maybe he can help me to heal. Really! Otherwise, why would he show up in my life?*

But I was terribly wrong. And not a little wrong, but a lot wrong. I found myself in the most dysfunctional relationship I could ever imagine. It was as if I was living in the movie *Gaslight. Was it my imagination, or was someone trying to make me think I was crazy?* It turns out that Peter was a deranged psychopathic narcissist, and I felt as if I were losing my mind. I doubted my judgment— always second-guessing my decisions and criticizing my actions. I was so shut down by my internal distress and panic that I didn't recognize I was in an abusive relationship, one that lasted far too long.

From a spiritual lens, this man was a perfect teacher. It's obvious I had a major lesson to learn and a huge karmic debt to pay. It was yet another challenge on my spiritual journey. Our relationship was especially disturbing because I was an empath and could feel this man's cruelty and pain, which, of course, he projected onto me. I learned the hard way that narcissists are drawn to empaths like moths to a flame and vice versa. Narcissists need constant love and attention because they feel unloved and rejected, and empaths want to pour their love and affection into them so they feel needed.

Dr. Judith Orloff, often referred to as the "godmother of the empath movement," explains that "empaths are able to sense the thoughts, feelings, and energy of those around them, and that they are able to use this ability to provide healing or comfort to others **if** they manage their condition correctly." **IF** is the operative word here.

Empaths are born with a sensitive nature, and more often than not, they have experienced trauma. ME!

Additionally, empaths come from a dysfunctional family where there are no emotional boundaries. ME!

67

Because I felt emotionally responsible from an early age to take care of my parents, I had no boundaries with them, setting my life to have no boundaries in relationships. It was difficult for me to even understand what a boundary was. The gift of being an empath works against a person until they learn boundaries.

One or both parents were narcissistic and suffered from addictions. ME AGAIN!

In addition, I was very bad at saying "no," always placing others' needs before my own. Hence, I spent years making bad choices in relationships, trying to take care of others to ensure their world was safe at the expense of my own safety.

Sadly, if an empath makes friends with an emotionally abusive narcissist, the empath can become unstable and unbalanced because they are feeling what the other one is feeling. They take on the other person's psychological moods, like their pain, anxiety, and anger.

Because I was highly sensitive and tuned into Peter, I could feel what he was feeling. I could sense he had low self-esteem, and I felt sorry for him and wanted to do whatever I could to make him feel better. Combined with my own unconscious fears, guilt, blame, and shame, my relationship with this man became lethal. Not only was I suffering from deep-seated trauma, I exposed myself to emotional abuse that piled on more trauma. I had feelings of overwhelming anxiety and depression. Emotional abuse is based on power and control, including rejecting, degrading, terrorizing, isolating, corrupting/exploiting, and denying emotional responsiveness. That was Peter 100%

You may be wondering why I couldn't leave such an abusive

relationship. I had often asked myself this question long after it was over. This relationship was unlike the ones I had with my husband, Craig, or other boyfriends. It took me a while to grasp what the heck was going on. In the meantime, I wanted to keep Peter happy, even though I was secretly in fear for my life.

Gradually, the relationship got worse. Peter became completely controlling—threatening many times to take Holiday away from me. This is the typical MO of an abuser. He would threaten, then apologize for his behavior, put on the charm, become affectionate, and all was well until the next time something disturbed him. It was an erratic and confusing situation.

Unfortunately, I felt helpless to do anything about it because Holiday was under his spell, too. Like me, she's an empath, and like me, she felt responsible in some way for Peter's enjoyment. Both of us were emotionally under his control.

While the abuse was going on in private, I was at work in a very masculine environment. Peter was jealous of my position and male colleagues. If I acted too aggressively to get ahead at work, there would be a price to pay at home. Not only did I have to do a balancing act at work, learning to get along with a room full of powerful men, but when I got home, I had to become dutiful, meek, and accommodating.

I was walking a tightrope, and it wasn't easy.

Chapter 5

MIND-BLOWING

What causes us the most difficulty in learning our lessons and working through our karma is our attachment to other people. This may sound rather strange, but what we often think is loving someone else is actually perceiving the other as a thing to fulfill our needs.

- Betty Bethards, *Be Your Own Guru*

As I have been saying, I had a lot to learn in this life, but I was thankful I had my spirit guides and unseen spiritual advocates to help me, even if I forgot that they were there working behind the scenes on my behalf.

In the midst of juggling my personal survival at home and my professional career, I was anxiously looking forward to a meeting in San Francisco with my first big account. It was also the first time I would be traveling on my own for business, and I was extremely nervous. I had to show everyone back in the office that I could do a good job—that I was a big girl who could hold her own in the boys club and that I was a very responsible and competent employee.

After the two-hour meeting was finally over, I found myself in a huge parking lot, aimlessly wandering around, looking for my rental car. I had been so wound up and focused on doing well that I had absolutely no idea where I parked or even the color and type of car it was.

Suddenly and without warning, it started to rain. Claps of thunder, streaks of lightning, and rain started to come down in buckets. Caught outside without an umbrella, I got soaked to the bone. My brand-new designer suit and shoes were ruined, and my curly hair hung down in front of my eyes. I looked like a bedraggled cat. I walked up and down every aisle of that parking lot, trying to locate my rental car to no avail. I was utterly lost, scared, and overwhelmed. So what could I do? The only thing that made sense at the time was that I sat on a step and started to cry like any normal woman.

As I sat trembling in the rain, I remembered the words of my wise and wonderful mother-in-law Shirley many years before. "If you're in any trouble, just ask your angels for help." I used to think it was a joke, as I had no belief in angels at the time. *Sure, angels!* But this was a time that called for desperate measures, and I was desperate. *Why not ask the angels?* There were hundreds of cars in this enormous lot, and I hadn't a clue which one was mine. Besides, every car looked like every other car. Still crying, I started to pray, asking angels, spirits, and anyone out there if you really do exist. P*lease help me.*

Suddenly, I heard a loud whistle and looked up at an enormous white van. A man with flaming red hair and the longest neck I had ever seen stretched his head out the window. "Is that your car?" He pointed to a gray sedan an aisle away. "What?" My head spun around to look at where he was pointing. *Who is this guy? How does he know where my car is parked?*

But he got my attention, and I got up and walked a couple steps toward the aisle. There it was... my car. I remembered because it had a sticker on the windshield. I turned to thank him, but he was GONE. It was then I realized that my prayers had been answered. From that day on, I knew that I could no longer doubt the spirit world, angelic beings, or whatever they were in. They had to exist—they were my invisible guides and companions. And more of them were yet to turn up in my life.

Oh, the "Joy" of Business Travel

After the mysterious intervention in the parking lot, I realized that not only is life interesting with its twists and turns, but that our souls are always revealing a plan, even if we are oblivious to the signposts often in plain sight. It may take us a long time after an experience to connect the dots. It certainly was taking me quite a while. Only then do we realize the answers are always present. It's as if the Universe is teasing us to wake up to the invisible force that surrounds us.

If we look back at our lives, I'm sure we've all experienced a situation where we said: *How did I survive that*? Or *Did that really happen?* That was my sentiment about the following incident.

My company colleagues, Bob and Phil, and I were on a business trip to Chicago. John, a business associate from a local marketing firm, met us at the airport. John was an older, happy-go-lucky guy, knowledgeable about the business, and everyone loved him.

It was a beautiful spring afternoon in the Midwest when John picked us up in his brand-new baby blue, four-door Cadillac Deville. The car was as big as a boat. Bob sat in the front with John, and Phil and I sat way in the back. We all buckled up, and off we went. John drove out of O'Hare Airport and headed west on the I-88 to our meeting in Aurora. Traffic was heavy, and John said, "You might be a few minutes late."

Phil and I were talking and laughing about something when, suddenly, the car veered into the next lane and began accelerating at an alarming speed. Phil and I were thrown back in our seats as the car sped up. In the front, Bob looked over at John and saw that he was slumped over with his foot on the accelerator. I began to pray like I never had before: *Please help us. I don't want to die and never see my daughter again.*

As if I were watching in slow motion, Phil immediately unbuckled his seatbelt, and from the back seat, he managed to push John over and reach for the steering wheel. At the same time, Bob pulled John's foot off the accelerator. Phil did his best to control the car as we weaved in and out of traffic. I closed my eyes. *This cannot be happening?* Finally, Phil was able to steer the car to the side of the interstate as Bob pushed his foot on the brake. The car stopped short, and we lurched forward. Then we all took a breath, relieved that no one was hurt. It was an absolute miracle.

Badly shaken, Bob, Phil, and I got out of the car together— glad to feel our feet touch the ground. I was literally shaking. John was still slumped over the driver's seat. We all assumed he had a heart attack. Phil started to walk to the emergency box when suddenly John popped up and asked, "Why are we sitting on the side of the road?" We stood there dumbfounded. John had no idea that we almost got killed. When we told him what had happened, he was so embarrassed he didn't know what to say, but finally, he admitted that he suffered from narcolepsy. *What?* Narcolepsy is when a person suddenly falls asleep at any time of the day or night, no matter where they are. John just happened to fall asleep while driving a car on the Interstate! *How in the world would John be allowed to drive a car with narcolepsy?*

Thank goodness I had my invisible friends watching out for me. Who knows what would've happened? And who would believe me? Bob immediately sat in the driver's seat, and we continued on to our appointment. We could see that John was terribly shamefaced, and I knew this group of men was not about to discuss the incident any further, well, not in front of me anyway. Since working in the corporate world, I learned about the male code of silence in such sensitive situations. But I couldn't keep this episode to myself. It might be okay for the good ole boys club, but it didn't work for me.

When we arrived at our destination, we were greeted by Mary, our lovely hostess, who had prepared a late lunch before our meeting. As I was a quivering wreck, I quickly took Mary aside and said, "I need a drink. And I need to talk to someone." Mary poured me a shot of whiskey, and I swallowed in one gulp. Then I told her what had just happened on the way over.

Mary sat and stared at me with her mouth hung open. I whispered, "We almost … died." (I threw in a few expletives as I spoke).

I'll never forget what she said. "Kellee, I don't know what your belief is, but you were saved by an angel. My neighbor just wrote a book about angels, particularly Archangel Michael, and I know he saved all of you." I learned that Archangel Michael is the top banana in the angel world. He is considered the patron of protection. *If that was you, Michael, a big thank you.*

As if on cue, Mary's neighbor came over holding a copy of her new book. Her dog, Michael, was at her side. I retold the story, and she shook her head, "It was Archangel Michael who saved you." I have to admit it was a reasonable explanation at the time. With all of the afternoon traffic and the car driving in excess of 90 miles an hour, it would have taken a team of angelic beings to save us. Whatever the mysterious forces at work on our behalf, I was grateful to them.

Of course, as we women contemplated the secrets of the Universe and the intercession of angels and archangels in our lives, the guys were outside sitting at the picnic table eating lunch and laughing as though nothing had ever happened. I'm sure at some later date, they will all get together and razz poor John. He will never live that one down.

If there had been a message to me from the Universe about this incident, it could have been, "Don't fall asleep at the wheel." This time, angels were there to save me, but could they save me from everything? And did I need to save?

Talking To Heaven

Soon after this experience, my dear friend Charlene told me

about an episode of *Larry King Live* on television. It was 1997, and his guest was medium James Van Praagh. As Charlene recounted, "I was mesmerized by this guy. He was talking to the air and telling callers about people they knew who passed on. Can you imagine? He was giving them messages from dead people."

Then Charlene exclaimed, "But that's not all. He said something that really freaked me out. He said, 'There's a man here who is playing with the zipper on his jacket. People called him Zip. He passed away three years ago in the hospital from an aneurism in his brain. He was 79 years old. I feel this man is Italian.'"

Charlene was getting excited as she spoke. "None of the callers knew who he was talking about. But I knew who it was. It was my Dad, Zip. They called him that because he was constantly playing with the zipper on his jacket. He did die of a brain aneurism in the hospital." Although Charlene had not phoned into the show, the message must have been for her. It was too bizarre for words.

After seeing James on TV, Charlene was on a mission to speak to him in person. She found out that he was going to be at the Bodhi Tree Bookstore in Los Angeles for a book signing. By then, the Bodhi Tree was a popular hangout for the New Age crowd, thanks to Shirley MacLaine and her autobiographical book *Out On a Limb* about reincarnation, mediumship, and meditation.

Charlene had to tell James that Zip was her father. She bought two copies of *Talking To Heaven* for James to sign—one for her and one for me. She waited in line for two hours until it was her turn. When she told him about the message from Zip, James explained, "Even though I was in the TV studio, Spirit has a way of reaching out to the person who's supposed to receive the message. Your father wanted to let you know he was still around."

It was another sign from the spirit world for me. Needless to say, I inhaled James' book, reading it more than once. Every word resonated in my soul. James described spirit guides and how simple it was to communicate with them. "Ask for them," he wrote. So, every single night before I went to sleep, I found myself asking to see my spirit guides. Even though my days were filled to capacity, I never forgot this important ritual. It was another one of my destiny points that would serve me well later on.

Is That What Happened to My Brain?

As I was inhaling James's book, I began to wonder: *Is the physical brain involved in any type of psychic phenomenon?* I didn't have to wait very long for a response. It just happened that a few months after digesting the book, Mom had a "chance meeting" at a party with a man who would change all of our lives. This was clearly another point of destiny arranged by Spirit.

Dr. Hamlin Emory was a neuropsychiatrist, which is a combination of neurologist and psychiatrist. He was a pioneer and specialist in applying EEG & QEEG (Electroencephalography and Quantum Electroencephalography) in the diagnosis of Neuropsychiatric Disorders. He used medication for brain disorders, not shock treatment, which was the norm at the time.

Mom was fascinated by Dr. Emory's process of diagnosis—it was cutting-edge in the 1990s. Dr. Emory's medical EEG/QEEG research identified diverse brain variations in persons who suffered from persistent mental disorders, substance dependence, and developmental/learning disorders. She wanted

Dr. Emory to do a baseline exam of the brain for each of her family members, including her patients. "Why would I need to do this?" I asked her. But Mom insisted until I agreed. It was a good thing I said yes. My EEG proved to be incredibly helpful.

As I sat in a recliner, approximately 25 electrodes were attached to my scalp with a special paste. I was asked to close my eyes and remain still. It took 45 minutes to complete the procedure. Afterward, I met with Dr. Emory, and he gave me a series of simple verbal tests that were easy for most but were not that easy for me. He read a paragraph and asked me to repeat it word for word. No matter how many times I tried, I couldn't. I was only able to sum up what he said very quickly.

The next test was really challenging. He asked that I start counting from 100 minus 7 all the way down to zero. I just couldn't do it. I managed to get to 93, but after that, my brain just froze. I told Dr. Emory, "I can't do it."

"You have to do it," he persisted.

Finally, I said, "Well, I can't do it your way, but I can do it my way."

He said, "What's your way?"

I answered, "Minus 10, add 3." I then proceeded to count until I reached the end.

Dr. Emory was impressed with my method. After reading my EEG and evaluating the tests, he announced that I had ADD or Attention Deficit Disorder. "I'm amazed at how far you've come. You definitely had to work twice as hard as most people."

I was truly blown away to hear this diagnosis. According to the dictionary, "ADD is a mental condition, beginning in childhood and often persisting into later life, that is characterized by persistent difficulty in maintaining attention and concentration, sometimes with a degree of impulsive or hyperactive behavior."

I had always associated ADD with 10-year-old boys who couldn't sit still. I had no clue that it was something that affected me. Dr. Emory said that my brain was like a computer with bad wiring, which meant I couldn't function in a "normal" way. I finally had proof that I was not "normal!"

Dr. Emory was a godsend and truly helped me to understand myself much better. I learned everything I possibly could about ADD and even ADHD—the H is for hyperactivity. At least I didn't have that. ADHD is a little more complicated and serious. Children with ADHD may have trouble paying attention, controlling impulsive behaviors, or having good judgment. Both ADD and ADHD are not negative behavior disorders or mental illness. They are brain impairments, simply "bad wiring."

To my way of thinking, ADD and ADHD are right-brained dominant as opposed to left-brained dominant. The left brain is verbal, analytical, and orderly, sometimes referred to as the digital brain, while the right brain is more visual and intuitive—sometimes referred to as the holistic brain. This answered so many questions for me. I was a left-brain person but had a strong, intuitive right brain, and it completely made sense with all of the "spiritual" experiences I had throughout my life. I truly believe part of my work in this lifetime is to balance both sides of the brain.

Dr. Emory prescribed medication that helped me to relax and focus. Once I began taking my meds, it was as if someone had turned on the lights in my brain, and I was able to think clearly without strain or anxiety. *So this is what it's like to be normal?* All my life, Mom was trying to guide me in the right direction. She would say, "Now, Kellee, here is the box. Stay in the box." It was her way of saying, "Be normal." But I just couldn't get there because I NEVER SAW THE BOX. This significant discovery has also helped me to identify clients with brain disorders like ADD and ADHD. It's often a relief when people understand that they are wired differently.

End of a Cycle

Work was going well. I was promoted and made more money than ever before. However, the abuse continued at home. I was in an endless cycle of fear, shame, and guilt with little freedom in my own home. I wasn't allowed friends or family to visit, so I became isolated. Very few people knew how bad my life was. Mom knew I was miserable. She never liked Peter, but she felt helpless in her efforts to get me out of the relationship.

I was in a persistent cycle of abuse: tension, incident, reconciliation, and calm, repeating over and over again. It was as if I was in *One Flew Over the Cuckoo's Nest* with Nurse Ratched as my partner. I knew I had to get out, but instead, I buried myself in my work; it was the only place I felt I had any control.

When Anheuser Busch closed down its food division, I was heartbroken. I loved the people and the work I was doing there. The thought of starting over in a new job didn't interest me at all. Besides, I was so emotionally beaten down by then. And to add to my misery, Peter was furious that I lost my job. His fits of rage made it difficult for him to keep a job, and so I became the sole support of the family. Again, I was responsible for everyone and everything, even my abuser.

Luckily, because of my ADD diagnosis and taking medication, the fog finally began to lift, and I started to think more clearly and make better decisions in my personal life. I knew my relationship with Peter was karmic. *Why else would I stay with him?* I didn't know how else to describe it.

I often thought about the incident in the San Francisco parking garage and how I prayed to get help. I knew with the help of my angels and guides, I could break free. After praying to them for several nights, I had a dream. In the dream, I was floating in the Universe and saw a beautiful angel shimmering with gold and white light. I listened as this celestial being explained that my relationship with Peter would soon be over, and my life was about to change. I woke up feeling that, *yes, I can do this!* I found the strength, courage, and the timing to get out. The karmic debt had been paid.

So, one day, when Peter was running an errand, Holiday and I left with only the clothes on our backs. I drove as fast as I could to Mom's house. Peter called many times, but he knew I was never going back to him. Ironically, on some level, he was afraid of my mother and knew once I had escaped, it was the end for us. Holiday was approximately six years old when this relationship began and 15 when we broke free from Peter's control. Nine years! That was some karmic obligation. I was so glad it was over. Both Holiday and I needed time to heal.

I don't know how I had the ability or the energy to fight for my life and also to work as hard as I had been doing. None of it was easy, but I had strong will power and unseen help. By now, I knew that Spirit had a bigger purpose in store for me. All these experiences were leading me to my destiny. I just had no idea what it was... yet.

Chapter 6

SIGNS AND OMENS

Not till we are lost, in other words, not till we have lost the world, do we begin to find ourselves and realize where we are and the infinite extent of our relations.

- Henry D. Thoreau, *On Man & Nature*

Mom was so relieved to "have me back." We talked day and night about my involvement with Peter. She helped me with the shame and self-condemnation that I carried inside for nine years. Needless to say, I had a lot of guilt about staying in that relationship.

"Kellee, I want you to see a therapist. You know I can't be your therapist because I'm your mother, and we're too close for me to be impartial."

She was right. I couldn't get through this immense pain and guilt by myself and knew I would have to see someone who could help me look at my life from an objective point of view. I began seeing a therapist named Susan, who came highly recommended. Susan understood the trauma of abuse. In our sessions, I told her that I felt completely vulnerable and that I was guilt-ridden over my past choices. "Will I pick someone like him again?" Susan quickly and emphatically replied, "No!"

Unfortunately, that was the wrong answer. The correct answer should have been: "Stay by yourself for at least one year and get to know yourself." The truth was I didn't know myself. I had so many misconceptions about who I was and what I was here to do. For one thing, I felt the heaviness of being responsible for everyone. The other thing was I was too empathetic to other people's feelings and had no boundaries. I needed to create boundaries within a relationship but had no clue how to do it. All I wanted was to be rescued.

I asked my ex- Craig if Holiday could stay with him and his wife Cheri for a while so I could take care of my own psychological self. I knew very little about my spiritual self, so I was unable to go that route to resolve my patterns. Craig kindly responded with a yes, and Holiday spent healing time with her father and his family. Craig had remarried years ago and had three wonderful children. I loved them all and was happy Holiday had siblings with whom to hang out. After a few weeks of rest at Mom's, it was time to find a place of our own and begin a new life journey of true freedom. On the bright side, I wasn't out of work long before a large meat company came knocking at my door with a lucrative offer I welcomed with open arms.

One day, when Holiday was visiting her stepmother, Cheri's parents, she happened to mention that there was a place to rent near their house. It was in a great area in Long Beach by the water. I took one look at the townhouse and was immediately taken in by its utter serenity—it was cheerful, bright, and beautiful. I knew it would be a healthy place for us to begin our new life and heal our emotional wounds.

However, because I had internalized the trauma from Holiday's fall and the more recent trauma of an abusive relationship, I still felt disconnected in many respects. I was unfamiliar with the term Post-Traumatic-Stress-Disorder or PTSD, but that was exactly what I had, and because I didn't know that I had PTSD, I couldn't really recover without a lot of help.

The Mayo Clinic describes PTSD as a "mental health condition that's triggered by a terrifying event either experiencing it or witnessing it. Symptoms may include flashbacks, nightmares, and severe anxiety, as well as uncontrollable thoughts about the event. Most people who go through traumatic events may have temporary difficulty adjusting and coping, but with time and good self-care, they usually get better. Getting effective treatment after PTSD symptoms develop can be critical to reduce symptoms and improve function."

So, instead of getting the help I needed, I used work as a coping mechanism whenever my anxiety intensified. I relied on the distractions of work to occupy my negative and misguided thoughts. Although the therapy helped me through the surface issues of the abusive relationship, it didn't go deeply enough, nor was it the type of therapy I needed. Trauma was so entrenched in my body that I couldn't crack through to the core. It was many years later that I found a therapy that profoundly changed my whole sense of it called Somatic Experience Therapy. I will explain more about this type of therapy later on.

Déjà Vu

The year was 1992, and I can't tell how much better Holiday and I felt living by the beach. Soon, I began to feel that life could be a wonderful adventure once again, the way I felt when I went to Paris for the first time. It was my high-powered job that certainly helped me to manage my insecurities. Traveling throughout the world and meeting all sorts of people while designing and creating menus for restaurant chains kept me busy. There was no time or inclination to analyze my feelings of shame, anger, and pain. I just thought those feelings would magically go away if I worked hard enough. To tell you the truth, they just got buried deeper within me. Eventually, I would need a large hoe and a shovel to dig them out.

Quite unexpectedly, however, I became a target of sexual abuse from a few male co-workers. It was something that I had never experienced in my previous employment. Although the fear of losing my job was great, especially because I was a single mother, somehow, I summoned the courage to report it. It was one of the very few times I could say that I finally stood up for myself. The past abusive relationship with Peter had one redeeming benefit—it made me stronger! This time, I won the battle, and to my surprise, the company handled the situation to my benefit. Soon afterward, its male-dominated policy changed. It happened quite unexpectedly and was a pivotal moment. For the first time in a long time, I felt in charge of my life, and it felt good.

But, in spite of my new-found sense of confidence, I repeated the same old pattern of jumping into a relationship before healing the wounds from the previous one. Remember, those wounds were deeply buried, so they were easily disregarded, and just because I wasn't conscious of them, it didn't mean they weren't alive somewhere in me. To add to my folly, my new guy was someone I met at work. I used to warn others, "never get involved at work." So much for heeding my own advice. Tom and I worked together, but not in the same company. He was the head of a large food chain, and I worked for the manufacturer that supplied products to his company. *Why in the world did I think that this time, the relationship would be different?* Unknowingly, I had more to learn and more karma to pay back.

Whatever nagging fears I had, I pushed aside because my fantasy of having the perfect life seemed to be unfolding. An incredibly brilliant and beautiful daughter, a handsome and successful boyfriend, a fabulous career as an executive, money in the bank, a house at the beach, an expensive car, and lots of travel. Dare I say, I was living the dream. Dare I say, it was all a fantasy. Apparently, any thoughts that rained on my parade were ignored—out of sight, out of mind.

I was ready for a new chapter. I've had enough of limitation and control. It was high time Holiday, and I enjoyed the freedom to do whatever we wanted whenever we wanted. And we did! We were like two kids in a candy store. We took lots of trips, partied with friends, and shopped till we dropped. We were finally free to be ourselves, and I loved every moment of our new-found freedom. At long last, I felt like I was the princess in a fairy tale, enchanted by all the trappings that life had to offer.

No matter the encounters I had with angels and spirits, nor the glimpses into an unseen world of unequaled peace and love,

I switched off my inner sight to focus outwardly on the glamor and glitz of the material world. Lacking a spiritual center cost me. Regrettably, I truly had no idea that the life I thought I loved was not what I expected it to be. *Was I that clueless? The answer had to be—Yes.*

Welcome to the Land of Fairies and Gnomes

As Tom and I ramped up our relationship, we planned a three-week European dream vacation together, spending the first week with our business friends, David, Kevin, Steve, and their wives in Ireland, and then traveling the last two weeks by ourselves in France and Italy. It was a romantic trip fit for a princess in a fairy tale.

Early in the morning on July 28, 2000, eight of us embarked on a short flight from county Galway to the Aran Islands in Ireland. The area was completely fogged in, and our tiny prop-engine plane took us over the Galway Bay toward our destination in Inis Mór. It was a white-knuckle ride to an island that time forgot. Known for its dramatic, massive cliffs and 2000 years of Celtic mythology, the island had a strong spiritual presence, and it was evident in the full-time residents, all 900 of them—mostly shop keepers, farmers, and fishermen.

We spent the day exploring sacred places, churches, cemeteries, and even a castle. We walked up to the magnificent Fort of Dun Aonghasa, built over two millennia ago. Afterward, we hovered over the intensely powerful cliffs above the Atlantic Ocean. None of us had ever experienced anything like it before. It was truly a magical, mystical adventure.

After a lovely late pub lunch of lamb stew, we walked a few yards to meet the van driver, who was parked in front of a cemetery. In a heavy Irish brogue, he said, "I have some errands but will be back in a wee bit." Since we had a few minutes to spare, we decided to walk around the ancient cemetery that looked like a set from a movie. Celtic crosses sat atop the gravestones that were spread out on rocks and overgrown grass.

Suddenly, the clouds rolled in, and a few seconds later, it began to pour. We all ran back to the parked van and waited for the driver to return. While standing under a portico next to the van, my eyes caught a glimpse of something down the road that took me by surprise. It was a small man about ten inches high, with a long pointy nose, wearing a red hat and overalls. He darted from behind a rock, stopped, and stared at me. I must have gasped because David, standing next to me, asked, "What KDub? Did you see a little person?" Then everyone began to laugh.

What was it? I wondered. *A fairy? A gnome?* I nervously laughed it off with everyone else. *Oh God, now, I was seeing little people. What else was in store for me?* There was no way I would ever admit it to my colleagues. They'd never let me hear the end of it.

I couldn't let on that. *Yes, I really did see a gnome—pointy nose, overalls, red hat, and all.* The question in my mind was: *Was he a good sign or a bad sign from the Universe?* It was as if I was in the Land of Oz—was he a good witch or a bad witch? Was he a harbinger warning me of the future? What did it mean? And what could I do about it anyway?

Another Foreshadowing

I didn't mention the gnome to Tom. He really would have teased me the entire trip about it, and I wanted to have a romantic time with him. We left our friends behind in Ireland and headed to Paris—my favorite place in the world. We spent a lovey-dovey week strolling along the Seine holding hands, sitting in cafes sipping wine, and visiting castles and museums. It was the perfect holiday for a princess in love with her knight in shining armor.

After a wonderful week in Paris, we flew to Venice. It was a first for both of us. After checking into our beautiful hotel, we headed to the legendary Harry's Bar in St. Mark's Square. They had a strict dress code, and Tom's shorts and sneakers didn't make the cut, nor did my spaghetti-strap sundress, so we were seated outside.

It was 10:30 in the morning, and we began celebrating with the bar's famous Bellini cocktails. We toasted to our new life together and marveled at the incredible beauty around us in the very heart of Venice. Suddenly, and quite shockingly, a pigeon dropped from the sky, landing directly between us, dead as a doornail.

I jumped up from the table and yelled for a waiter. Several men came running out. They all made quite a commotion, "Morte—morte!"

"Yes, I know he's dead," I said. "Surely, with thousands of birds around here, this must happen every day!" Every waiter shook his head, "No. Never see this before."

I didn't believe any of them. This had to happen a lot. But I was wrong. Not one waiter had ever seen a bird drop dead from the sky. I felt a knot in my stomach. *What's going on with me? Why are these things happening? Irish gnomes. Dead pigeons.*

I had no inkling that animals could be some sort of spiritual messengers, but according to Native American and Celtic beliefs, animal totems play huge roles in our lives. I read that they aid in our path of self-discovery. They assist us in the present by showing us our past. If we are attentive, animal totems can reveal glimpses of our future and the lessons we have yet to learn.

So what was the dead pigeon trying to tell me? In the book *Animal Speak*, the author explains that pigeons denote love and the security of home. "Are we falling into old patterns we vowed to remember and change?" *Was I stepping into another landmine with Tom? Was the dead pigeon an omen? Was I lost in a relationship that would disrupt my home life?*

The old fears started to bubble up from the deep where they had been lying low. Somehow, I knew in my heart that this incident had significance, and it had something to do with Tom. I believe it was clearly a foreshadowing of the future and the downfall of our relationship. More wake-up signs in the Universe.

The Day My World Turned Upside Down

Finding answers to all the signs and omens from Spirit seemed a bit daunting, especially as I was a busy executive and a single mom shouldering many responsibilities and obligations. I had been out of the country for five weeks at business meetings— two weeks in Hong Kong followed by three weeks in Europe. To say I was exhausted and strained when I got home was an understatement. I was extremely jet-lagged, and all I wanted to do was to sleep for the next few days.

Nevertheless, I promised my sweet 15-year-old daughter Holiday tickets to see Sting in concert at the Greek Theatre in Los Angeles. She had been looking forward to the concert, and I couldn't disappoint my darling daughter, especially since I had been away from her for so long. The Greek Theatre is an outdoor venue, so my best girlfriend Charlene suggested we make it a picnic. She was bringing the goodies, and I was bringing the tickets, along with Holiday and her friend Sam. It promised to be a fun night, and I only hoped I could stay awake for the next few hours.

It was August 10, 2000, at about 4 PM, when we walked into the parking garage. I noticed it was very dark and assumed the electricity was out or someone had turned off the lights. Remember, I was already tired and disoriented, so the darkness didn't help the situation. As the three of us approached the car, my cell phone rang. It was Charlene checking to see if we had left yet. Not paying attention to what I was doing, I opened the car door, cell phone at my ear, and suddenly, the doorframe smashed into my head with full force.

My knees buckled, and for a moment, everything went black. My head felt on fire, as if blood was swishing around in my brain. I lost my balance and held on to the car door for dear life.

Holiday yelled at me, "Mom, get in the car, or we'll be late."

I yelled back, "I just hit my head on the door. Am I bleeding?"

She answered, "No, there's no blood, but there is a tiny bump."

So, reluctantly, I got into the car, thinking that I'd be okay in a few minutes. But that was a big mistake.

The theatre was over an hour's ride from our beach condo. As I drove, I became confused and lost my bearings. I thought, *Where am I? Am I in the car?* I had no idea how to get to the concert. I tried to get control of myself, but I couldn't keep it together. Instead, I began to scream. Holiday and Sam didn't understand what was happening. "Mom, are you okay. What's the matter?" We were on the freeway driving 60 miles an hour, and I was screaming like a banshee. Both girls were scared to death and did their best to calm me down.

How we got to the concert is anyone's guess, but we did. I was so full of rage that I just kept screaming. It was horrifying. Even Charlene couldn't figure out what was wrong with me. Nobody knew what to do. I felt like my head was on fire, and all I wanted to do was lie down and sleep.

The only memory I have of the concert was yelling at Holiday to drive home. She had just turned 16 and had recently gotten a driver's permit but had never driven on the freeway. At that point, I didn't care. I just wanted the pain in my head to stop. I didn't even ask if they liked the concert. I was totally dazed and confused, and all I could do was shriek, "Get me home." And by the grace of God (and probably a few angels), we arrived home safe and sound.

Towering Rage

For days, my head ached. But it wasn't like a typical headache. Instead, it felt as if my brain was burning. I had no idea that hitting my head could be a serious thing or even deadly. To my way of thinking, a head injury happened during a football game when a player got tackled or in a car accident, not by a car door slamming into you. It never occurred to me that I should see a doctor or go to the ER or that I might have suffered a concussion or maybe a severe head injury.

Since I never went completely unconscious, I figured it couldn't be that bad. It is strange how limited my thinking was back then, and it is hard to believe that I could be so dumb. But remember, I had PTSD that was left untreated. The rage I felt had been buried deep inside me, and I had done nothing to set it free. Besides, all I could think of was all the responsibilities I had at work and at home. Responsibility was at the uppermost level in my mind, especially when it came to taking care of holidays. She always came first, so what was a little bang on the head?

After speaking with Mom the next day, she said, "Kellee, you need to see a doctor or go to the ER and get a scan of your head. You may have a concussion." But I simply ignored her advice.

"If I get worse, I'll see a doctor," was my reply. For whatever reason, I never got myself checked. Again, it was pretty dumb on my part, but I was pretty stubborn back then, so I buried this new trauma deep down along with the rest of the trauma I had been through.

I went to work as if everything was normal. My job entailed a lot of traveling, and I continued at full throttle. But to my bewilderment, everything made me angry. I never had a temper before the accident, so the change in my behavior was noticeable. It became very obvious to all who knew me that my personality had changed. My friends and family thought I was exhausted from all the travel. How they excused my behavior, I'll never know. My co-workers thought my demanding job and difficult clients had finally pushed me over the edge. There were many possible reasons, but no one, **especially me**, ever thought that the bang on my head could cause such intense change and rage.

A few months after my head injury, another milestone occurred in my career. The company I worked for decided to shrink my territory, taking away a huge portion of my business. I thought: *Wait a minute. I'm so dedicated and have worked so hard to sustain this company. Are you taking back what I helped you accomplish?* I'm not sure why it happened or whether my occasional outbursts had anything to do with it, but the decrease in work clearly added to my rage. *Why didn't I see it coming?* So, I decided to file a lawsuit against them.

The head injury had affected me, but I hadn't noticed that my work environment was an indication that something might be wrong with me. So, having to file a lawsuit only added insult to injury. All these events kept piling on top of me, and I was deeply in the dark, or maybe *asleep at the wheel*.

The Same Old Pattern

As the lawsuit dragged on, I sat at home feeling irritable and miserable. After the last nightmare of a relationship, I thought Tom was an amazing guy. He appeared to be my savior and hero—my one and only. He made grand gestures of love and romance, and I fell for every single one over and over again. He would say, Darlin' this and Darlin' that, and I thought *Darlin'* literally meant I was his "darling." Little did I realize that he called every woman Darlin'. It was his way of diminishing the female sex. How precious he was and how foolish I was. Like my previous partner, Tom "love bombed" me, and I couldn't see through the charade.

In time, it became clear that everything revolved around Tom. He was an alcoholic, a selfish narcissist, and had not an ounce of human compassion. Sound familiar? The only thing Tom cared about was Tom. He didn't care about me or what was happening to me. And that angered me even more. When I sacrificed everything, including work and my daughter, to be with him, all was well. The moment I asked for anything or had to change plans, I was in danger of rocking his fragile boat. The rage inside me kept building.

Little did I realize at the time that my relationship with Tom was another karmic one and that we had been together in a previous lifetime. According to the book *Karma and Reincarnation*, "If you make mistakes in a romantic relationship and hurt someone else, you will have to come back in a future life to work things out with that person, usually in a similar romantic situation. Some people feel unlucky in love, and this can most definitely be karmic."

Déjà Vu all over again! Another karmic relationship to work through.

On the outside, I tried to keep it together, but there were times when my anger inappropriately roared its ugly head. I was seething on the inside and couldn't explain it. Everyone chalked up my outbursts to the impending lawsuit. And I went along with their opinions. *Maybe when the lawsuit is over, I'll feel like my old self again.*

One day, as I was sulking, Tom asked if I wanted to escape

for a vacation in Tahiti. It seemed like a wonderful idea—a chance to regroup and recharge. It would be a much-needed change of scenery, even if it included Tom. Maybe it would even help our relationship.

PART 2

THE GREAT AWAKENING

Chapter 7

SPIRIT CONTACT

Every soul has to withstand great pressure and be well-tested.

- White Eagle, *The Quiet Mind*

In July 2001, Tom and I flew to Papeete and from there to the island of Rangiroa. We stayed at a beautiful hotel on a lagoon for a couple nights, and I could feel all the tension slowly leaving my body. I must admit Tom picked the most chill spot for a vacation. The next stop on our Tahitian adventure was a small motu or reef islet called Kia Ora Sauvage. Early in the morning, our boat sailed to what I can only describe as a true island paradise.

As we docked, the French Polynesian host of the tiny motu greeted us. We were amazed at the beauty and serenity of the tiny private island. It was as if we were castaways in a make-believe world—*Gilligan's Island* meets *Fantasy Island*. It was hard for me to curtail my excitement. All my anger and fury vanished into thin air, replaced by a feeling of timeless bliss.

Meeting My Spirit Guides

As the host escorted us to our hut, he explained, "There is no electricity here on the motu. There are only oil lamps to light at night." Then he showed Tom how to use them. As I gazed around the hut, I noticed how rustically simple it was. There was a queen-size bed a bathroom designed with lots of seashells, along with bamboo shutters and grass-covered walls. No phones, no TVs, only a 180-degree view of the most stunning turquoise water that I had ever seen.

Our first day and night were heavenly. Eating fresh fish, swimming in the tranquil sea, and basking in the sun was exactly what I needed. By the second day, I was completely de-stressed, as if I had been on this island paradise my entire life. Occasionally, we would see other couples, as there were only a few huts on the island. Sometimes, in the stillness, we could even hear someone sneeze on the other side of the motu.

After another fabulous candlelit dinner, Tom and I walked around the Motu and stopped directly in front of the most incredible orange-colored full moon. It was so large and so bright that it seemed like it was sitting on the water, and we could reach out and touch it. I certainly felt a million miles away from all my troubles. We had no idea about time, nor did we care. With only the light from the moon to guide us, we carefully walked back to our hut. It didn't take long for us to fall asleep as soon as our heads hit the pillows.

A few hours later, I woke up to go to the bathroom, which was unusual for me. I hardly ever got up in the middle of the night. It was pitch-black, and I had to wake Tom so he could light the kerosene lamp. As soon as I sat up, I saw an Indian man floating about three feet directly in front of me. He reminded me of the Indian psychic I met in New Delhi so many years ago. Even in the blackness, he was clearer than anything else in the hut. He had a white turban atop his large round head and was wearing something like a black-and-white genie outfit. He was beaming with light and radiated pure love.

I started to shout at the top of my lungs, "There's an Indian man here! There's an Indian man here!" My jaw trembled, and my teeth chattered uncontrollably. Tom jumped up and down on the bed, repeating, "No one is here! No one is here!"

But I continued to scream, pointing to the foot of the bed, "He's right there. Can't you see him? It's an Indian man!" After I precariously ventured into the bathroom, I returned to the bed and shut my eyes, but I could still see the Indian floating in my mind. It didn't matter if my eyes were opened or closed. The Indian was still there. After a few minutes, he finally disappeared.

I was about to breathe a sigh of relief when suddenly a Jamaican woman appeared. I began to shout all over again, "Now, it's a Jamaican woman!" Poor Tom. He was jumping up and down, barking, "Kellee, Darlin', no one is here! You must be dreaming."

Like the Indian man, the woman radiated enormous love. She also wore a white turban but was dressed in orange, yellow, gold, and white robes. After about a minute, she, too, disappeared from my inner sight.

At that point, Tom stopped moving and, completely out of the blue, said in a monotone voice, "Those are your spirit guides, darlin'. You were awfully rude. You should apologize."

I lay motionless in bed. *What is he saying? How in the world did he know they were spirit guides? How did he even know what a spirit guide was?* It was too absurd. Was I delirious and hallucinating? Did my head injury cause a brain tumor? I didn't know what to think, and I especially didn't know what to think about Tom. He didn't have a single spiritual thought in his mind, let alone mention something as mysterious and mystical as spirit guides.

Something else was unusual. I was yelling bloody murder, and not one single person came to check on us. If we could hear someone sneeze in a neighboring hut, someone had to hear me screaming at the top of my lungs. The next morning, when we gathered for breakfast with the other couples, I thought for sure someone would say something about my shouting in the middle of the night. But no one on the tiny motu, not even our hosts, mentioned a word. It was definitely strange.

One would think this unusual incident would warrant a discussion between Tom and me. But no. Although I tried to bring up the subject on several occasions, Tom didn't want to talk about it. *Now that's the Tom I know—totally closed off to all things supernatural.* He just said, "Let's move on," as if I was annoying his enjoyment of our trip. And that was that. We never spoke about it again because it was of no interest to Tom. That's when I thought, *This is not someone I could share my life with. He couldn't care less about what was happening to me or how I felt.*

Luckily, I brought a set of watercolor paints with me, not because I was an artist, but because I thought I would use them to capture some of the beauty of our trip. I was glad I did because I painted a picture of my two spirit guides on hotel stationery as a reminder of what I saw on that very special night when they appeared for the first time in our little hut.

As my friend James Van Praagh explains, "Our guides occupy an infinite array of spiritual dimensions and may have never incarnated at all. Whoever they may be, guides have a keen interest in your development as a soul, and they work with you as personal teachers to inspire, influence, motivate, protect, and direct you throughout your lifetime."

Who would've thought that my first glimpse of my spirit guides would be on some remote island in the Pacific? It was sort of magical and wonderful.

As I continued on my journey, I later realized that these two guides had been with me in a variety of lifetimes and would probably be with me in many other lifetimes as well. I was and will always be very thankful for them. I only wish I might have seen them earlier on in my life, but it became obvious that when I was younger, I wasn't in a receptive state for them to make themselves known to me.

Only when I was totally relaxed and at peace as I was on that island were they able to appear. I appreciate the fact that they waited until I was ready. As the ancient saying goes, *When the student is ready, the teacher will appear.*

The Tyranny of Egos

After spending three relaxing weeks in Tahiti, transported to a realm of utter peace and tranquility, I returned home to face a host of business problems and the infuriating lawsuit. Big egos took over my world, and that only fueled my uncontrollable anger even more. It was a struggle to transcend the limitations of the external world thrust upon me after experiencing the profound loving energy of the spirit world.

The lawsuit was set for mediation in mid-October 2001. It was only a month away, but I carried on with my work responsibilities without admitting defeat because I still wanted my territories. I had a business meeting planned for Chicago on September 11. But, suddenly, the night before, as I was packing my bags and checking my itinerary, an inner voice clearly said in my mind: *Don't go. Something is not right.* I thought to myself, *Was it the lawsuit? Am I getting cold feet?* I tried to rationalize the thought, but the inner voice became stronger: *Don't go.* It was extremely intense, but this time, I didn't argue with the advice. I actually heeded the inner foreboding and canceled my trip. I had to make several phone calls to Chicago and felt a little foolish when I didn't have an acceptable excuse for changing my plans. I merely told everyone I couldn't attend because of the pending lawsuit.

Early morning of September 11, 2001, I was still asleep in bed when my friend Charlene called. "Turn on your TV!" She sounded frantic. "Hurry up, Kellee, turn on your TV." I jumped up and grabbed the television remote. *Oh my God, what is happening?* I watched in horror as the planes hit the Twin Towers. I began to cry; I could feel the pain, the horror, and the anguish of these poor people attempting to flee the buildings. Then, instantly, the whole world seemed to go up in smoke! Fear, panic, death, and destruction played out right in front of me.

As an empath, I felt overwhelmed by the devastation of human life. Planes were hijacked, and people were terrorized. As the news continued, I saw that any plane in the air, which would have been the one I was taking to Chicago, had to quickly reroute to the nearest airport. I felt the terror those in the air must have experienced as their plane was sent somewhere else. I closed my eyes and said a prayer. I thanked my angels and guides for giving me their counsel. I was grateful to be on the ground. It was another wake-up call for my soul. I was being given information, and I had to start paying attention to what Spirit wanted me to know.

By the time my lawsuit got underway in mid-October, I felt as emotionally and factually prepared as possible. My legal team and I were ready for mediation. Tom flew in from Denver to be my emotional support. He knew I was extremely nervous and that the company was being unfair and discriminatory towards me.

The mediation turned out to be a mess—cruel and completely partisan. Don't forget, I was a woman working in a male-dominated business, and besides, I didn't stand a chance against the legal machinery of a large corporation. In the end, they offered me a small amount of money to go away, and they bullied me into signing a non-compete agreement stipulating that I could never again be employed in the food business. *Never! What was I going to work at, if not that?* It was the only business I had ever known. Part of my life and career had come to an abrupt end.

That in and of itself was brutal, but what Tom did next was even worse and bordered on surrealism. After the mediation ended, all the parties involved headed to the elevators. There we were, silently standing together, waiting. I said to Tom, "Let them go first, and we'll catch the next elevator."

"Oh, no, Darlin, you don't want to appear weak. Stay tough."

I was starting to feel the rage well up in me. *How could I stand tough when these men totally took away my livelihood?* As we all got on the elevator, I was seething. I wanted to lash out and say something, and just as I was about to, I was interrupted by one of the men turning to Tom and asking, "How about a round of golf next week." And without a moment's hesitation, Tom automatically replied, "Sure, let me know where and when." I might as well have been invisible. It was the good ole boys showing me that everything was "just business."

I felt so betrayed by the man who claimed to love me. His lack of respect and insensitivity struck me to the core; I couldn't believe he had no regard for my feelings, especially after the drubbing I just went through. Tom was all lip service—he had no intention of really supporting me. He just kept repeating, "Darlin', you'll get another job."

The Love of Jesus

For days after the mediation, I was down in the dumps. I couldn't get myself out of bed. It was a painful pill to swallow. I had no job, no career, and nothing I could do. I didn't have the wherewithal to think it was the work of Spirit guiding me to travel another road. If I had known that then, I would have probably said, *No, thank you. I like the road I'm on. I can find a new job in another company.* But who was I kidding? I hadn't a clue what else I was capable of doing.

At first, I was full of rage. All the abuse I had suffered over the years was churning inside me. As time went on, my anger turned inward, and I grew more and more depressed. Days turned into nights, and nights into days. After a while, I had no idea what day it was or what time it was, nor did I care. I barely had enough strength to get up to eat. Besides, I didn't have much of an appetite. I was truly in the land of lost souls. My only escape was in bed with the covers pulled over me.

Everyone, even Mom, thought I was suffering from the strain of the lawsuit. I thought so, too, but there was something else going on because I simply couldn't shake off feelings of desolation and despair. I didn't realize it, but I was clinically depressed.

I was at another crossroads; I didn't know what to do anymore. I was so far into the weeds that I didn't understand what anything was for and what life even meant. *What kind of job could I get?* I kept looking for my answers in the outside world. All the while, Spirit was urging me to go within and seek the truth.

Early one morning—not quite dawn, I opened my eyes and saw the outline of a man floating above the bed. He had long dark hair, bright eyes, and the most radiant smile. I felt a tremendous amount of love emanating from him. This time, I wasn't shocked, nor did I scream like I had in Tahiti when I first saw my spirit guides. I somehow knew this presence was here to help me and that he had the answers to all my questions. This holy figure hovered at the foot of my bed, smiling at me, and instantly, I felt peaceful, even blissful.

Although I was sort of in and out of my body, I knew I wasn't dreaming—I was wide-awake. My curiosity kicked in. *Who are you? Why are you here?* He reached over to me and held a small jar to my nose. I leaned down to smell whatever was in the jar, but the scent was unfamiliar. "Please, do it again," I said. He smiled and moved the jar closer. This time, I took in a breath and recognized the aroma. It was frankincense—it had a woodsy yet sweet bouquet. One whiff, and within seconds, I fell back on my pillow and was sound asleep.

Because I had no religious upbringing, I never looked at myself as a spiritual being or was very interested in spirituality because I thought it had to do with religion. Even though there were signs from Spirit, having faith in the unseen didn't come easily to me. But I knew with all my heart that this transcendent presence had to be Jesus, and I also knew that he was there to help me. *But why me?*

I took everything in life at face value, so to me, Jesus was a myth—a good man who did miracles. *Had such a person ever really lived on earth?* But after this experience, I can tell you without a doubt that there is a Jesus, and he is real. As Joel Goldsmith once said, "Jesus who left this experience in full illumination still exists and lives. He does not live in any place. He lives in, and as consciousness, and since consciousness is infinite, he lives and exists in your consciousness and in mine." I can say, in all honesty, that Jesus entered my mind and heart that fateful morning, and from that moment on, I knew my healing was about to begin in earnest.

The Hand of God

Although the visit from Jesus comforted me, I continued to sleep most of the time. *Could I still be upset about the lawsuit, or was something actually wrong with me?* Around 9:30 AM, I was awakened from a sound sleep by a very loud voice in my mind practically shouting, "Get up, Kellee. You have a serious brain injury. Get up and call Dr. Emory right now. He will see you today."

My neurologist, Dr. Emory, was the one who years ago administered EEGs to my entire family and diagnosed my ADD. He was extremely busy, traveling, lecturing, and seeing patients. It was almost impossible to get an appointment with him on such short notice. I knew that it would take at least a month to get one.

I answered the voice out loud, "You're kidding, right? I'll never get in to see Dr. Emory today. He's a busy guy."

Suddenly, I felt something like a hand under my rear end propel me from a prone position to a sitting one, leaving me with my feet dangling over the side of the bed. The voice grew stronger and demanded, "Call Dr. Emory now! He will see you today."

"Okay," I responded. "I'll call him, but I won't get in today. You'll see."

The voice didn't sound like a Spirit Guide, nor Jesus, nor an angel. To this day, I could swear it was the voice of God. It was so commanding. I have never heard it again since then.

I hopped out of bed, picked up my phone, and dialed Dr. Emory's office, knowing full well there was no way I could see him. *Only God could get me in to see Dr. Emory*, I thought.

His assistant answered the phone. "Jan, this is Kellee White. I hit my head, and I need to see Dr. Emory today."

Jan answered, "Well, I'm sorry to hear that, but we don't have any time today. The soonest availability is in two weeks. Do you want me to schedule an EEG and a visit with Dr. Emory? It's the earliest I have."

I wanted to say, "But God told me to call Dr. Emory and see

113

him today," but I knew that probably wasn't going to fly. I didn't want to sound like a complete nut job. Instead, I pleaded, "I'm having a lot of problems. I really need to see him today."

She repeated, "I understand Kellee, but he's booked. Let me set up an appointment in two weeks."

I persisted. "Look, I know it sounds crazy, but he'll have a cancellation today. And when he does, please call my cell. I live two hours away, so please let me know as soon as possible."

She wasn't fazed. "Yes, but he'll not have a cancellation today. He never does."

"I just have a hunch. Please call me when he does," I said and hung up the phone.

I began to get back into bed, thinking, *She's not going to call,* when the voice once again instructed, "Get up! Take a shower, get dressed, and drive to Dr. Emory's office right now!"

I jumped. "Okay, okay, I'll go." I had been in bed so long that getting washed and dressed felt insurmountable. But I made the effort to get out of bed, get showered, and wash my hair. I had something to eat to get my blood sugar up. By noon, I left the house, stopping for gas, and began the 65-mile drive to Dr. Emory's office (in LA traffic, which equals at least a two-hour drive).

At five to two, as I was exiting the freeway for the doctor's office, my cell phone pinged. It was Jan. "I just had a last-minute cancellation. Can you be here in five minutes?"

"Yes!" I shrieked into the phone. "I'm right around the corner. I'll be right there."

If I had waited at home for the office to call, I would never

114

have made it there on time. God, indeed, works in mysterious ways.

Because my mom had insisted three years earlier that I have a baseline picture of my brain, Dr. Emory was able to compare my brain from before the bang on my head to my new EEG. He was shocked to see the difference. He immediately picked up the phone and called Mom.

"Kellee has to get to UCLA as soon as possible," Dr. Emory insisted. "She has had a traumatic brain injury, and it looks like her brain has had significant hemorrhaging. She may need surgery."

A week later, I had an appointment to see a traumatic brain specialist at UCLA. Spirit was on a roll to get me moving onto the right road. To say there was a lot going on behind the scenes of my physical life would be an understatement. Strange and unexpected events began to happen continually. I was now in my mid-forties, and there was no time to lose. I had to wake up and carry out my contract with Spirit. It's what I came to Earth to do.

I See Dead People

While waiting to see the neurosurgeon, every day became more and more of a struggle. My house became difficult to navigate. I had four flights of stairs in my condo. FOUR! The bedroom was on the bottom floor, and my kitchen was upstairs. If I wanted anything from the kitchen, I had to walk upstairs, and it was becoming tougher for me to do. My balance was completely off, and I would often fall. It got to the point that getting up the stairs was so strenuous that I just sat at the bottom and watched my beloved cat, Phil, race to the top on all fours, daring me to follow. One day, I decided to follow his example and crawled on all fours up to the kitchen. It was the easiest way to keep my balance.

Like any cat, Phil had a distinctive personality. He would make a game of racing up the stairs and staring at me from the top. As he waited, he would wash his fur as if to infer, *Poor girl, you're so slow*. By mid-week, I got the hang of crawling up the stairs on all fours. Phil was already waiting at the top, but this time, he was frozen in place, staring at a corner below me.

"What are you looking at, you silly cat?" I said as I turned to see what he was staring at.

I gasped. There, at the bottom, was a shadowy man huddled in the corner. His face was bright red, and he smelled like a brewery. He seemed to be shaking in fright. I knew he was an apparition because I could see right through him. He scared me so much that I basically raced up the stairs.

When I looked back down, I saw that the spirit was still there. *What in the world is he doing here?* I wondered. *This is a fairly new home, not an old one like the one in Toluca Lake. Why is there a ghost?* Then I remembered what my mother said years ago when I saw similar apparitions: "Just tell them to go to the light, Kellee, and they'll leave."

At the time, I had no idea what she meant, but I heard myself say out loud, "Go into the light." I repeated it over and over. And, suddenly, I knew everything about the man. His name was John. He was an alcoholic. He was abandoned by his parents when he was young, and he grew up to be a bully. Next to him was a light-filled opening, like a portal, and his grandmother stood there waiting for him.

"Your grandmother is here. Don't be scared. She's here to help you." I told him. "Go to her in the light."

"I'm afraid. I want to stay here," I heard him answer in my mind.

I didn't know what to do, and then, just like that, he disappeared. I didn't see him again, so I assumed he went into the light with his grandmother.

By then, my cat Phil was long gone—the proverbial scaredy-cat.

I chose not to tell Holiday about this disturbance because I knew it would upset her. Plus, I thought that this incident was a onetime occurrence, but I was wrong.

Later that night, I sat on the balcony overlooking the marina and thought about the man in the corner. *Why did he, of all people, show up in my townhouse?* Suddenly, the Indian psychic who read my thumb in Delhi came to mind, and I recalled his telling me about being a psychic and that I may or may not choose to use this gift in this lifetime. Seeing the spirit made me think. *Was I supposed to use this gift now? Was I supposed to tell him to go into the light?* I said out loud to Spirit. "What are you doing to me? Do you want me to be a psychic?"

I thought I was alone, but I looked over at the next balcony, and there stood an elegantly-dressed woman, perhaps in her early eighties, and she was smoking. She waved, and I waved back. I was a little embarrassed by my outburst, but she didn't say a word. I stood on my balcony hundreds of times and had never seen her before. I wondered if m*aybe she just moved in.*

117

Every evening for the next week, I went out on my balcony, and there she was—the elderly woman standing and smoking. She always waved to me, and I always waved back. She was always beautifully dressed in those expensive St. John suits.

The following Sunday afternoon, my sister Carol came to visit. Carol was in the mortgage business and noticed a "For Sale" sign in the complex. "Let's take a look," she prompted. The townhouse for sale was in the building next to mine, so we walked over. When we entered the condo foyer, I noticed that the place was completely empty. "I guess the owners already moved out," I said to Carol. I walked out to the balcony to see the view and recognized it as the same balcony where the elegantly-dressed woman stood and smoked every night.

I looked for the sellers' agent. "Did an elderly woman live here? I used to wave to her every night from my balcony," I asked.

"Yes, that was my mother," he said. "She died several months ago."

Months? I caught my breath in surprise. Then, I noticed a rack of beautiful knits being wheeled out of the room. "Did your mother wear St. John suits?"

He said, "Oh, my mother was a very classy dresser. She loved clothes and was forever shopping in Beverly Hills."

"I know this sounds strange, but did your mother ever smoke?"

"Smoked all her life. Unfortunately, she died of lung cancer." Then he showed me her picture. I was bowled over. It was my nightly companion.

That evening, instead of wondering about my future, I actually spent time thinking that Spirit was definitely trying to communicate something important. *Was the Indian psychic right about the Akashic Records? Was I really a psychic who was supposed to help people? Was I a medium who could see the dead? Was Jesus trying to get me to wake up to my true calling? Was Spirit showing me what to do with my life?* Talk about arriving late to the party.

Deadly Serious

On Monday, November 19, 2001, I met with Dr. V., the brain expert at UCLA. He was short, dark-haired, in his mid-thirties, and deadly serious. He asked a litany of questions like, "Explain how you hit your head? What were you like before you hit your head? How are you different now?"

I answered everything very carefully, beginning with the time the car door slammed into me and knocked me for a loop.

"Do you have or have you had any hallucinations?"

I quickly responded, "No!" *How could I explain what I was seeing?* Nor did I dare tell him that his grandmother was right there standing over his shoulder, saying she paid for his medical school education. I could imagine two large men in white coats carrying me out the door and into a van, and off we'd go to the looney bin.

Dr. V. agreed with Dr. Emory that I required further brain imaging. He scheduled an MRI, a Doppler Brain Scan, and other lab work. I spent several weeks at UCLA taking tests, and the results were disturbing, to say the least. They showed a subdural hematoma, which is blood slowly leaking through layers of the brain, causing pressure in the brain and damage to brain tissue.

119

Along with that, there was a 5mm puncture in my frontal lobe that was of uncertain significance. I was flabbergasted at the diagnosis. All this time, my brain was slowly bleeding from some unknown puncture wound. No wonder my behavior was strange. It wasn't a mere bang on the head; what I had was life-threatening!

Instead of having surgery to stop the slow leaking, I opted for medication as a treatment plan, hoping that the medication would also control my erratic behavior. My episodes were extremely persistent, first spiraling downward into depression and, without warning, suddenly becoming full-blown mania. I was filled with rage and would rant and rave for no apparent reason. Moreover, I had absolutely no control over these fits. It was as if energy was expanding and contracting in and out of my body. I was definitely in uncharted territory.

A Series of Strange Occurrences

After all the tests were done, Holiday invited her best friend Shannon for lunch. They were eating in the dining area that overlooked the ocean. I walked, grumbling about something that upset me when suddenly, the forks on the table floated up and began flying across the room. The poor teenage girls had no idea what was happening. They jumped up from their seats and started screaming. Stunned by the sight of flying forks, I screamed along with them.

Unfortunately, it did not stop there. At the very same time, the refrigerator door opened, and a large mayonnaise jar on the top shelf flew out, hovered in the air for a few seconds, then crashed onto the tile floor. Glass and mayonnaise splattered everywhere.

Again, we all screamed. It was like living in the movie *Poltergeist*.

I soon realized that my emotionally-disturbed energy was the root cause and could trigger such bizarre happenings. Like my grandfather, the physical medium, I could make objects shake and dance as well. Only I didn't know how to control it like he did. It was unnerving to see the silverware drawers open and shut by themselves and forks and spoons flying around the room. *Thank goodness the knives stayed in the drawer.*

If that wasn't freaky enough, there was another problem. Every morning, seagulls crashed into the living room's huge glass windows. The banging birds shook the entire house, almost like tiny earthquakes. Eventually, a few of the windows cracked from the constant barrage. Glad to say the birds managed to stay intact. I have to say I wasn't sure how this happened or what my energy was doing to cause it.

For some odd or not-so-odd reason, I could handle all of these crazy, surreal phenomena, but it was extremely difficult on holiday. She wanted her home and mother to be normal like the rest of her friends, but I wasn't a normal mother. Later, when Holiday was a grown woman, everything came to light, and we both understood, but I couldn't explain it at this juncture.

To add to all the strangeness, and completely out of the blue, I found myself going into yoga positions and stretches. It was odd because I knew nothing about yoga, nor did I ever practice it. But I couldn't stop myself. When I went into a position, I could feel the energy surge up and down my body.

With each position came a vision of a past life situation. For instance, I remember being a 14-year-old boy on an island in the

Pacific. A volcano erupted, and I ran to the village to warn everyone. Then I ran into the ocean and drowned. This could explain why I love being by the ocean but am afraid of being in the water.

Another very clear past life was as a strong and brave 30-something male Native warrior. The tribe was somewhere in the Great Plains. I was on horseback alongside two other warriors, keeping watch over our territory. I recognized the two men with me as my two siblings, Danny and Carol. We were trying to keep peace among white people and neighboring tribes. Out of nowhere, the three of us were ambushed. I was shot in the back by an arrow, fell off my horse, and died. The other warrior was also hit by an arrow and died. The third fellow managed to get away. The white people responsible for the attack were, sadly but not surprisingly, the people I worked with in the food business, including my boyfriend, Tom. This vision gave me a new perspective on the people in my present environment, and many of my life events were really starting to come into focus.

Besides the physical manifestations of a brain injury, there was something happening on a deeper level. Because I was very clearly seeing and hearing spirits and recalling past-life attachments, it seemed as if the head injury had unlocked a door to a profound spiritual plane of existence. I didn't understand it, but my vibration was moving from a lower frequency to a higher energetic frequency.

Falling Down the Rabbit Hole

At a certain point, my balance was totally off, and I had

difficulty speaking, hearing, and seeing. Memories of my teen years to the age of 40 just disappeared. The only solution was to take my medication and get plenty of bedrest.

After a few days of medication, I would feel better, so I would skip the next doses. Subsequently, my short-sightedness created a hellish nightmare of hypomania and insomnia, and I began writing and writing for days without end. If anyone tried to help me, I would ignore them. No one could stop my manic episodes. I was having a Bipolar episode caused by the head trauma, but I wasn't aware of it... yet.

Bipolar disorder is sometimes called manic-depression. People who have it may spend weeks feeling like they're on top of the world before crashing into a deep depression. The length of each high and low varies. When a person is manic, they think they can do anything. It's hard for them to sit still. Their thoughts race, and they don't sleep. Usually, it leads to reckless behavior. Add that to my ADD, and I become Dr. Jekyll and Ms. Hyde.

The following Mother's Day after my diagnosis, everyone was at Mom's to celebrate. Even Tom flew in from Denver to be with us. Because of the yet unknown and undiagnosed Bipolar One situation, I began to feel invincible and went into full-blown mania. I drank a full bottle of champagne, followed by vodka shots. My sister-in-law Josie tried to calm me down while my sister Carol furiously shouted, "Stop it, Kellee, or we'll put you away."

In my manic state, I wrote a Mother's Day play about God with parts for everyone. Then I insisted everyone read their parts. It's embarrassing to look back at all my erratic behavior. At the end of the day, everyone left the party, and although I had too much to drink, I drove Tom to the airport. He couldn't wait to leave.

On my way home, I stopped to get gas. Holiday was asleep in the back seat. Suddenly, I heard a voice in my head telling me to take the pump, pour gas over my head, and light myself on fire. I was ready to do it, but when I saw my daughter sleeping peacefully in the car, I stopped myself. One look and my love for her broke my maniacal trance. I went home immediately and took my medication. My spirit guides were obviously working overtime to keep me safe.

Early the next morning, I called Mom. "I'm hearing voices and thinking of killing myself. Am I schizophrenic?"

She replied, "Kellee, come over to my office right now."

I couldn't get there fast enough.

Mom said nothing to me about my behavior at her house. Apparently, she and Marc talked about it all night, trying to process my unrestrained performance. Mom recognized that something was tremendously off with me, yet at the same time, she was overwhelmed to see me in such a condition. Sometime later, she admitted to me, "Kellee, you scared me to death; I was terribly shaken. I really thought the brain injury had caused you irreversible harm."

I arrived at Mom's office. We sat on the couch together. She had been formulating a plan to help me. She was totally calm and composed. She couldn't let her feelings show, or I probably would have had one of my panic attacks.

"Kellee, you're having manic episodes, but it's not as bad as you think. It has to do with your brain injury. You have to take your medication every day, even on the days you feel okay. It's the only way you can get through these disturbances."

I knew she was out of her mind with worry, but she put on a good face to keep me balanced and grounded. She was like that with all her patients. If someone was having a mental breakdown, even if it was difficult to observe, she remained objective. But when it came to me, it was hard to be objective because it was so very personal and extremely disheartening.

After these horrific bouts of mania, I never missed taking my medication again. Anger came up occasionally, but it usually involved Tom.

Although Tom and I lived in different cities, we took turns flying back and forth, me from Los Angeles and Tom from Denver. My anger toward him was palpable, and yet I kept the relationship going. Why? I think it was because I had lost so much independence, and somewhere in the back of my mind, I still naively believed he could help me. After all, I lived in the fantasy that he was supposed to rescue me. At this point in time, after losing my job, my career, and, to some extent, my mind, losing Tom would have been too traumatic. In reality, all I could think was that we hadn't finished our karmic commitment, and so our relationship dragged on.

Chapter 8

AKASHIC RECORDS

And I have felt a presence that disturbs me with the joy of elevated thoughts, a sense sublime of something far more deeply interfused, whose dwelling is the light of setting suns, and the round oceans and the living air, and the blue sky, and in the mind of man; a motion and a spirit, that impels all thinking things, all objects of all thought, and rolls through all things.

— William Wordsworth

Being on medication was actually a Godsend. I became more clear-headed and lucid, much like the dream state I experienced at night. Before too long, I started to have more and more lucid dreams. A lucid dream is a type of dream in which a person is aware that she is dreaming while in the dream state. Each night, I became more conscious of my lucid dreams. It also seemed possible to be in control of what I was dreaming.

Night after night, I traveled to a great library in my dreams. I recall visiting what appeared to be massive buildings of learning and creativity. I didn't realize it back then, but I was actually visiting the Hall of Akashic Records. The first time I heard the term Akashic Records was in India. After my encounter with the Indian psychic, I learned about the Akashic Records. It is a compendium of all universal events, thoughts, words, emotions, and intent ever to have occurred in a soul's past, present, and future existences. It must be the biggest storeroom in the Universe.

During my dreams, I remember my two spirit guides from Tahiti walking alongside me and ushering me through a secret door into this enormous library. To be allowed into such a hallowed place was, to say at the very least, quite special. I was directed to bookshelves that housed various scrolls. I was able to read these scrolls and information about people I would meet in the future. It was extraordinary to gather such details that one day would be helpful to people with whom I would come into contact. I also studied the past lives of people I had never met before. All this knowledge expanded my perceptions of the world in which I lived and the worlds beyond.

When I was on the other side, I felt I was in my true home. It was comforting and peaceful—nothing like my life in the physical world. I also loved the fact that I could relax and learn at my own pace and that much of what I studied had to do mostly with karma and destiny. While in the dream state, the light beings from the other side were helping to lift my vibration to higher levels, not only to purify and heal myself but to heal others in my sphere as well. After all, my major lesson in this current lifetime was to learn about all aspects of responsibility.

Then, one night, as I traveled my usual way to the secret

entrance of the great library, I was taken aback to find that the door was not there. I was locked out of the great hall. A voice whispered, "You have all the information you need for the time being. When you need more, you will be given entry to the library once again."

I cannot begin to describe the sheer sadness I felt; I cried for a week, feeling alone and confused again. It was as if a veil dropped over my mind, and everything became fuzzy. I was desperately trying to understand what was happening to me, but my mind persisted in fearful thoughts. However, I did know something big was happening to change my life from the mundane to the spiritual. I just needed to remember to take it step by step and be patient as I continued on my path.

Grasping At Straws

By now, I assumed that Tom wanted to get away from me as often as he could because he had begun to travel out of town frequently. It was obvious that he could see that I was inherently changing, and he didn't like the person I was becoming. Because my mind was still gripped by doubt and fear, I felt I had no control over any of the changes in my life. All I wanted was Tom's acceptance. His abandonment felt like another loss, and I couldn't bear any more loss in my life. I had always focused on material security and stability, not the unknown and mystical, which always seemed to be unreal. If I could have prevented my spiritual awakening at that time, I probably would have. I really desired to have my old life back, but I knew in my heart it was gone and gone forever.

As I changed from Tom's business peer and partner to someone he didn't recognize, both of us realized that we had very little left in common. He was too self-involved, and his ego didn't allow for a relationship that had anything to do with my sudden spiritual growth. Even though I had a loving family, without a man, I began to feel very alone—living in complete solitude. It would take me many, many years to figure out why a MAN played such an important role in my life—if I was ever to find out at all.

Depending on my mental state and physical disabilities, I found it increasingly difficult to travel. However, Tom insisted on my flying to Denver so we could "Get back to normal." I went along because he paid for my trips—I still couldn't say "no." Tom had little compassion or tolerance for me. He kept telling me that I was going through a phase, and soon I would get back to "normal." There's that word again. "Kellee, just look for a job. Your life will get back to normal if you could just get a job."

In my warped mind, I agreed with him. *He's right. I just need a job to be normal again.* But I cringed in horror every single time I heard the word "normal." *What is normal anymore? I was never normal. I will never be normal!*

Because the food business was all I knew, I didn't have the capacity to give my all and look for a job in another area of business. Besides dealing with my ongoing physical imbalance, limited sight, impaired hearing, and long stretches of sleep, I knew that I wouldn't be able to work the way I once had. There was no way I could return to corporate life, work long hours, travel, and, most of all, pretend to be someone I wasn't—normal.

It was my ego that was so embarrassed and ashamed by

what had happened to me, and I hadn't yet made the break with my ego. That was the hardest part of all. I was so tied into how my job defined me. I felt a deep sadness at losing my old way of life. The mental anguish and pain were constant and consuming. My heart was aching to be the person I used to be. How could I explain my feelings to anyone, even my mother? Instead, I decided to grieve alone. No one could begin to understand the magnitude of the loss I felt. It was the death of the old Kellee, and I felt like I was in a bottomless pit.   I begged the Spirit to let me see some kind of insight into my future.

A Glimmer of Hope

Finally, the Universe answered my prayer. Early one morning, while I was still in bed, and the sun was just peeking through the window shades, I felt immense energy radiating around the room. Still not fully awake, I opened my eyes, and at the foot of the bed stood someone that I could only describe as a very large angel with wings and all. He had long dark hair and was surrounded by a cobalt blue light. Immense love and peace emanated from this light being.

"I am Michael, and I am here to help you," I heard him say in my mind. "There are many changes coming to your life. You will get through them all."

He explained that I was a Light Worker and that he would guide me through the changes. "There is a new era on Earth, and you will be a part of it." He said that I would help to bring Heaven to Earth. That was my mission and my RESPONSIBILITY in this lifetime.

"There will be other Messengers that will be by your side to help. Don't be afraid." Michael assured me that I would be okay. He looked and felt so familiar that I had no fear, only peace of mind. A mental and physical calm came over me.

He went on to say, "I will see you in your dreams and bring messages to keep you strong. Don't lose hope. You are never alone." Little did I know that Archangel Michael would be my savior and had been my savior so many times before.

But it was puzzling. *Why are all these religious symbols showing up in my life?* No one in my family every talked about God or celestial beings. My father was a musical pragmatist, and my mother was a scientist and humanist at heart. The only time I had an inkling of the supernatural was the time I spent at the farm with my grandfather. But, I believed the angel who appeared was Michael, although I cannot begin to explain why I believed it. I can only guess that my grandfather had his hand in my spiritual awakening.

Because of this celestial visit, I finally began to "see the light" at the end of the tunnel. There was a road ahead for me, and it had a powerful purpose. I did have a mission, although I didn't know how, what, or when it would all play out. At that moment, I felt huge relief and comfort by Michael's message.

The thoughts that followed: *How would I explain all of this to Tom, and did I want to?* After all, we had reached a fork in the road, and I was going one way, and he was heading in another direction. I knew our life together had no legs, but not how and when it would end.

Looking at this relationship in hindsight, I realize that psychics may see the future for others but not very well for themselves. Even though we may see visions and predict outcomes for clients, the same doesn't apply to our personal lives. I can only surmise that as we learn through our experiences, we get better at helping others learn from theirs and, in turn, get better at helping ourselves.

A Message from Joe

Even with Michael's message, my ego had a strong hold on me, and feelings of insecurity and doubt kept creeping back into my mind. *How could I be with people and act as if nothing was wrong with me?* It seemed every time I went somewhere, something bad happened. Besides, I was still having so many physical problems.

My dear friend Laury often asked me to dinner, and I always declined. Finally, I gave in and agreed to meet her and her friends for dinner. The restaurant was close to my house, so I knew that I could make a quick escape if I got overwhelmed, which often happened.

Laury was so happy when I arrived. It was a beautifully warm night, and we all sat outside on the patio. Her friends were nice and friendly to me, and everyone seemed to be having a pleasant evening.

I began chatting with Pam, a middle-aged woman next to me. It was a normal conversation, nothing deep, just small talk about her latest travel adventure. Then, as I dreaded, something spontaneously occurred that I couldn't control. The cheery mood was broken as I looked up and saw a man with dark curly hair floating three feet above Pam's head. He sat in a lotus position and began telepathically talking to me. "My name is Joe. I'm her brother."

I really didn't want to say anything. Nor did I want to cause trouble for my dear friend Laury and the entire dinner party. But the spirit wouldn't leave me alone, so I knew I had to convey Joe's message to this woman, even though it might upset her. In the softest voice, I said, "I'm so sorry if this scares you, but for some reason, I seem to have this gift of seeing dead people, and there's a man floating above your head who says he's your brother Joe."

Pam's eyes widened, and her mouth fell open. I continued speaking to her. "Your brother looks like the singer Jim Croce with dark curly hair. He says you were young when he died, and your family couldn't get over the shock of his untimely death. He's saying he was speeding on his bike, hit a bump in the road, fell off, and hit his head on the concrete. He said it was quick and painless. He wants you to know that he watches over you, your sister, and your mom, and he's with your father."

Although shocked, Pam handled the information better than I expected. She said, "I was 10 years old when my brother Joe died. No one knew exactly how it happened, but we were told that he had a severe head injury that caused his death." Even though she appeared to be somewhat skeptical, she thanked me for giving her the information.

The rest of the dinner party stopped talking and looked at the two of us, wondering what was going on. One person in particular, Steve, asked, "What are you two whispering about?" Pam explained what I just said to her. I could see the annoyed look on Steve's face. "Why don't you mind your own business," he rudely replied. I could feel the energy in my body start to vibrate, and I knew I had to hightail it out of there before anything weird happened. Besides, there was no way to explain something I didn't understand myself, so I felt it best to leave.

"I'm sorry," I said to Laury as I got up from the table.

"Don't worry. They'll get over it," she answered. Laury was good at not making me feel bad.

Some people have an extreme dislike for anything spiritual. That was my take on Steve. So, after that night, again, I felt extremely vulnerable and slowly began to withdraw from society. I never knew what I might see, what I might say, or what might happen. I thought everybody would want to know that their loved ones were watching over them, but I was wrong. People were terrified of death, or maybe they thought people like me were fakes and seeing spirits was plain nonsense. I decided it was better to stay inside rather than venture out and be subjected to ridicule and hostility.

A Son Bringing Comfort to His Mother

Two years before the incident with Laury and her friends in the restaurant occurred, the movie *The Sixth Sense* was released. It was so popular that communicating with the dead piqued public interest. Mediums like James Van Praagh had already written several books about his contact with spirits. In 1995, he was a frequent guest on the short-lived TV series *The Other Side*. In 2002, his TV show *Beyond*, in which he connected with spirits for audience members, first aired. Another popular medium, John

135

Edwards, had a similar TV show called *Crossing Over*, and psychic/medium Sylvia Browne was a regular guest on The Montel Williams Show.

Although people were becoming familiar with spirits and "ghost" stories, I was still unsure about my ability to communicate with them. This kind of thing was new and very strange, and it wasn't easy to think I could do it with any accuracy. Because I was so hesitant, Spirit sent me another opportunity to test my skills.

One Sunday, Holiday's best friend Shannon asked if I would go with her to the Laguna Arts Fair. I have always adored Shannon because she was someone who seemed to understand, or at the very least, did not judge me or the strange occurrences in my home. It was the middle of summer and a perfect day for a slow stroll along the Pacific Ocean.

As we stopped at each artist's booth to admire the paintings and sculptures, I was drawn to one artist's colorful ceramic vases. It's almost as if I was pushed into that particular stall. The pieces were visually stunning, with vibrant turquoise blues and bright yellows. An older woman in her sixties sat behind the counter, quietly reading a book. She was so engrossed in her book she didn't notice Shannon or me standing there.

Suddenly, directly behind this woman, a tanned young man in spirit appeared. He was in his early twenties with light brown hair. He seemed to be rubbing the woman's shoulders in the most loving way. He glanced at me, and I could see his beautiful green eyes. That's when he sent me a telepathic message.

"I'm John, and this is my mother." He continued, "She has never recovered from my death, and now she has breast cancer."

I asked, "How did you die?"

"I was surfing over at Victoria Beach, and an enormous wave took me under. I never came back up." Then he showed me what had happened and, unfortunately, revealed his bloated body, which was something I wished I hadn't seen.

I whispered to Shannon that I was seeing a young man standing behind the woman. She looked but did not see anyone. *Oh, Shannon, of course, you can't see him. He's a spirit. I'm the lucky one who can see him. Ha.Ha.* I could tell from Shannon's expression not to say anything: *Don't go there, Kellee. Let the woman be.*

But I couldn't hold myself back. He was right in front of me, and he wanted his mother to know how he died since his body was never recovered. I could feel the enormous grief she carried inside her, and add to that, she had cancer to boot. I wanted to comfort her in some way.

John pleaded with me. "Please, she needs to know that I'm okay. Tell her I'm always nearby. I'm not gone."

I walked over to the woman behind the counter. I felt nervous and self-conscious and didn't want to disturb her, but I knew I had to take a chance. It might be the only time this soul could get a message to his mother.

I broke her concentration by asking her about some of the vases. "They're quite beautiful. Are they yours?"

She closed her book and looked up at me. "I'm not the artist. They're my son's. He created all these incredible pieces."

I couldn't help myself, so I blurted out, "Your son John is standing right behind you, rubbing your shoulders. He said you've been undergoing treatment for breast cancer, and you're in a lot of pain in your neck and shoulders. He said he used to rub your shoulders when he was alive. He's deeply sorry that he left you so suddenly. He was surfing early in the morning and was hit by an enormous wave knocked off his surfboard, and drowned. John says he's so sorry for putting you through this torment. He insists I tell you that he's okay now. He's been with his Grandpa Bill."

I took a deep breath and waited for her reply.

The woman stared at me in utter shock as if the wind had knocked her out of her. She could barely get the words out. "How could you possibly know this?" she asked.

With nothing to lose, I felt I needed to be honest and tell her about myself. Without skipping a beat, I told her about my traumatic brain injury and why I was able to see and hear dead people everywhere.

Then I described her son. "John has piercing green eyes and long brown hair. He's a sweetheart. He feels really bad about leaving you. I didn't want to let this opportunity go by without saying something to you."

Visibly shaken, the woman sat down. "I don't know how to respond. Please go. I can't listen anymore. It's just too much."

Shannon put her arm around me, and slowly, we walked back to the car. She said, "Kellee, I love you. You mean well, but not everybody is ready to hear what you have to say." Shannon's kindness and compassion helped me to not sink into a hole of sadness and despair.

As I turned on the ignition, John's mother came running up to the car. I rolled down my window and looked into her eyes. With tears streaming down her face, she said, "I'm not sure I believe what just happened, but I want to thank you for the message from my son. It's a great comfort to me."

I felt a huge wave of relief as tears welled up in my eyes. *You did good, Kellee*, I said to myself.

As we drove home on the 405 freeway, an old woody wagon with a turquoise surfboard on top passed next to us. The driver was John, and he was smiling. Then he waved and disappeared.

I was grateful that John's mother was kind enough to thank me. I was always concerned about how to present messages from the other side and worried that I would do more harm than good. With all the different belief systems in the world, the last thing I wanted was to hurt another person. This encounter was a blessing in disguise. It was finally dawning on me that I was doing the right thing at last. *Thank you, spirit world.*

Chapter 9

HEALING BEGINS

Whether we like it or not, we have all been born on this earth as part of one great family. We all desire happiness and do not want suffering. When you recognize that all beings are equal in this respect, you automatically feel empathy and closeness for them. Out of this comes a genuine sense of universal responsibility, the wish to actively help others overcome their problems.

> - The Dalai Lama, *His Essential Wisdom*

By the spring of 2002, I was almost 45 years old and about to embark upon my brand-new destiny. I had to surrender to Spirit and go with the flow, something that, by now, you know didn't come easily to me. By this time, I had received and experienced visions of various spirits and even more insights and amazingly detailed dreams from my spirit guides.

One particular night, I had a lucid dream of two Native American men living in New Mexico. One was an older medicine man, and the other was younger, tall, and movie-star handsome. Innately, I knew that both of them were assisting me to heal. I was at the very beginning stages of opening the shades of my mind to trust the inner wisdom of the Spirit. It was this trust within my heart that led me to believe these men held the solutions to any doubts and uncertainty I still kept inside. Seeing spirits, as well as the sudden energy bursts that caused things around my home to move, often left me in a depleted and dazed state. I definitely needed help, and I knew that the spirit world would lead me to these two healers.

The next morning, I called my cousin Sandy and described my dream vision.

"Will you go with me to Santa Fe and help me look for these men?" I asked.

"Of course, I'll go with you, but instead of Santa Fe, let's try Taos first. I'm more familiar with Taos. Since you're not sure where in New Mexico to find them, let's start there."

Since I had never been to New Mexico, I agreed to go to Taos. Besides, Spirit promised to guide me, and I was eager to follow Spirit's direction. I flew into Denver, met Sandy, and without delay, we drove to Taos. During the five-hour drive, I was jabbering the entire time. I couldn't contain my excitement.

"I just know these two men are going to help me with my seeing and hearing." My new-found abilities were thrilling, and I was eager to explore what else I could do. The down side was that I had no idea when, where, or how they would kick in, nor how to control them, so I definitely needed help and guidance in that department.

Sandy made arrangements for us to stay in a lovely bed and breakfast inn with separate cottages. It was a serene spot surrounded by majestic mountains. The owners, Frank and Tina, greeted us when we arrived. Frank was middle-aged, quiet, and all business, while Tina was sweet and friendly. They lived in the main house while we were shown a cozy cottage with a wooden porch and two rustic rocking chairs. After unpacking, we sat on the porch with a glass of wine to admire the incredible mountain views.

Afterward, we walked to the main house to ask about dinner recommendations. As we approached the inn, we spotted two young children, about 8 and 10, running around the courtyard. Tina came outside, and without warning, a teenage-girl spirit about 16 years-old holding a white dog showed up. She hovered about three feet off the ground next to Tina. She turned towards me and began giving me a message.

Telepathically, she said, "Tell my mother I'm okay. I grew up in Heaven, and I'm a teen now. I watch over my little sister and brother all the time. Tell her it was an accident. She has to forgive herself. Tell her it was an accident." She seemed very emphatic about "accident."

I completely stopped in my tracks by this spontaneous visit from the spirit world. I wanted to help Tina, but I also knew that it wasn't the right time to share the information. Telepathically, I promised the daughter, "I'll talk to her when it's the right time."

Sandy and I left for the restaurant, and at dinner, I explained my spirit vision to Sandy. I tried to enjoy our evening, but all I could think of was this poor mother who had suffered the loss of a child.

I didn't know the circumstances at the time, but I knew I could help her.

Sandy agreed, "You're right, Kellee. She would want to know about her child." I decided to speak with Tina the next day after we returned from the Taos Pueblo, the tribal land of the Native American community.

A Past Life Connection

Sandy and I got up early the next morning, had our coffee, and immediately headed to the Pueblo. I was beside myself with high expectations, hoping to find my two Native healers. I described exactly what the two men looked like to Sandy, and she declared, "Don't worry, we'll find them."

As soon as we arrived, the place looked familiar. I felt very connected to it. I sensed its high spiritual vibration and knew I had lived in this village in another life.

I had a vision of the Pueblo in one of my yoga positions as my energy surged through my body. As I stood there in the small village, I began to have visions of my life in the Pueblo, making adobe huts with straw and mud and sitting in a circle grinding corn with other women.

There were many small tourist shops in the town, so Sandy quickly went off to shop. My mission was to find the two healers, and I went from store to store looking for them. I could feel their presence, but after covering nearly every inch of the Pueblo, I became discouraged. Sandy, however, was full of energy and coaxed me to follow her into a shop. "C'mon, Kellee, this one looks interesting."

I didn't want to go into a trinket shop—*there was no way these spiritual healers would be in a souvenir store.* But I was hot and tired, so I followed Sandy into the store. As soon as we entered, I saw the handsome man from my vision behind the counter. I walked up to him and said, "I saw you in a vision." He replied, "I know."

We hugged, and I started to cry. He said, "My name is Henry. Go see Howard Bad Hand. He is the one who will help you. Here's his phone number. He's expecting your call."

I called Howard immediately. He said, "I was waiting for you to call. Come to my home tomorrow at 10 in the morning." I cannot describe the elation I felt in finding these two men. My vision was correct. Finally, there would be someone who could help me to understand the changes that have been happening to me.

Healing A Mother's Pain

We arrived back at the inn just in time for a glass of wine and a view of the sunset. I was in a beautifully blissful state—finally feeling good about my newfound gifts. I thought about all the wonderful possibilities the future held and thought that I would be using my gifts to help others.

Our host, Tina, invited us into her living room. "I love meeting new people," she said. Sandy replied, "Your inn is so homey and wonderful. The view of the beautiful mountains at sunset is so special."

At that moment, Tina's teenage daughter's spirit reappeared. She was sitting next to her mother and looking at me. Frank was not around, so I felt this would be the best time to speak. If Frank was around, I suspected my vision would cause some trouble, and that's not at all what I wanted.

I had my opening when Tina asked, "What brings you two to Taos."

"I'm recovering from a head injury," I replied. I felt I needed to speak quickly. "As a result of my injury, I can see dead people." Tina stared at me with a perplexed look. "I can see your daughter, who is about 16 now. She has blonde hair and a white dog—I believe the dog's name is Fluffy, and your daughter is Sara. She's sitting next to you."

At that moment, Frank came into the room. Tina's eyes welled up in tears. "Yes, that's my daughter, Sara," she said. "She would be 16 now."

Even though her husband was staring at me, I went on. "Sara says it wasn't your fault. It was an accident. She's a guide to you and the children. She loves you all very much."

The husband cried out, "That's enough! I want you both out of my house now. Pack up your stuff and get out of here. You're no longer welcome." He was livid; his face turned red, and for a moment, I thought he was going to hit me.

Sandy and I ran out of the room while Tina sat sobbing on the couch. Shaken and dazed, I felt confused. I thought I was doing the right thing for this mother and her beloved daughter. As with anyone I meet with a message from the other side, I felt Tina may never again have an opportunity to hear from Sara. Instead of acceptance, we were being thrown out.

Sandy and I hurried back to our small cottage. I apologized profusely to Sandy about our hasty departure. She was great about it; I love her for being so understanding. "Don't worry, it's an experience I'll never forget." She knew my heart was pure and full of love for this woman and the loss of her young daughter. I never intended to make the situation worse.

As we threw things into our suitcases, there was a knock at the door. Both of us stood frozen in place. I thought it might be Frank wanting to slug me or give me a piece of his mind. When I opened the door, Frank and Tina stood there holding hands. Both faces were wet with tears. "I'm sorry I yelled at you," Frank said. "I was trying to protect Tina. She's already been through too much. She told me what you said and that you mentioned Fluffy, the rescue dog I gave Sara." *It was the DOG that got him.* "It happened a long time ago. There was no way you could've known about Fluffy."

Frank explained their tragic story. Sara was two years old and riding some sort of scooter in the courtyard. "Tina was backing out of the driveway and didn't see Sara behind her and accidentally ran her over. Fluffy, her dog, died soon after it happened." It was a tragic moment that lived in their minds every day!

I empathized with Tina. The guilt she felt must have been immeasurable. I reassured her. "It was an accident. Sara knows that and wants you to be happy. Most of all, she wants you to know that you will see each other again. She's never far away."

Tina hugged me. "Thank you so much for telling me. It has been the darkest time of my life." Frank again apologized and thanked me for helping them see some good out of a lifetime of deep sadness.

I saw how important Spirit's gift was, not only for Tina but also for me. It showed powerful healing on both sides for mother and daughter. To this day, I think of Tina and the painful guilt she must have carried for so many years.

Thankfully, Tina and Frank had a lot of community support. After reading with them, I learned that they created a foundation in Sara's name to reward people for mentoring young children. Out of the most painful situation, an amazing light was lit that led the two of them to help others.

Howard Bad Hand

The next morning, I couldn't wait to meet my new mentor, Howard Bad Hand. From my vision, he was the older Native American man. I knew I needed to do this part of the trip alone, so Sandy stayed at the inn. I drove her Jeep the few miles to his home in Taos, right outside the Pueblo. It was a modest one-story southwestern-style house with a flat roof and covered porch.

Howard was in the front yard waiting for me. He had a big smile on his face. "I'm happy to meet you. Don't worry, I will help you." We hugged, and without any warning, I went into a fit of crying. *Finally, someone will help me figure out what to do.*

We sat on his front porch. He poured a glass of cold water on each of us. I didn't want to waste his time, and more importantly, I didn't know how he would respond to the wild account of my past experiences, so I hurriedly described my situation. He listened to every word and nodded very patiently as if he knew and understood my ordeal. It felt good to explain the supernatural events without someone judging me. He got it instantly. What a gift he was to me.

Howard explained, "I'm Lakota Sioux medicine man. I have helped others like yourself." Being curious, I asked, "Wow, there are others like me?" And he said, "Yes. A few special ones. Some have had dangerous illnesses, and some have suffered accidents usually involving head injuries like you."

He continued. "Your brain injury forced an opening. Your vital life force that lay coiled at the base of your spine has been aroused." Howard explained how my energy was making things move around in a room. "It is a powerful life force that we all have, and unleashed quickly, it becomes chaotic and out of control. This energy is also very sacred, and once awakened, it conveys higher consciousness and enlightenment."

He went on, "I can tell your third eye is wide open. Your head injury was a blessed experience. This is why you are seeing ancestors, spirit guides, angels." Howard treated me with kindness, compassion, and respect. It was something I had not experienced very much in the last year, and it was the very first time on my journey that I didn't feel so all alone. Someone finally understood exactly what I had been going through. I will always be grateful for the time I spent with Howard.

I Had No Veil

Howard and I worked closely for the next two days. He taught me the importance of being grounded in Mother Earth. He told me that in earlier times, when someone had an awakening like mine, the elders would watch that person for weeks, months, and sometimes years, helping them through the transition period from the onset of the initial trauma to the culmination of deep spiritual wisdom.

He taught me how to open and close my third eye. He showed me how to connect with the Spirit through my crown chakra. This is the 7th chakra at the very top of the head. This particular chakra's meaning is all about spiritual connectivity. Howard had me imagining my crown chakra opening and then closing. We practiced this visualization for two days. He taught me how to control my energy and to stay balanced.

Howard referred to "the veil," a thin, permeable barrier between the Earth's world and the spiritual realms. It is a gateway, a window, so to speak, to the other side. Think of the veil as a curtain between our three-dimensional, physical world and the divine unlimited consciousness. The veil drops over our minds at birth to allow us to experience earthly challenges without remembering our past lives, our soul plans, and even our divine source. Without this veil, people would literally go insane.

But because this "veil of forgetfulness" drops over our minds, we have a limited view of life in the physical body. In my case, the veil had lifted, and I was able to see all possibilities of consciousness with the divine source. That was why, at times, I thought I was going crazy.

Howard was so positive and upbeat, and more importantly, he was encouraging. "You will be okay. You are on Earth to make a difference." And I believed him. The time spent with Howard was incredibly significant. I cannot describe how liberated I felt. In a way, I felt like I was coming home and well on the road to healing.

At the end of two days, it was time to leave Howard. I was sad but grateful. I returned to the inn and picked up Sandy, and we drove back to her home in Denver. Like so many people in my life, Sandy was another living angel, and I was grateful for her love and support. Tom, on the other hand, was no angel, and he stayed away from me as much as possible. Mostly, he was out of town on business trips. Since he wasn't home, there was no reason for me to stay in Denver, so I flew back to LA. This time, I had more confidence, knowing my soul was on a mission. I learned a very valuable lesson—that I should never doubt that still small voice within.

Chapter 10

SECOND SIGHT

It is not you who is speaking but the Holy Spirit who speaks
through you.

- *Matthew 10:20*

By the time I arrived back in LA, I realized that I had to give
up my home because I had no job, no money, and no prospects
in sight. I managed to put all my possessions into storage. Holiday
began living with her now ex-stepmother because, by this time,
Cheri and Craig had divorced after 15 years of marriage. I was
very grateful to Cheri for caring for Holiday, but I was, sad to say,
homeless.

My relationship with Tom was on its last leg, slipping away like
all the others. Although Tom was incredibly wealthy, and it wouldn't
have been a burden for him to help me out financially, he never
offered any support, either monetarily or emotionally. Again, I
picked a partner who only looked out for himself.

My wonderful mother invited me to live with her and Marc.

Since I was traveling light, it was easy to pack up my clothes and stay at her place. I told her it would be temporary as I didn't want to be the third wheel in their relationship. I was grateful for her moral and financial support. I was still at a very low point with regard to getting a job and taking responsibility for Holiday and myself.

Since I had so many angelic and spirit encounters, I decided it was time that I signed up for some metaphysical workshops. The first one I enrolled in was a class on angels in Orange County. It would be the first of many outings into the paranormal universe. I felt freer than I had ever felt. I was finally beginning to understand who I was from the inside out. Since I had no job or timetable to keep me busy, my time was my own, and I had plenty of time to explore who I truly was.

That particular weekend, Marc was away on business, and Mom was at home busy working on her taxes. Before I left the house, I said to Mom, "Let's have a nice, quiet dinner when I come home from the workshop. I'm sure I'll have plenty to talk about." Mom was also eager to learn more about the paranormal world.

As I drove from Beverly Hills to Orange County, my excitement to finally be among like-minded, spiritual people grew with each passing mile. Perhaps there would be someone to point me in the right direction for the next step on my inner journey.

When Is a Psychic Not Psychic?

It was a two-hour drive to the seminar, and it was amazing that I managed to arrive on time. Traffic in southern California can be hit or miss. When I arrived, the room was filled with over 100 people. The presenter was a well-known psychic in the area. After her discussion of the "angelic realms," she asked us to pair up for an exercise. I felt like I finally found my niche because I was thoroughly enjoying the entire experience.

But things turned dark when the psychic began explaining extrasensory phenomena and mediumship. She literally made my skin crawl. I knew that she was making things up. *How could you?* I thought to myself. After learning from Howard that my "veil" had been lifted and I was opened to unlimited consciousness, I knew that her readings with people in the audience were flat-out wrong. They were so off the mark that I could hardly control myself. Even the colors I saw around her were gray and cloudy. She had no connection at all to the spirit world. I was mortified. She told one woman that her beloved son would not come home from the war. Wrong! That's when I completely lost it. She had no clue about the woman's son. He wasn't dead. I wanted to jump up and say something, but instead, I left in the middle of the demonstration. I couldn't get out of there fast enough. I was so mad that this woman was causing harm to these trusting people. She was no help to them at all.

Besides myself with anger, it was a miracle I could drive home safe and sound. In fact, I didn't remember the two-hour drive at all. As I entered Mom's house, I was still shaking with outrage. Before I reached the landing, Mom opened the door and asked, "Kellee, are you all right? You look upset." I answered, "No, Mom, I'm not okay. I'll tell you all about it, but I have to lie down first."

Mom had an unusually strange look on her face. She said, "Kellee, can I show you something before you go upstairs?" I was exhausted—my energy had been zapped from my body. It was going to be a chore just to climb the stairs, but I said, "Yes."

We walked into the living room where she had been doing her taxes. She was working on a large coffee table (5-foot square, 350-pound Italian glass and steel). She told me, "Just before you came home, I finished with the taxes, gathered all the paperwork, and went into my office to put them away. When I returned to the living room, something strange had occurred, and I was confused. Look at the coffee table."

I looked at the table (it had taken three men to carry it inside the house). It had moved five inches on all sides. The crystal vase and books on top were in place, but I could tell the table had shifted. *How could this be?* Mom certainly couldn't move it by herself. Then I realized: *It must have been me.* It was my uncontrolled energy that had something to do with it.

Obviously, the coffee table freaked Mom out. "Kellee, do you have any idea what happened here?" I knew she knew it was my doing.

Speaking very rapidly, I vented my upset about the psychic. "That woman at the seminar provoked me. She was giving people the wrong information, and negative energy started to pump through my body. I was so mad at her. I'm sorry. I guess I carried that bad energy home with me."

I was so ashamed of myself; I broke down and cried. Mom forgave me. She was always supportive. The only thing I wondered was, *Why that table?*

For the record, the next day, my mother called her friend Jim, who had been a structural engineer and, more recently, an attorney. He was a very rational, intelligent guy. She asked him, "What would cause this table to lift up and move all the way around? You can see from the indentation on the rug where it had been."

Jim looked at the table. "I have no idea," he said.

After carefully studying the table for a while and ruling out an earthquake or uneven floor structure, Jim just scratched his head.

Then Mom explained, "Well, let me tell you about Kellee." As I mentioned, he was an engineer and an attorney, very left-brained and logical. He shrugged, "Well, that's as good a reason as any."

It Runs in the Family

The next afternoon, Mom suggested we sit outside, have a glass of wine, and chat. It was a lovely day, and the scent of jasmine filled the air. I knew she was concerned about the table and didn't want any more erratic-spirited activity in her house.

"Did I ever tell you about my father?" She said.

"What do you mean?" I asked.

"When I was growing up in Indiana, my father would gather his family around a large table. He would put his hands on the table, and people would ask questions, and the table would actually lift up and tap out the answers. It was our Sunday ritual."

"What?" This is how and when I learned that my grandfather was a physical medium.

Mom continued. "I used to think my father was a warlock, you know, a male witch because he could find water on the land when no one else could. Sometime later, I realized my father was actually a psychic healer, and he used his telekinetic ability to help people in that small rural area." She continued. "I think you inherited your psychic gifts from him."

In this particular instance, with the living room table, I believe my grandfather was trying to get Mom's attention and let her know that he was still around, and maybe he was communicating that I had telekinetic power like him. Not only was my grandfather psychic, but I always felt that Mom was psychic as well. She just couldn't bring herself to acknowledge it. It didn't fit in with her left-brain, logical, and professional protocol.

Although she never claimed to be psychic, Spirit always seemed to come to her aid when she needed it the most. I was curious, so I asked, "Did anything unusual ever happen to you?" Her eyes lit up.

"When I was in college—this was before I met your father—I took a course in paleontology. I was the only female in the class. My professor, a real chauvinist, asked me a very obscure question." She smiled. "He waited for me to answer. He wanted to prove that women are not cut out for anything scientific. By then, every man in the class began to snigger."

She continued, "My mind was literally a blank until suddenly the word 'trilobite' came to me." So I answered, "Trilobite." (Trilobite was a form of insect that existed millions of millennia ago.) "The whole class let out a groan." Mom laughed, "I certainly outsmarted them. But I got lucky that Spirit interceded right at that moment."

Then she told me about another incident that happened years later while she was taking her oral exams for her Ph.D.

The California oral exams for psychotherapists were held in

San Francisco in front of a board of five psychologists, and back in the 1970s, they were, as you can expect—all male. It's hard to believe now, but back then, and it wasn't that long ago, there weren't many female licensed psychologists. Mom was one of the very few exceptions.

Everyone dreaded the oral part of the exam. It usually lasted about four hours and was quite subjective. If the examiner didn't like you for some reason, you usually didn't pass. Most people failed the first time. Mom had known several people who failed many times. It was such a frightening experience that some people never received their license to practice, and some didn't bother to take the orals at all.

At the time, Mom sat in the room with the all-male examiners and answered all of their questions, many of which were complicated, often tricky, and designed to catch a person off balance. All the answers were recorded on an audio tape machine (no such thing as CDs, DVDs, or streaming).

"I could feel those five men judging me; they didn't want to pass me, a woman." One judge sarcastically asked why I had such a large practice? He said, 'You're merely a psych assistant and not yet licensed.' He really wanted to intimidate me."

Mom continued. "All of a sudden, at the very moment the head psychologist was about to announce whether I passed or failed, the tape machine, which was sitting on a side table next to the judges, toppled onto the floor, and the tape began to unravel. It was all over the floor. I had to hide my amusement." The judges were stunned.

Mom laughed, "They had to pass me by default since the tape

was completely unwound and too twisted to review. I knew it had to be Spirit that caused the tape to unravel."

If Spirit had not intervened, Mom's destiny, and probably mine as well, would have turned out very differently.

I Needed Grounding

After my chat with Mom, I knew being a psychic was my destiny. It had to be. As the Indian in New Delhi said—it was up to me whether I would choose to do it again in this life. *What other confirmation did I need?* At this point, I had nothing left and nothing to lose. I decided to put my heart and soul into my new calling.

Even though I learned from Harold Bad Hand how to move the kundalini energy up and down my body, I still had trouble controlling it. Hence, everywhere I went, there was some sort of chaos. Glasses would break, computers would go on the fritz, and things would fly around the room. I felt sorry for anyone unlucky to be in the room with me when it happened.

I remember one night in particular when my energy was quite chaotic. Everyone in my family made arrangements to meet for dinner at a fancy French restaurant in West Hollywood. My sister Carol arrived in a bad mood because something happened at work that made her mad. Her anger escalated with every word she spoke. It became so intense that I had a hard time concentrating on the menu.

"Carol, can you please calm down," I asked her.

"No, Kellee, I will not. I have a right to my feelings," she snidely replied.

Mom saw that I was shaking. "Carol, settle down. Let's have

a nice dinner."

However, the more Carol talked about work, the more I could feel my energy rising. Mom looked at me, and I frowned back at her.

Marc interrupted the conversation and brought out a special bottle of wine for the occasion. Our waitress gently placed lovely, long-stemmed wine glasses around the table. By then, unfortunately, I could no longer contain my energy, and suddenly, the wine glasses exploded one by one until all six glasses shattered on the table.

A large chandelier above our table began to shake. I knew that if I stayed any longer, the chandelier would be next. Poor Mom. She was afraid that the big chandelier would drop right down on my sister's head. At that point, Mom turned to me and quietly asked me to leave, and I did.

As I continued to struggle with my energy, my good friend Charlene came to my rescue. She explained, "I have a way of grounding energy that I think will work for you." I needed something and hoped it would do the trick.

We went outside in bare feet, and Charlene began the visualization. "See the energy at the top of your head flow down and drain out through your feet into the earth." You can do this in the dirt, sand, or on the grass. Visualize your energy flowing from the top of your head down your body and out through the feet."

I did the exercise over and over until I could actually feel the energy easily flow through my body and out my toes. I shouted to Charlene, "It works!" I could feel the energy in my body settling down until I was relaxed.

161

To this day, I follow Charlene's advice, and it's something I share with all my clients. Grounding was a necessary step to keep my erratic energy contained. If I wanted to connect to the infinite, unlimited consciousness, I needed orderly, disciplined, and stable energy. That became my goal.

The Third Eye

As Howard Bad Hand explained in Taos, "When you hit your head with great force, your pineal gland cracked open." Dr. Emory explained that only 3% of the population with my type of frontal lobe injury actually survive. Most people die within 17 hours if they don't receive help. That was quite an illuminating tidbit of information, and I admit that I was glad to be one of the people who survived. It became clear that Spirit had planned the accident on the other side, and my guides had a hand in saving me.

The pineal gland is located in the center of the brain between the left and right hemispheres. In metaphysical terms, it is known as the *Third Eye* or the 6th chakra. It is where spiritual insight resides and usually how mediums communicate with souls who have passed on.

Because my third eye was wide open, I became very aware that I was a spiritual being with extrasensory capabilities. As an empath, I could usually tell how people felt and what troubles they were having. But with my third eye wide open, I also knew if their traumas were from this life or a past life. I could see way back to the beginning of their time on Earth, their present circumstances, and even their futures. That's another thing I learned—I realized there was no such thing as time; time is an illusion of the physical dimension. As Albert Einstein theorized, everything is relative, even time.

Besides knowing time is an illusion of this dimension, I also gained an understanding that everything is made of vibrating energy—people, pets, houses, tables, chairs, planes, trains, food, liquids, everything made of matter. Energy vibrates at certain frequencies. Everything is in constant movement with millions upon millions of different rates of vibration. This was particularly noticeable with the awakening of my third eye, which caused my energy vibration to rise to higher levels. Because of this phenomenon, I was able to see spirits, angels, and spirit guides, as well as people's auras—the vibrant colors around them. More importantly, I learned that no one is ever alone, and although we cannot see the spiritual world, it is not separate from us. We are one with it—like all the matching pieces of one giant puzzle.

As a person becomes more spiritually adept, there will be signs that demonstrate a person's vibration is rising to a higher level. I found out the hard way, kicking and screaming through all the spiritual happenings in my life. These signs include mental clarity, a sense of purpose, a positive outlook on life, an oneness with all things, feelings of love and peace, and, while acknowledging the ego, seeing all things from a spiritual or higher self.

Energy can fluctuate depending on our thoughts. Remember, thoughts are real things. So if we are angry, fearful, revengeful, etc., our energy vibrates in our lower/ego self, and we can become destructive to ourselves and others. Fortunately for me, Spirit had been sending a ton of help to raise my energy vibration, and the most important way came in the form of spirit doctors.

Psychic Healing

From 2001 until the end of 2003, around the age of 45, I began an intense healing process. With little warning, maybe a minute or two, and no matter how much sleep I had the night before, I would get very sleepy. An inner voice would tell me, *Lie down, we are going to work on you.* Right away, I had to find a place to lie down—a bed, a couch, or sometimes the floor. There was no particular time of day or night when these healings would take place.

Once I was in a prone position, I fell into a twilight sleep. Psychic doctors would surround me and work on me. In a dreamlike state, I would catch glimpses of these healers, hear voices, and feel tugs and nips to my body. I could tell that they were using light energy to fix my brain and energy centers. The whole procedure lasted about two hours. Afterward, I slept for quite a while. When I woke up, I knew I had been rewired.

During that healing time, I felt like I was between two worlds—the earthly dimension and the other side of the astral world where my spiritual awakening was taking place. I saw visions of people long dead and knew about their lives without knowing who they were. Although my third eye was wide open, it was not yet working exactly right. The healers were helping to restore the pineal gland so I could clearly see through my third eye and communicate accurately with the other side.

This intense psychic healing contact lasted about six months, and it would have burned me out if it kept going much longer than that. It was a phenomenon I found difficult to explain to people. Although it may sound like a fantastic voyage into the various spiritual realms, like being on a psychedelic trip, to exist between two worlds would eventually and quickly blow out one's circuitry. It would cause mental and emotional disabilities that would make it difficult to function in a normal way.

Instead, today, I rely on my lucid dreams and spirit visions for insight, but they are nothing like the experiences I had during that healing time. Due to the incredible celestial doctors' help and learning how to center my energetic vibration and stay grounded, at last, I was in control of my psychic energy and ready to take on the world.

Disturbing Premonition

After my healing sessions were over, I realized that my relationship with Tom had to come to an end. In fact, it was hard to believe that Tom and I were still together. I was sure that by now, he would have left me. After all, I had no job, no prospects, no money, and no place of my own—not the kind of arm piece he'd like to have. How Tom and I justified our relationship would be hard to understand. Unfortunately, we simply pretended everything was status quo.

So, with business as usual, we planned a trip together that would stop in London, Paris, and Rome. This time, we decided to bring our daughters. Tom's daughters Melody and Holiday were the same age, and they were excited about the trip abroad, as Tom was. On the other hand, I wasn't too sure. My visions began to multiply, not only while I was sleeping but also in the waking state. At first, it was all so odd because the visions seemed to come out of the blue—like watching videos streaming in my mind. I couldn't help but wonder if these visions would be a major problem on our trip. I looked up to Heaven and sent out a "please help me" prayer.

It was exactly one week before our European vacation. As I sat alone in my kitchen enjoying my morning coffee, a vision came to my mind. A lone gunman was at the ticket counter in the International Terminal of Los Angeles Airport. Shockingly, I could see him randomly shooting at people as they were running for their lives. I was even able to see the date and time—July 4, 2002, 11:30 AM—the day of our trip. We would all be in that very terminal at that precise time. I panicked. I didn't know what to do, so I called my mother and described what I saw.

She advised, "Kellee, call Tom right now and tell him to cancel the trip." She was always my "go-to" when these visions happened. I was so glad that she believed in me and was receptive to these revelations. I agreed with her and immediately called Tom.

He said he was in a meeting and couldn't talk. I didn't care; it was urgent. I screeched into the phone. "We cannot go to Europe." I heard him say, "We'll discuss it later," which infuriated me even more. So I shouted even louder, "There will be a shooting at LAX that day. We cannot go there." Before I could finish, Tom had already hung up. A few hours later, he called back, and I explained my vision in great detail. I could tell he was thoroughly annoyed with me. "Now, that's just ridiculous, Darlin'. We already paid for this trip, so we're going."

"Holiday and I are not going," I replied. "You can take Melody, but I will not put Holiday and myself in jeopardy. We absolutely will not go."

This blow-up certainly didn't help our relationship. After a lot of unpleasant back and forth, he finally agreed to see if he could get his money back and put it towards a cruise to the Caribbean. "NOT Europe!" I stressed.

Luckily, Tom was able to find a last-minute deal. Instead of leaving on July 4, Holiday and I would fly out of LAX on July 5, and Tom and Melody would fly out of Denver. We would all meet in San Juan to board the cruise.

On the morning of July 4th, as I was packing for the cruise, there was a news alert on TV—a shooting at LAX at 11:30 AM at the ticket counter of El Al Airlines. Several shots were fired, and three people were dead, including the gunman. Several others were injured. I nearly fainted.

Immediately, I called Tom. "Turn on the TV now." I would like to say he was, at the very least, shocked by the news, but he wasn't. Instead, he was only irritated and fed up with the new version of me. "Darlin', just pack and let's hope this cruise goes smoothly. I don't want to hear any more about your freaky fantasies."

Foretelling a Detour

As planned, Holiday and I boarded the plane to San Juan. Since it was a last-minute change of plans, we couldn't get a direct flight, so we had a stop in Dallas. The first leg of the flight went fine. We were seated towards the back of the plane with an empty seat between us. Once the plane reboarded in Dallas, a young man sat in our row. I gave him my seat by the window and sat in the middle next to Holiday.

About 45 minutes into the flight, I had another vision. This one was not as dire, but I saw us landing in New Orleans instead of San Juan. I was in an odd state of mind; thoughts were racing, almost as if I was in manic mode.

I turned to Holiday and said, "When we land in New Orleans, do you think we can get off the plane and go to Bourbon Street and get some Lucky Dogs?"

She looked at me as if I had lost my mind, "What are you talking about, Mom? We are flying to San Juan, not to New Orleans."

"Oh, I know we're headed to San Juan, but the plane is going to make a stop in New Orleans first," I said.

The man in the window seat got very upset. He said, "What are you talking about? I have to get to San Juan. I haven't seen my wife in months, and we're meeting in San Juan. This plane has to go to San Juan."

I explained, "I'm aware we're flying to San Juan, but there's a man up front about to have a heart attack. When he does, we'll be making a detour to New Orleans to get him help. It'll take several hours, and that's why I was wondering if they would let us off the plane."

The man by the window practically jumped out of his seat. I added, "The man who's about to have a heart attack is having an affair, and he's so stressed that his wife will find out about it that his heart is going to beat very fast and very irregularly."

These last details were quite unnecessary. My seatmates stared at me with their mouths open. Poor Holiday. She explained to our fellow passengers that I was psychic and sometimes had visions of the future. The poor guy was completely shaken, understandably so.

From the back of the plane, a flight attendant began running up the aisle, calling out, "Is there a doctor on the plane?"

I turned to my daughter and said, "The man just had a heart attack, so we should be landing in New Orleans soon."

The man next to me was shaking his head. I thought, *I hope his guy doesn't have a heart attack, too.* I tried to comfort him. "We'll only be delayed a few hours. We'll get to San Juan today, just later than anticipated." Needless to say, nothing I said helped.

The pilot addressed the passengers and asked everyone to fasten their seat belts. "One of the passengers is having a medical emergency, and we're landing at the nearest airport to get him assistance. Stay in your seats. We'll get back in the air as soon as possible."

I asked our flight attendant. "Can we get off the plane when we land?"   "Absolutely not," was her reply.

We sat on the plane in New Orleans for about three hours. I called Tom with the update. He and Melody were waiting for us at the San Juan airport. When I shared my vision about the man with a heart attack, Tom was furious, as if it were all my fault. He started to rant about my psychic "mumbo jumbo."

"We'll meet you at the hotel," I said, abruptly cutting him off. I still didn't get it through my thick skull that the less I said to Tom, the better.

Seeing An Old Friend

Our plane finally landed in San Juan at about 11 PM. Tom had reluctantly waited for us at the hotel. Judging by the look on his face, it was easy to see that he had a few drinks. He didn't care about my welfare, only his own.

The next morning, we boarded our ship. Holiday and I were excited about the cruise. Since it was a last-minute booking, I wondered about the kind of room we would have, but surprisingly, it was a lovely two-room suite with a large balcony. Melody and Holiday were 16, and they were thrilled to learn that their room was on a different floor.

Somewhere in my delusional state, I had hoped things would get back to normal between Tom and me and that the cruise would be a jumpstart to a more intimate relationship. But, no pun intended, that ship had already sailed.

As the ship was ready to leave port, Tom and I went up to the pool deck to see the view. That's when I saw the spirit of Harry, the father of an old boyfriend of mine and Marc's cousin. Harry had been dead a long time, and yet there he was, happily lying on one of the lounge chairs. I always liked Harry, even if he was a little rough around the edges.

Many years ago, while I was driving along the freeway in LA, I saw a Rolls Royce parked on the shoulder. Its hood was up, and there was a man sitting in the car. I recognized Harry's personal license plate and pulled over in my yellow Volkswagen Bug to see if there was something I could do to help. Harry loved that I stopped, and from that moment on, we were friends.

I wondered. *Why would Harry be on this cruise?* I knew better than to let Tom know about my visitor, so I didn't say a word. I only prayed that Harry would be the one and only spirit I would see that week.

Tom suggested we get cocktails. "I'll wait here," I said. "Bring the drinks, and we can watch the sunset together as the ship heads out to sea."

While Tom made a beeline for the bar, I had an opportunity to visit with Harry. He wore white shorts and a flowered Hawaiian T-shirt. He still had his twinkling blue eyes and a big smile. We communicated telepathically.

"I just want you to know that I'm enjoying life over here. I miss my family, but we'll all be together again. Don't forget to enjoy life and eat lots of hot dogs." I smiled. When Harry was alive, he loved going to Dodger games and eating ballpark franks.

When Tom returned with our drinks, Harry wished me luck and told me, "I'll be around, so we'll probably bump into each other again." Then he disappeared.

As Tom and I enjoyed the sunset, I asked, "Do you think we could have hot dogs for dinner." He was appalled at the suggestion. "God! No! Hot dogs?! We have reservations for a formal dinner."

A Valuable Lesson

The next day, the four of us disembarked the ship and took the tender that ferried us to an island paradise. We spent the day swimming, lying in the sun and relaxing.

For the greater part of our relationship, Tom kept his daughter pretty much away from me. He flat-out told me, "Don't you dare ever discuss your psychic nonsense with her." So, while Tom was in the water, I was surprised when Melody asked, "Kellee, can you tell me my future? Will I get into San Diego State? Will I get married and have children?"

I was uncomfortable answering. "Melody, I would love to have this conversation with you, but it would really upset your dad."

"Oh, he'll be okay. He won't get mad. I'm just curious about the future."

Despite my misgivings, especially about teens not being able to keep secrets and having no boundaries or the ability to just say no, I gave in. I genuinely thought if I could assist her with any future insight, she wouldn't have to worry so much. But, looking back now with the knowledge I had gleaned over the years, I might not have been so outspoken, realizing there would be unpleasant consequences.

"Yes, Melody, you will get into San Diego State. You'll meet a boy in one of your classes, and a few years later, you'll marry him. Both of you will be schoolteachers and live in San Diego for many years. You'll be very happy."

It was all positive information, and Melody was thrilled to hear it. Several years later, I heard from a reliable source that my prediction had come true.

When Tom came back and sat on a beach towel next to us, Melody couldn't contain her excitement, so she told him everything I had said.

To put it mildly, Tom was livid. "How could you tell her that? What if she doesn't get into San Diego State? What if she doesn't meet a boy? Why don't you keep that crazy stuff to yourself? I should've never let you get near my daughter."

He was so mad; he made us all miserable, and we left the beach early. I never saw him that evening, not even for dinner. Around 4 AM, a drunken Tom staggered into our suite and passed out on the bed with a mighty thump.

At 6 AM, I woke up to the presence of three spirits—Harry, his sister Nan, and Ben, Nan's husband. I always loved the three of them and was glad to see Harry again. The spirited trio came together and manifested a vision. As I looked over at Tom, he quickly morphed into a baby. The vision was Immediately followed by the thought, "He's a baby and not yet prepared for your wisdom. Let him be." I let out a screech.

When Tom heard me, he jumped up from a dead sleep. Groggily, he stared at me with his mouth wide open. He shrieked, "What is it? What are you screaming at?"

Harry, Nan, and Ben looked after me, and they taught me valuable lessons. Not everyone is ready to understand the spirit world, and it was NOT my job to make them. Everyone learns in their own way and in their own time. Once again, I felt that Tom and I had come to the end of our journey. With that knowledge, I was able to take a big sigh and slowly fall back to sleep. I understood that I was not only protected by Spirit but that I could never force another to see the light.

After that night, I didn't see much of Tom for the rest of the cruise. He was usually getting hammered in one of the many bars on the ship. In a way, it was a relief, and it gave me the freedom to spend most of my time talking to Harry and learning about the other side.

Everywhere I walked, I saw loved ones floating above passengers, trying to get my attention. On one of my walks, I stepped into the ship's library and noticed an African American woman sitting alone, staring out the window. Her spirit mother was next to her. It was so clear in my mind I had to say something. Besides, at this point, I still had no discernment.

I walked up to the woman. "Hi. I hope I'm not bothering you," I said. "I know this may sound strange, but I can see your mom sitting next to you. She says she's sorry she had to leave without saying goodbye. She had a heart attack in the grocery store and left her body so fast she didn't know what was happening. She was supposed to be with you on this cruise, but she's so glad you still made the trip without her."

I wanted to continue with more messages, but the woman looked at me and snarled, "How do you know this information?" I explained that I could see spirits and that most of them wanted to let their families know they were okay. She kept staring at me with an intensity I had not anticipated. My inability to create boundaries usually landed me in hot water. *Maybe this wasn't such a good idea after all.*

Finally, she spoke. "My mother did die unexpectedly while shopping in the grocery store. It happened a couple of months ago. We made plans to take this cruise together. I miss her terribly. I guess I needed to hear that Mom's all right. Knowing she's here on the cruise gives me great comfort. It would be like Mom trying to get a message to me. She wouldn't want me to sit here all day in the library. Thank you for stopping and telling me." What a relief! I smiled at her and was happy to be of service.

When we arrived back home, Tom was thoroughly fed up. He told me he had had enough of "whatever you think you're doing" and "to just get a job." He emphatically stated, "No more crazy talk. Either everything goes back to normal, or I'm leaving you."

That was my cue to say, "Good riddance," but I was too insecure about my future to chuck it all away. Besides, I couldn't admit to myself that my old world was totally over; I still felt so fragile. How could I accept that in less than two years, I went from being a powerful corporate executive with all the luxuries of the good life to a homeless, broke psychically without a plan?

Chapter 11

HEAVENLY MESSENGERS

The Moving finger writes, and, having writ, moves on; nor all your Piety nor wit shall lure it back to cancel half a line, nor all your tears wash out a word of it.

> — Omar Khayyam, *The Rubaiyat*

In April 2003, Tom and I were still seeing each other, but I assure you it was coming to an end. It's still unbelievable to me that I could stay in relationships well past their due date. Of course, I'm sure much of it had to do with living through the never-ending theme of RESPONSIBILITY for others. I knew there was one more issue to resolve before the karmic contract between Tom and me came to an end. And the following incident was the final straw.

Tom had recently bought a brand-new Mercedes and wanted to take it for a long drive, so we drove from Denver to Albuquerque to visit some of his friends. When Tom was around me, he always drank way too much, and his behavior towards me bordered on belligerent. That weekend was no different. Tom treated me with very little respect, flirting with every woman who walked by him. Being a typical woman, you might think that his behavior would have been enough to end it right there and then, but I wasn't a typical woman. I had a miserable time, and all I wanted to do was to go home.

On the drive back, Tom began a tirade. "Kellee, I told you to stop with your psychic nonsense." He shouted, "BE NORMAL," over and over again. As he got louder and louder, the car went faster and faster. He never raged at me before, but he did drink a lot, and his drinking always changed his behavior. By now, we were going 90 miles an hour, and I was scared to death.

I begged him, "Tom, please stop yelling at me. You're going too fast. Please slow down." But he continued to berate me.

Suddenly, I felt Archangel Michael's presence. I could see him in my mind, surrounded by the cobalt blue light.

"Tom, please stop yelling at me." I pleaded. "Archangel Michael doesn't like it when you yell at me." The words came out of my mouth before I could stop them, and they ignited Tom's fury even more.

"Stop talking about Archangel Michael," he shouted. "You're crazy, and I can't take it anymore."

Suddenly, at 90 miles an hour, the windows in his brand-new Mercedes started going up and down. The air conditioning turned up full blast, and the sunroof kept opening and shutting.

Tom screamed at the top of his lungs, "What the hell is happening?"

"Archangel Michael doesn't like it when you're mean to me." I cried. "He wants you to stop yelling at me!"

He screamed even louder, "I'm not yelling at you!"

And then he grabbed one of his ears and shrieked, "My ears. My ears."

Both his ears were being pulled, and I could tell he was in a lot of pain. Meanwhile, the windows and sunroof kept opening and closing, and the air conditioner stayed at full blast as we sped along at 90 miles an hour.

Because he was in so much pain, he begged, "Tell him to make it stop."

"He wants you to apologize to me," I muttered.

"What?"

"He wants you to apologize to me," I repeated.

"Okay. I'm sorry."

"He says that's not good enough."

"Ok, I'm very sorry!"

In an instant, everything went back to normal.

Tom pulled the car over to the shoulder, opened his door, and practically fell out.

He sat down on the dirt and lit a cigarette.

The responsibility I felt for keeping this relationship alive was completely gone, and any feelings I had for Tom were over. At that moment, I felt an overwhelming relief of accomplishment. I finally reached the expiration date, and I felt nothing for him and only peace for myself.

Messages from the Ancient Priesthood

When I returned to LA, I knew I had to see Mom. She was always a safe place of comfort and upliftment. Spirit always seemed to arrange for Marc to be out of town whenever I was at Mom's house. It was uncanny yet necessary, as Marc couldn't have handled all the high-spirited activities going on around me. He was a left-brained attorney with a religious-based belief system and was skeptical of the paranormal or anything psychic. But over time, his worldview began to extend beyond his analytical perception.

Mom, being the complete opposite and psychic in her own right, was continually fascinated by all the supernatural incidents. She thoroughly enjoyed the surreal visits from Spirit, although there was a limit to any more flying objects around the house.

The one thing that did bother Mom was her morbid fear of sleeping alone in the house. She had night terrors her entire life and always needed someone to stay with her when Marc was gone. I never understood how this brilliant psychologist, who had literally helped thousands of people, had such a profound fear. She claimed she had no idea how and why such a fear derived, but she had always been afraid since childhood. In fact, sometimes her fear got so bad she would scream out loud, "Help me, help me, help me," in her sleep. The screams could be heard all over the house. So, when Marc was out of town, Carol, Danny, or I would sleep over Mom's house so she wouldn't be alone.

This time, when Marc was on a trip, I had Mom all to myself. Early one morning, while Mom and I were both asleep, Mom suddenly sat straight up in bed. She was awakened from a deep sleep and could see three men with long white beards and piercing blue eyes floating above my head. She was overwhelmed at the sight of these apparent apparitions and quickly turned to me and shook my arm.

"Kellee! Kellee! Get up." Mom sounded frantic.

I turned over and opened my eyes. "What's going on?"

"Can you see those men with white beards and long purple robes? They're talking to you."

"Yes."

"Who are they?"

Knowing they were part of my team of guides, I told her, "I'll fill you in in the morning," and I settled back into bed. "I have to go back to sleep."

Clearly, these guides wanted Mom to witness their existence and to show that these occurrences were not figments of my imagination. I knew she believed me, but I guess they wanted her to see for herself.

Mom was so shaken she stayed awake until it was light. Finally, she couldn't take it anymore.

"Kellee, are you awake now?" she asked.

"Yes, Mom," I said, giving up on sleep. "I'll get up. I'll tell you who they are."

I got out of bed, and we both headed downstairs to the kitchen, where I had left a book on angels on the table. In the middle of the big fat book was a picture of three men with scarlet and white robes, long white beards, and piercing blue eyes. I called them the "ancient ones."

I pointed to them. "Are these the men you saw, Mom?"

181

"Yes, that looks like them. Who are they?" she asked.

"Moses, Abraham, and Lord Melchizedek," I repeated the caption under the picture.

"Oh my God," Mom shuddered.

"Mom, are you okay?"

"No," she said. "My head is reeling. Did you say, Moses?"

"Yes. Moses, Abraham, and Lord Melchizedek."

"Did you know they were working with you?" she asked.

"Yes," I replied. "I'm amazed they let you see them. I guess they really wanted you to know that they were helping me."

"Oh, Kellee. I know Moses and Abraham, but who is this Melchizedek?"

I pointed to the book. "He was considered a high priest and a kind of savior. He's in the Old Testament."

After my visit with the "ancient ones," Mom realized that something more miraculous than mere psychic phenomena was taking place. It was way beyond table tipping or dousing to find water that my grandfather brought about. It was more than having answers to tests that Mom experienced. Powerful beings were teaching me in my sleep and transforming my mind.

Heavenly Music

On Sunday evening, the night after Mom saw my three ancient guides, Mom and I were happy to be alone in the house making dinner and drinking wine. I could tell that she was still confused by that nightly visitation.

She said, "I could tell they were talking to you. I wasn't afraid, only mesmerized—it was fascinating to watch those spirits working with you. I really had no idea about what you were going through. It just seemed too hard to understand. You know me, Kellee, I'm a very practical and no-nonsense."

As we prepared dinner, suddenly, we heard classical music coming from somewhere inside the house. It sounded like a heavenly chorus. It reminded me of monks chanting sacred music.

"Kellee, do you have any idea where this music is coming from?" Mom asked nervously.

"I don't know. I'll go check outside."

Mom's home overlooked Sunset Boulevard, and it had an incredible view of Los Angeles. On a clear day, you could see all the way to the ocean.

I ran up to the 4th floor of the house and opened the rooftop terrace door. I walked outside. It was quiet. The music was not coming from outside. To make sure, I ran downstairs and opened the front door. Again, no music. Then I ran down to the garage and opened the garage door. No music. But inside the house, the music was blaring.

Mom called down to me. "Kellee, where is the music coming from?"

"What?" I yelled. "I can't hear you."

The heavenly chorus became almost deafening.

"Tell it to stop, Kellee. I'm getting a headache." It was at this point I believed that Mom had reached her limit of supernatural manifestations.

I checked every room, and the sound was definitely inside the house, but from where or what? I had no idea, nor did it help that neither of us knew anything about the stereo system in the house, which was quite elaborate.

The music continued for at least an hour. Mom was overwrought.

"Kellee, please call it off."

I wasn't sure how, but I closed my eyes and prayed to Archangel Michael to stop the music. The music abruptly came to an end. *Thank you,* I said into the ethers. I'm not sure why the music started or stopped, but my only thought was that, once again, either the angels or my spirit guides wanted Mom to witness how real the experiences were happening around me.

The Winds of Change

My final visit with Tom happened the following weekend. At the end of my trip to Denver, Tom dropped me off at the terminal, put $200 in my hand, and drove away. No words, no hug, not even a kiss goodbye. It was the last time we would ever see each other. I stood outside the terminal and began to cry. It was one of the most painful experiences of my life.

At this point, I was not only homeless and penniless, but my so-called friends had stopped calling because I no longer fit into their lifestyles. I felt very alone. In my heart, I knew that the Spirit had stripped me of all the significant involvements that were delaying my spiritual progress. I knew Mom would let me stay with her forever, but my energy was too temperamental and disturbing, and I didn't want to cause her any more problems.

In the meantime, Holiday had just begun college at UC San Diego. I was so proud of her. But at the same time, I felt depressed that I couldn't provide any monetary resources for her schooling nor have a place for her to come home to. I felt an enormous amount of shame. After all, she was my responsibility; I was supposed to take care of her.

Although chaos seemed to follow me wherever I went, I was fortunate to have angels, both celestial and human, who would come to my aid just in the nick of time. My girlfriend Charlene kindly invited me to stay with her and her mother. Unfortunately, I didn't stay very long. Once again, the unsettling supernatural occurrences that happened around me created more trouble than she could handle, and she politely asked me to leave.

On my last night at Charlene's house, I had another lucid dream with Archangel Michael. "I will send someone to take care of you so that you are not alone. You will be okay. You have work to do."

Michael was true to his word. The next day, my dear younger brother Danny called and asked me to live with him. "I'll take care of you, Kellee. We have plenty of room." Danny and his girlfriend Josie, later to become his wife, welcomed me with open arms. Danny and Josie had just bought their first home in the Hollywood Hills under the famous HOLLYWOOD sign. Danny, a director in Hollywood for many years, and Josie, a mortgage broker, were used to working long hours and were keen on the idea of my being at home during the day.

Having no children and only a cat named Tiger, Danny and Josie's home was neat, spacious, and attractive. It felt good to have a comfortable room and a safe space to call my own. I was so grateful to these two angels; they will never know how much they helped me in my time of need.

185

The day I arrived, Danny showed me around the house. We walked down to the bottom floor, where there was a long hallway. Beautiful paintings lined the walls. My bedroom was on the right of the hallway, and Danny and Josie's room was on the left. Danny began pointing to each painting and describing it. Then he turned to me and said, "Kellee, I'm so happy you're here with us. I promise to take care of you. You'll be safe and secure, and if you have to, you can stay forever." It was one of the sweetest things that anyone had ever said to me. It was a wonderful moment.

Suddenly, a mighty wind, seemingly out of nowhere, tore through the narrow hallway. Since I was new to the home, I figured the wind came through a door or window. It was so fierce it knocked some of the paintings sideways, and the two of us held onto each other for dear life.

Danny cried out, "What's happening?"

I screeched, "Shut the door. Shut the window."

"There are no windows in the hallway," Danny said.

Crazy as this may sound, I told my brother, "I think it's Archangel Michael. He's happy you're taking care of me."

Danny smiled, pulled a chain from under his shirt, and showed me a pendant by Archangel Michael. He said, "Funny you should say, Michael. I love him, too. He's my champion. I keep him close to me." He turned and yelled into the air, "Don't worry, Michael, I'll take good care of Kellee."

And just like that, the wind stopped, and a new chapter of my life was about to unfold.

PART 3

A TRANSFORMED MIND

Chapter 12

FORGIVENESS AND ACCEPTANCE

… and in the meditation, don't meditate upon, but listen to the voice within. Prayer is a supplication for direction and understanding. Meditation is listening to the Divine within.

- Edgar Cayce, *from his readings*

Staying with Danny and Josie set my mind at ease, and I was grateful for their help. During this critical period in my life, while it appeared I had nothing, I was given one of the greatest gifts of all—the much-needed space and time to heal. Every day, I would sit for hours in the stillness of connecting to a higher source. I slept when I felt the need. I ate very little and constantly hydrated with a lot of water. I could feel my old self slowly slipping away. My spiritual future was unclear, but for the first time in my life, I DID NOT have anxiety.

Usually, I would be racked with worry and concern because I couldn't take care of my earthly responsibilities. In the past, I let my ego control my life. I was finally secure in the knowledge of who I was and where I was going. Instead of asking: *Who am I really? What is my purpose in life?* I let go and let Spirit take control. Somewhere deep within my soul, I knew there had to be a reason for my existence, and the ego was not part of it.

After a few months of searching within to overcome my grievances and find peace of mind, I felt a wave of tremendous sadness take over. My heart was heavy with the loss of all that I thought was real in this world, like hard work, money, control of my future, and, of course, my responsibility to others. I couldn't stop weeping. I think that through this grieving process, a new awareness has unfolded. I realized that my brain injury was essential in order to rearrange and reset my way of thinking. I may not have understood it, but it was Spirit's inimitable way of waking my soul.

Finding My True Self

Even though I may have appeared "normal" on the outside, I was far from that on the inside. There was a tug-of-war taking place between my head and my heart. I didn't know how to move on, and yet I had to accept that I had to change my life. I couldn't be stagnant any longer, and yet I yearned for a moment of calm.

Suddenly, I felt the unmistakable presence of Jesus and was overcome with compassion for myself and what my soul had been through. I became aware that the only way for me to heal was to forgive myself. Forgiveness was the key to freeing myself from the sudden change in life direction, along with acceptance of all that had occurred in the past. Forgiveness and acceptance would be my constant companions as I began to travel the long road ahead to my spiritual destiny.

I called my mother. "I'm never going to be the same anymore." And I then cried.

"Yes, I know Kellee. It will take time to heal, but together, we will figure out who you are becoming."

It was important to know I was not alone on this journey. I had my beloved and brilliant mother by my side. Intuitively, I knew that the two of us had planned this shift in consciousness long ago on the other side. At least I felt comfort in knowing Mom would help me through this enormous life transition. I was in between losing my old self and finding my new self.

Most people with traumatic brain injury have this experience—losing the life they once had and going in a totally different direction. Even though I didn't know anyone else dealing with the exact situation, I wasn't alone on this road. There were many others who had experienced this type of grief and loss. Somehow, I found comfort in knowing that. Looking back, it was so important that I wrote my master's thesis on the subject.

As a psychotherapist, one of the first questions I ask a new client, particularly one with rage and anger issues: "Have you ever had a head injury?" Usually, the answer is "No." So, I continue. "Have you ever fallen out of the tree, or banged your head against a door, or were in a car accident? Sometimes, a client will remember such an incident, but usually, no one makes the connection that it might be a traumatic head injury like a concussion. Symptoms may include loss of consciousness, memory loss, headaches, difficulty thinking, concentration, loss of balance, nausea, blurred vision, sleep disturbances, and mood

191

changes. That was the gist of my experience. Knowing this could be the case, which helps clients understand their behavior.

Although I grieved the loss of a good chunk of my memory, I believe it was to make room for my newfound psychic ability and communication with the spirit world. Psychologically speaking, it was quite a reframe.

Meeting the Guru

After my mentor, Harold Bad Hand, gave me the initial guidance to travel a new road, I looked for someone who could help me learn how to accept and forgive what had happened to me. At this point, I needed a mortal guide who could steer me in the right direction through my profound spiritual journey. At the very least, I needed someone with understanding and compassion.

It was about this time that I met two new friends who claimed to be healers. We all seemed to be in the same spiritual boat together. My friends had been following a guru from India who was teaching meditation and raising people's energy.

"Do you want to meet her?" one of them asked. My eyes lit up. I jumped at the chance to meet a teacher.

"Yes, of course," I answered. Could it be another destiny point?

The guru was a woman from India. Even though I had traveled to India and met a seer, gurus were unfamiliar territory. I only knew that a guru was a person who had gained some self-mastery and could lead others on their journey toward enlightenment. Again, I was naive and undisciplined in any type of spiritual practice, so I hoped the guru could help me understand my gifts and give me direction on how to use them.

But I soon learned that is not the way it works. The guru didn't tell me anything that could help with my visions or seeing spirits. Instead, I observed a cultish atmosphere of devotees surrounding the guru. People were totally dedicated to her, giving up their lives to be with their guru. Simple chores like laundry and housekeeping seemed important steps to enlightenment. I was told that they were considered the highest form of service to the guru.

Although everyone seemed genuine, to me, it seemed a little much. Many followers gave gifts of enormous value to the guru. Some traveled along with her on her lecture tour throughout the world. It was as if people lost their own sense of self and blindly followed this woman. I found out that many of her disciples had been estranged from their families and were looking for someone to fill the void, perhaps a mother figure to love. Clearly, I didn't understand their particular way of life; it was unsettling.

However, I was interested in learning a spiritual practice and attended many retreats with the guru. Although I didn't appreciate the cult-like atmosphere, I did value the guru's greatest gift— teaching meditation. I genuinely enjoyed the meditation and the profound peace it gave me.

I remember one retreat in Palm Springs. I invited Mom and my new boyfriend, Don, to share the experience with me. Mom was ever curious about new ways of thinking, but when she saw all of us dressed in white gathered devotedly around the guru, she was flustered. Of course, Indian traditions are very different from our Western culture, so I could understand Mom's uneasiness.

I was happy to set up a private meeting for Mom and Don with the guru, but after it was over, both of them grabbed me, packed me into the car, and off we drove back to LA. Mom was uncomfortable to begin with, but after an audience with the guru, she was even more so.

She confided, "Kellee, I had such a peculiar feeling sitting next to her. I can't really say why, but I don't think this group is for you." And just like that, I stopped attending meditation classes with the guru. I have to say it was quite an experience, but one that was short-lived.

Meditation

Like most things in life, if we pay attention, we can learn from our experiences. Although I had been meditating for a while, meeting the guru and following her method of meditation helped me to stay in a deeply meditative state longer. It was so important to go inward and be still. It enabled me to curb my wandering thoughts and to control the psychic activity.

The benefits of meditation are enormous. It helps to calm us, enabling us to make better choices. It causes us to have more compassion for ourselves and one another. It slows down our racing minds so that we can think before we act. It also helps to lower our blood pressure. I suffered from anxiety and depression on and off my entire life. Little did I know how much meditation would supplement my medication and give me the ability to focus my thoughts and think clearly.

After a year of daily deep meditation practice, I went to see Dr. Emory for my annual checkup and EEG. Imagine his surprise when he read the EEG and found that my brain waves were in complete Theta. I had the brain waves of a Tibetan monk! I explained I had been meditating daily for several hours a day. Dr. Emory was impressed by the results.

Meditation has the ability to balance the brain, and in my case, it was life-changing. I was able to slow down my brain waves and thereby change how I felt. I have a profound appreciation for the dramatic change in my brain that came from my daily practice of meditation.

Meeting The Real Deal

During my existential crisis, I have never forgotten James Van Praagh and his work as a ground-breaking medium. I had virtually inhaled all of his books up to that moment, from *Talking To Heaven* to *Heaven and Earth*. His books were manna for my soul. I intuitively knew everything he wrote to be true. Oddly enough, in 1997, I somehow sensed, when Charlene gifted me with his first book, that one day our paths would cross, and James and I would become friends. And that's exactly what happened.

In 2004, at around the age of 46, I knew the only person who could possibly understand what I was going through was James Van Praagh. I told my mother, "I need to meet James." Mom had heard of him and actually had discussed him with her celebrity clients. Out of the blue, she remembered that a dear friend of hers, Madeline, someone I had known for many years, also knew James. Mom called Madeline and asked if she would introduce me to James.

Happily, Madeline was very open to the idea. "I'd be delighted to give him a call. He's a fun guy, so let's see what happens."

Imagine my surprise when, two days later, James called me from Italy. He was on one of his seminar cruises, and while in port, he phoned. We spoke for more than an hour, and he was very attentive. I explained my circumstances and the supernatural events I had experienced, and he quickly understood my predicament. As a medium, he knew exactly how I felt seeing the spirit world, and he promised to call me as soon as he returned home. And he did—we spoke for hours. He was incredibly encouraging and helpful, and we have been the dearest of friends ever since.

I was extremely fortunate because James took me under his wing and showed me how to improve my skills. He became my private tutor and mentor. When I was ready, I sat with other psychics in his weekly development circle. As James says in his books, "The purpose of a development circle is to assist like-minded people in developing their natural psychic abilities and connections to the spiritual realms. The spirit world vibrates at a much higher frequency than our world, so participants must increase their individual vibrations in order to integrate the thoughts, feelings, words, and sights of spirit beings."

It was not long after my studies with James that he opened his spiritual school, the James Van Praagh School of Mystical Arts. Students are able to study many spiritual, paranormal, and psychic classes, including mediumship, contact with spirit guides, healing grief, meditation, and personal transformation.

If it were not for James, I would not have had the courage to demonstrate my gift of mediumship in public. He is the bravest person I have ever known. All mediums owe a debt of gratitude to him for kicking down the doors and making it possible for so many of us to do this important work.

After training with James and other like-minded individuals, I began a new chapter in my life. The year I spent living with Danny and Josie seemed to fly by. Every day was spent in meditation, practicing Kouk Sun Do, a form of meditation, as well as yoga, Qigong, and Tai Chi. All these ancient mind-body practices helped my mental and physical health. I was able to get the much-needed sleep I needed, during which time my broken spirit was in full healing mode.

At this juncture, I knew that my life had taken a 180-degree turnaround. I embraced my spirituality with open arms. No more doubt or anxiety about not knowing what to do. Spirituality wasn't foreign to me anymore. Finally, I felt at peace within my soul. I knew I was on the right path and going in the direction Spirit had planned for me all along.

Being stubborn, it took quite a while to recognize that life is not about getting or having things. Life is about knowing that we are spiritual beings having a temporary existence on Earth. We are here to learn and grow from our experiences, the good, the bad, and everything in between. Kindness, compassion, generosity, love, trust, and patience are the characteristics we need to cultivate. Everyone has these qualities, but few choose to express them. To quote the guru Paramahansa Yogananda, "The secret of success and happiness is inside you. If you have found success and prosperity outside but not inside, you are not truly successful."

It is a natural tendency for everyone to gravitate to the ego's qualities of fear, anxiety, anger, and havoc. I hoped that by now, I was done with those. I was ready for true happiness.

Chapter 13

RESURRECTION

Step out of your cave: the world waits for you as a garden.
The wind plays with the heavy fragrance that seeks you, and
all the brooks would like to run after you.

- Friedrich Nietzsche, *Thus Spoke
Zarathustra*

By late spring, I was feeling stronger mentally and spiritually,
so I decided to make an appointment with a headhunter. After all,
I needed to get a job and pay my way. Even though Danny and
Josie gave me carte blanche with their beautiful home, I knew I
couldn't live with them forever. I was a responsible person and
able to work, so I made an appointment with a head hunter,
although I was still uncertain about the kind of job I could do and
apply for.

My daughter's best friend, Shannon, who is like a daughter to
me, had been staying with me at my brother's house during her
summer vacation. Holiday had taken the summer off and was
traveling through Europe with a friend, thanks to a generous gift

from my mother. After all the upheaval of the last few years with my hitting my head, things seemingly flying around the room, and dreams of angels, Mom felt Holiday needed a break from all the unexpected and weird happenings to feel "normal" again.

As I was getting ready to leave the house for my appointment, I couldn't find my car keys. By this time, I had lived such a simple life, having few possessions or distractions. Finding my keys should have been easy because they were always in my Louis Vuitton handbag. It was my one and only favorite purse that I saved after I let go of my former self. Although I checked my bag over and over, I couldn't find them.

Sharon and I began to search the house from top to bottom for my lost keys. We checked the kitchen cabinets, the bathroom cabinets, under my bed, the laundry room, the garage, and even the refrigerator, but still no keys. We were the only two people in the house during the past week, so it would be impossible for Danny or Josie to have them. After an hour of hunting for the keys, we gave up. I called the head hunter and canceled the appointment.

At this point, I felt completely discouraged. Nothing was going the way I had planned. It didn't dawn on me at the time that Spirit must have had another plan for me of which I wasn't aware. Again, it was a tug-of-war between my spirit self and what my ego wanted.

Looking for car keys made us hungry, so Shannon and I went into the kitchen to make lunch. We brought our turkey sandwiches into the den, sat on the big Lazy Boy couch, and turned on the TV.

A movie was just starting called *Alaska*. It was a Disney movie that neither of us would normally watch, but as soon as we heard the lyrical Native American flute musical score, we were drawn in. The music was so compelling and otherworldly that we were transfixed and transported to a magical place.

At the end of the movie, we waited for the credits to roll across the screen to find out the name of the person who performed the music. And there it was—*Native American Flutes by Don Markese.*

After the movie, Shannon and I went to my bedroom to make another attempt at finding my keys. Imagine our surprise when we saw them sitting on top of my purse. We both shrieked. *How can this possibly be?* Then I sensed that my spirit guides must have moved my keys. I could only surmise that they did not want me to meet with the headhunter as they had more significant plans for me.

That same night, my sister Carol called and invited me to join her and a client for dinner the next evening. She had given this particular client some valuable advice, and he wanted to repay her with dinner. For some strange reason, she asked if she could bring me along. At first, I hesitated. It was so out of character for my sister to include me in her social sphere. Besides, having dinner with a stranger was the last thing I wanted to do. I only hoped that he would not ask, "Kellee, what do you do?" Do I answer—*I see spirits and angels!* Oh no. That would upset Carol, and I would never hear the end of it.

Just to be safe, I called Josie, who was out of town on a business trip and asked her opinion about the dinner. She said,

"Kellee, you need to go. You need to get out and have a good time for a change. Just go."

I decided to take a chance.

A Match Made in Heaven

Our dinner reservation was at The Palm, a well-known celebrity and movie industry hangout in West Hollywood. I didn't want Carol to pick me up, so I drove there myself just in case something unusual happened at dinner, and I needed to make a quick getaway.

I walked into the restaurant and spotted a handsome-looking man sitting at the bar watching the Lakers game on TV. When he turned around, our eyes met, and he got up and walked over to me. "You must be Kellee?"

Startled, I answered, "Yes."

He said, "My name is Don Markese. I'm happy to meet you and so glad you were able to join us for dinner."

I was knocked over. *Was this the same Don Markese whose name appeared on the credits for the movie Alaska?*

I didn't ask because, at that moment, Carol entered the restaurant, and we were ushered to our big red booth. Carol and I sat on one side across from Don. My sister wanted to talk about business, and I kept quiet as she went on and on. When there was a lull in the conversation, I finally spoke up.

"Are you a musician?" I asked.

"Yes, I am," he said. "Are you?"

"No." I blushed. Then said, "I watched this movie, *Alaska*, and the music was so beautiful. I waited for the credits to roll and saw

Flutes by Don Markese. Is that you?"

He simply said, "Yes."

I was thoroughly surprised. Then I wondered If the "missing keys" incident was about him.

After dinner, Don remarked, "I had a great time. Let's do it again soon." Carol begged off, saying she was swamped at work. But I didn't hesitate and said, "I'd love to."

Thus began my relationship with Don. I must say, it began in a unique way. Because of my ADD, head trauma, and the unusual episodes that occurred in my presence, my family kept a close guard over me. As a result, our first eight dates were chaperoned! Can you believe it? I was in my mid-forties and had to have a chaperone. To say it was very odd to have my brother Danny, or Mom and Marc, or sometimes Holiday as part of the date is an understatement. Don and I were literally never alone! Our conversations were limited for good reason—my family was afraid I would scare the poor guy off. But in my heart of hearts, I felt that he was sent by the spirit world, and he took the menagerie of dinner companions with a grain of salt.

By our ninth dinner date, we were finally left on our own. Thank God. Don was patient, interesting, and truly appeared to be captivated by me. He immediately gave me a feeling of safety and belonging. So safe, in fact, that right before our salads arrived that evening, I looked up and saw his sister hovering over his shoulder. She was talking to me telepathically.

"When you were about five years old, were you called "Dutes," I asked.

"What did you say?" Don looked up at me.

203

"When you were about 5 or 6, did your father call you Dutes?"

"Who told you that?" He turned around to see if someone was there.

"Your sister Marie," I replied.

He was completely bewildered. "How do you know I have a sister named Marie?" I began to explain when he interrupted. "You know, with your family always around, we haven't had a chance to talk about our past very much."

He seemed somewhat unsure to say anything, but then he spoke. "My sister Marie passed away five years ago."

"Yes, I can see her. She has dark hair and says she was five years older than you. She is the one telling me that you used to be called Donny Dutes."

Don stared at me in disbelief. "But you couldn't possibly know that. I didn't tell you about my sister."

It was my turn to feel uneasy. *Oh no. I blew it again. He thinks I'm a nutcase. My family was right. They should never have left me alone with him.*

He continued to stare at me but eventually relaxed. "How do you know about my sister and my nickname? No one knows that name from my childhood except close friends. What aren't you telling me, Kellee?"

This time, I felt safe enough to explain. I began slowly and softly. "I have this gift, and it may seem very strange to you, but I can see spirits, like in the movie. That's why my family was always with me. They were concerned that some weird thing would happen around me and frighten you away. They really like you, Don. And sometimes, it's hard for me to control what I see and what I say to someone. My family was only looking out for my welfare... and, in a way, yours."

Don smiled, and I felt the tenseness in my shoulders leave. He asked me a lot of questions about my psychic abilities. It felt good to be myself, to express my feelings, and to give him some personal background. He seemed so curious and focused on my every word; it was amazing. We talked until the restaurant closed. It was the beginning of a beautiful friendship.

Around 2 AM, Don dropped me off at my brother's house. When I opened the door, I saw Danny waiting for me. I was so grateful that there were people concerned for my well-being. It was a far cry from the years of abuse and turmoil I had endured.

Ever since meeting at the Palm, when Don and I looked into each other's eyes, I knew he was someone who could relate to me and vice versa. Don was and is creative, genuine, easygoing, and an all-around nice guy with a sense of humor. No more misogynistic, ego-maniacal corporate, unethical executive types who were never going to "get" me. Our two worlds came together as one. Thank you, Spirit. It was a match made in Heaven, and knowing what I know now, it definitely was.

Don and Me

There were so many "coincidences" with Don. First of all, like my father, he was a musician—a horn and flute player who loved jazz. Not only did he play in Neil Diamond's band, but he also accompanied many celebrities like Aretha Franklin, Linda Ronstadt, Brian Wilson, Liza Minelli, and so on. Secondly, Neil Diamond's band is called *The Archangels*. Huh!? That blew me away! Third of all, he was a spiritual person who didn't think that anything I said was strange. Actually, he was totally fascinated that I could tap into the spirit world. He was a nature lover and spent any time off from work in nature. Even his music reflected his spirituality—one of his albums is titled *Spirit Flows*.

I wasn't sure I would ever be in a relationship again. I had no idea where my life was going or what the road looked like ahead for me. Before all the intense spiritual experiences, I had always been sure of my life and where I was headed. Anyone who knew me thought of me as fearless. But spirituality was all new territory. I was in such an emotionally fragile state and so vulnerable. I was so afraid of being blind-sighted and betrayed by a man yet again. And beyond my fears was the feeling that I had absolutely no idea who I was anymore. It's hard to be in a new relationship when you don't have a sense of self. That's my warning to everyone. Know yourself before you get involved!

I was petrified when meeting Don because I wasn't sure of what to say. I knew my name and where I lived and knew who I had been. But... who I was at that particular moment in time was a mystery. How could I explain my visions or my conversations with the dead? What would he think of me?

But Don was not what I had expected. In fact, I had never met anyone like Don before. When I looked into his eyes, I saw only one thing—kindness. I don't think I had ever experienced that feeling with any man before Don. To hear him tell the story of our first encounter, he said, "When I first set eyes on you as you were walking into the restaurant, light poured out of you." He added, "I thought you were an angel."

Years before meeting Don, I had a dream—I was in a park in Chicago surrounded by what appeared to be male relatives—people I didn't recognize but who I knew—grandfathers, uncles, and cousins. It was this group that introduced me to a man who looked a lot like Don. I'm quite sure this is why when I met Don, on a psychic level, I knew him. It was as if we had already met before, and yes, we probably did in another life or lifetimes. There was a deep soul connection that I couldn't articulate. It was uncanny but very real.

Although Don was a working musician, which was familiar territory to me, at the same time, I couldn't imagine that I would EVER be with a musician. Most of the ones I knew were wildly narcissistic, drug addicts or alcoholics, and I just couldn't be in that type of relationship again. For sure, I had my share of narcissists and alcoholics.

But Don was different. Really different. I found out that he had NEVER had alcohol in his life. And he had never done drugs. It was mystifying and confusing. How can anyone be a musician in Los Angeles their entire life and NEVER use alcohol or drugs? It just made no sense to me. Go figure. I found the ONE UNICORN musician.

It was Don's beloved mother, Blanche, who explained Don's unexpected behavior. She told me, "When Donny was young, I drummed it into his head—no drugs and no alcohol." Blanche was a fierce force to be reckoned with, so apparently, Don followed her admonition and did what he was told. I'm sure he must have had some tempting moments, but I think in the back of his mind, dealing with Blanche would have made having a drink not worth the trouble.

Don was a hard-working musician. When he was not on tour with Neil Diamond's band, he was playing in sets for movie soundtracks, commercials, and record albums. He was a top musician in LA, which meant he literally worked non-stop. Don was also consistent. If he said he would call me, he did. We saw each other every single night when he was in town.

I also loved that Don was so family-oriented. He told me all about his family, and I couldn't wait to meet them. They all lived in Wisconsin on farms. That was a completely new adventure for me. Because Don was so busy either in LA or on tour, our first trip together to the farm was on December 26, 2004, for Christmas. Imagine Christmas on a farm! A dream come true. Don's family warmly embraced me, and we have been close ever since. The two of us would try and plan to be on the farm three or four times a year. Don wanted me to see it in different seasons. It was always beautiful, and I always felt sad when it came time to leave. The farm was one of the very few places where both Don and I could relax.

In all the years we've been together, it was Don who taught me what love really was. He was always there for me. He shared his hopes and dreams with me. He was good-hearted, loving, and loyal, and I grew to trust him. Another trait that was foreign to me was that Don was a man of his word. I never felt anxious with him like I did with so many others. His patience, kindness, and understanding of me were more than profound. Don't let me be me exactly as I am. He was unwavering in his support for my work and honored my path.

I also changed Don's life. Before me, Don had been married for many years, and it was a difficult relationship. Because we were both caregivers, we both understood how to care for one another. I was so happy to take care of this man in any way possible. We were so grateful that we found each other. There were no games or hidden agendas. Just love.

Although he performed in front of thousands of people, ironically, Don was an introvert. I helped to bring him out of his shell and make him feel comfortable around a group of people. He was always a spiritual person, and my insight and experiences helped to open him up to a wondrous world beyond. His compassion has helped so many of his friends who are going through difficult life situations. And Don never shies away from spiritual conversations!

I thank God every day that our relationship is loving and joyful and not filled with angst and trauma like my previous unstable relationships. It took me a while to work through the karma of the past. I guess you could call me a "late bloomer."

My life was changing for the better. Not only was I in a loving relationship with a truly beautiful human being, but I was on my spiritual path. As I continued my spiritual journey with Don by my side, I had a new life and a positive direction. It took me half my life to find myself, but there was no going back and no stopping me from moving forward. I was reborn.

Chapter 14

FINDING PURPOSE

Do not look to others to do the work for you. Every man is his own savior, and every man is the savior of all mankind.

- White Eagle, The Still Voice

Way back in 1995, before I began entering the therapeutic world working with Mom, I was still running ragged in the corporate world. That's when Dr. Shirley Impellizzeri entered my life and found her way into my heart as a true confidant and trusted friend. She seems to have the natural effect of love with everyone she meets. I could truly say that Shirley is my one and only soul sister.

Shirley had many dreams when she was growing up in Argentina, and one of them was to work in a place she heard about as a child, Beverly Hills, California.

Like many other psychology students fresh out of UCLA grad school and attempting to go into private practice, Shirley had to obtain a psychotherapy license. In the state of California, that meant 3,000 hours of supervised experience. Unbelievable huh?

My incredible mother had a knack for seeing the potential in others and had decided to risk her license and her busy practice to make Shirley her intern.

Let me start at the beginning, or what I consider the fun part. When my mother asked Shirley how she happened to come upon her office out of all the ones in Beverly Hills, Shirley said, "First of all, I knew I was supposed to go there. I had been dreaming of being in Beverly Hills since I was a little girl. As I drove around the streets with all the glitz and glamor I expected, I saw your building and stopped the car. *This is it,* I thought to myself. It felt familiar, so I knew it was the place for me. I can't tell you how I knew. I just knew. So, I parked the car and walked into the building. As I suspected, it was filled with doctor and therapy suites. I was sure to find the right psychology office for me, and whoever answered the call bell, I would ask to be their associate."

Of course, Shirley had to be living in "fantasyland" for all this to happen. But I knew, and I'm sure my mother had an inkling, that the spirit world was unfolding Shirley's destiny plan.

Only six square miles, Beverly Hills, like the rest of LA, is known for its many celebrities, its luxury stores, and its nightmarish traffic. Finding a parking space in a town overrun with tourists is almost inconceivable. But not, I guess, for Shirley. She drove from east Los Angeles and somehow managed to find my mom's office/medical building and a parking spot right in front. As if on a mission, Shirley stepped impulsively into the elevator and pushed "3". When the elevator doors opened, she headed straight to a suite of psychologists' offices at the very end of the hall. When Shirley entered the suite, she pushed the button under the name of Dr. LaWanda Katzman, and out stepped Mom, who asked, "Do you need help?"

Pretty remarkable, to say the least. Moreover, Mom was in session, so the odds of her leaving her patient and answering the door were unimaginable. Shirley quickly launched into her rehearsed speech. "My name is Shirley Impellizzeri. I graduated from UCLA with my Ph.D. in psychology, and I'm looking for someone to supervise my hours. Would you consider being my supervisor?"

Mom softly answered, "Well, that's good honey, but I don't know you, and I don't take psych assistants anymore. It's a big commitment." She was about to close the door when Shirley quickly blurted out, "But I'm excellent in hypnosis."

"Well, that's great to know," Mom said. "I'm always looking for someone who can use hypnosis with patients, but I still don't know you. Let's set up lunch, get to know each other, and see if we're a good fit." Long story short, Mom became Shirley's supervisor and eventually one of her closest friends.

Psychologists, Spirits, and One Medium

Shirley moved into my mother's large suite of offices. When the lease came up for renewal, Mom no longer wanted the responsibility of a large suite, so she and Shirley found a beautiful space with three offices in a building two blocks away. It was a perfect place that fulfilled all their needs.

Funny how life works out. When Mom and Shirley moved into their offices, there was a windowless office they could never seem to rent out. That's where I come in. One day, they both commented that perhaps that windowless office would be a perfect setting for me to do mediumship readings. So when I finally left the corporate world and began my spiritual journey, I often wondered, *How could I possibly do my work as a medium in an office setting?* Previously, I would do readings in people's homes or sometimes sat with Mom or Shirley with their patients in their offices. Wow! How did the spirit world set this up perfectly? I could be around the two people I admired most and simultaneously become enriched by changing people's lives and by creating a safe space of love. The intelligence of the spirit world never ceased to amaze me. I was all in.

I began to work with a few of my mother's selected patients who had suffered a loss. For sure, I wasn't everyone's cup of tea, but the ones who believed in an afterlife were open to spiritual contact with their loved ones. I could tell that these patients made great headway by viewing their problems from two different perspectives. Not only did the patients improve and get better, but Mom and I learned more every day about loss, grief, and mental disorders and how all of it affects a person's life in a variety of areas.

One day, while I waited to see a patient with Mom, a young woman sat in the reception area waiting for Shirley. She was in her late 20s with long dark hair and very sad eyes. It's not uncommon for a psych patient to look sad. But I saw a baby girl about two years old in Spirit right next to her.

Shirley greeted her patient, and I watched the mother and baby go into her office. The connection between the mother and baby deeply affected me, and I had to discuss it with Shirley afterward. When Shirley said goodbye to the young woman, she looked at me. "Did you see anyone with her?"

"Yes, I saw her baby daughter. She never left her mother's side."

Shirley shook her head in acknowledgment.

On the next visit, Shirley escorted the young woman into my office. I could sense her loss; it was enormous. It surprised me that the woman was even able to function well enough to see a therapist. I began by describing my vision. "I see something about the wrong medicine from a pharmacy. As a result, the pharmacy has been closed. I believe your baby angel in Heaven had something to do with the pharmacy closing to prevent the wrong medicine from hurting other children."

At that moment, the young woman took a deep breath and let out a moan.

I continued. "Your baby girl is your spirit guide, and she'll grow up in Heaven. She will always be a part of your life."

The young woman broke down and cried. When she stopped crying, she looked at me. "I'm so grateful to you. I know my baby is safe. Now I can move forward."

"Your baby is telling me that you will be together again, and she will be with you whenever you need her."

From that day forward, I worked with many of Shirley's patients, often with Shirley in the room. She was always moved by the progress a person made after meeting a loved one in Spirit. It was as if a heavy burden had been lifted off their shoulders. All the dread and depression dissipated, making space in their hearts to love and be loved again. I will always be indebted to Shirley for believing in me and letting me share my work with her patients.

The Ballroom

At this point, my mornings were spent practicing Sundo, a combination of meditation, yoga, Tai Chi, and Qigong. This daily practice helped to balance body, mind, and soul. My main goal was to heal all the hurts, pain, and confusion of the past. I found a Sundo studio in Hollywood near my brother's house, and every day I attended classes. Our master teacher from Korea was instrumental in bringing me back to my center. I will forever be grateful to Master Young. Sundo has given me much peace of mind and enabled me to move forward with quiet confidence.

After class, I would sit and meditate for hours in silent solitude. Several days a week, around 5 PM, I would drive to Beverly Hills to pick up Mom from her office and chauffeur her home. At this stage in her life, Mom found driving difficult. I coveted our time alone as we discussed all things mystical and paranormal. Other than Don and Holiday, she was the only one with whom I could safely share my spiritual progress.

My evenings were spent with Don. He was one busy guy, always working on his music, but the evenings were our time together. After work, he would pick me up at my brother's house, and we would go out for Italian food. Don was Italian, and his favorite foods revolved around pizza and Caesar salad. We went to every single Italian restaurant in Los Angeles. It was so much fun!

Late one afternoon, as I was waiting in the car to drive Mom home, I noticed that it was taking longer than usual for her to leave the office. I started to worry. Finally, she appeared. "I'm so sorry, Kellee. My patient was late because she couldn't find her car keys." *That sounded familiar.* "I wanted to give her a full session." It never occurred to me that "losing car keys" was one way the spirit world gets us to change direction.

It was typical of Mom to wait for her patients; she tried her best to accommodate them. As we drove to her house, I tuned into the patient with the lost keys and saw an unexpected situation at her home. The patient's house was filled with spirits, and they were all dancing. A little spirit girl about six years old had taken the patient's keys to get her attention. I told my mother about my vision.

Mom turned to me, "Kellee, are you saying that a six-year-old girl in the spirit world is moving the keys to get her mother's attention?"

"Yes. That's exactly what I'm saying. She wants her mother to know she's there." My mother was dumbfounded.

I continued, "Also, at one time, the house had a large ballroom because I see spirit people dancing in the main room. And by the way, their young son sees the dancing spirits, too."

Mom stared at me. She never said anything about this patient, her family, or where they lived. I knew nothing, and yet I seemed to know more than her.

When we arrived home, Mom quickly went to the den and said, "I need a drink. Honey, I can't imagine that you can see so clearly. May I repeat what you just said to my patient? Her name is Liz."

By this time, the scenes in my mind had vanished. Frankly,

these visions came in waves, and I never knew what was coming next. "Be my guest," I replied.

The next day, Mom spoke with her patient, and Liz asked her, "Can I see your daughter?"

Liz preferred that I go to her house, and I agreed. She lived in Beverly Hills, not far from Mom's house, so it was easy to find. I parked the car and walked up to the enormous gates. I pushed a button, and the gates opened. I walked up the driveway and saw Liz waiting at the front door along with her ten-year-old son, Matt.

Liz led me into the living room, and immediately, I saw spirits dancing above me. They were elegantly dressed from another era. Apparently, back in the day, this home was a place where many parties were held. I told Liz about the dancing spirits. Matt quickly chimed in, "See, Mom. That's exactly what I've been telling you. I see them too!" He was happy to be validated.

When Matt went outside, I told Liz, "There's a little girl upstairs in your closet playing dress-up with your shoes. She tells me you're her mother. It appears she passed away when she was two."

Like the little girl in Taos who grew up in Spirit, this little girl was now six years old. She, too, was growing up in Heaven.

Liz was visibly shaken by this information. "Chloe was so small when she died of cancer. We couldn't talk about her passing with anyone. It was too devastating for all of us. I tried to close that chapter of my life because it was so painful. I thought if I just kept quiet about it, it would somehow disappear."

It was obvious that she kept it quite hidden. She didn't even tell my mother, her therapist.

I understood Liz very well. Like her, I tried to hide my hurt and pain, hoping it would vanish, and I used work as a way to cope. I'm not sure how Liz escaped the pain, but I knew that she needed to explore her feelings with my mother; otherwise, the pain would never go away.

Matt was six years old when Chloe passed. Even he couldn't talk about it. I suspect he was in pain, too. The spirit dancers in the ballroom were trying to get the family's attention—to make them recognize that it was important to acknowledge that Chloe did exist. Matt tried to let his parents know, but eventually, he gave up.

I visited the family a few more times to help them reconnect with their daughter. Liz continued to see Mom to work through her grief. The keys never went missing again, and the family began the most important thing of all—the healing process.

From that time on, Mom asked me to help her with patients who had suffered a loss. I brought a powerful lens to these sessions, and the results were dramatic and valuable to the patient's health, bringing change, even transformation. Mom realized that there was more to therapy than just talking about problems.

My role in her sessions played a prominent part in changing the customary way Mom worked with her patients. These sessions with Mom's patients became the foundation for the work I do today with my clients.

The Plane Crash

Often, the spirit world will spontaneously reveal itself to me

219

when someone is in dire need. This happened one day as I sat in the reception area once again, waiting to drive Mom home. A young woman was leaving Shirley's office, and she was not alone as she walked out. An entire spirit family—mother, father, and sister—followed her, and they made quite sure I could see them.

As soon as we were alone, I said to Shirley, "That young woman who just walked out of your office needs my help. Her whole family is around her, and they're reaching out to me because they have messages for her. I should see her."

Shirley was taken off guard. "Really?" She hasn't talked to me about her family, but that's because she is quite shut down. I'm having a difficult time breaking through. Yes, she does need to see you," She then said. "I'll ask her if she's willing to talk to you, and if so, I'll arrange a session." I was hoping that Shirley could persuade the young woman to see me as I knew her family wouldn't rest until they had a chance to communicate with her—they had a lot to tell her.

By this time, Shirley and I had a mutual understanding, so to speak—she's not to tell me anything about a patient, and I won't ask any questions about the person's circumstances. If I know the patient's background beforehand, it muddies the water. I want the information I receive to come straight from Spirit and not from some information I may have stored away in my mind.

A week later, I met Shirley and her patient, Nicole. She was understandably nervous, but Shirley assured her, "It'll be okay. Kellee's going to help you."

Nicole, Shirley, and I went into my small office. Nicole sat down, and I could tell she was a little hesitant, so I suggested she take a few deep breaths to relax. I wanted to get clear messages from the spirit world, and often, a person's anxiety can and will block communication.

When the room became very still, I began. "I see a large plane—looks like it's in New York or Long Island. The plane is headed for Paris. Your family is on the plane. Your mother has short hair like a Pixie cut, and your father is a bigger-than-life kind of man. He has a strong personality, as if he was the head of a company. He certainly shows he's the boss. And your little sister is with them—she's a lot younger than you—maybe six or seven years old. They're indicating that you didn't want to go with them to Paris. No matter how much they begged you, you were adamant. You had just turned 14 and were crazy about boys, and one boy in particular. You wanted to stay with your best friend's family so the two of you could hang out with the other kids, especially this boy you had a crush on."

Nicole's eyes widened, and she nodded she understood.

To my dismay, in my mind, I saw the plane explode upon taking off and all the parts scatter in the water. The explosion appeared as an enormous bright light, almost as if a bomb just dropped. I explained to Nicole what I saw, and both she and Shirley gasped. Nicole looked down. I could see she was trying to hold back her tears.

I paused before continuing. "Nicole, your mother doesn't want you to feel guilty that you weren't on that plane. You weren't supposed to be. It was not spirit's plan." Nicole sat in silence as I continued.

"Your mother is saying that she is proud of you and how well you are doing. She sees you volunteering at a church shelter. You're helping to make meals for the homeless."

Nicole was trembling. "She can see me at the shelter?"

I replied, "Yes, she's watching over you. She loves that you are following your dream of becoming a chef. She's saying that she wants you to come out of your own shelter and live your life. She says you have enormous talent, and one day, you'll be running your own restaurant."

After some more details about her family and some loving words from her father, Nicole put her hands to her face and sobbed. Shirley and I sat there, knowing that Nicole was finally able to start grieving for her family in Heaven.

I continued, "Your mom is saying that she will be your guide. She promises you'll all be together again."

That plane crash took place in 1996 on a flight from New York to Paris. The encounter with Nicole took place 10 years later. Suffice it to say Nicole needed to hear from her family to begin her journey of healing. The session opened her heart and gave her hope. Shirley worked with Nicole on the psychological trauma—helping her to release the burden of her misplaced "survivor guilt" and the regret and remorse she felt that chained her to the past.

Taking Care of Mom

Mediumship became my life's purpose, and I had a busy schedule doing readings for many clients who came to Mom and Shirley's office. My life was in full swing. No longer was I concerned about getting a job or wondering why spirits were all around. I truly felt my life force function in a profound way. I had awakened to my true life's purpose, and this was the responsibility I had come back to Earth to fulfill. It was awesome!

Along the way, Don and I moved in together. Although he was on tour most of the year, I felt safe and secure with him. Our relationship was filled with laughter, lots of friends, and good times together.

It was 2007, and I had just turned 50. Mom was in the hospital for a second hip replacement surgery. The first was 20 years ago due to a skiing accident. Unfortunately, the radiation treatment she underwent when she had breast cancer had taken a toll on her left lung. As a result, any new surgery was considered life-threatening.

Luckily, the surgery went well, and I thought she was out of the woods. However, in the middle of the night, her oxygen level fell below normal. Mom began to act strangely. When I stood by her bed, she began telling me that she was seeing her father, mother, and brother. I thought to myself, *What the heck is going on? She's seeing spirits! She's very close to the veil. Oh my God, is she about to die?*

A Code Blue was called, and all the doctors on the floor raced into her room with the crash cart. Doctors worked to revive her. She stopped breathing and slipped into unconsciousness. That's when I realized her oversight. Because the hip surgery happened so fast, she didn't tell the hospital about all the medicine she had been taking to keep her lungs and brain functioning. *How could she forget that? How could I forget it?* That mishap took a hit on my sense of responsibility.

Thank God, the Spirit intervened at that moment. Mom was delirious and on her way out when I picked up the phone and called Dr. Emory. Because of her radiation treatment for cancer all those years ago, she had only the use of one good lung. The other one became paralyzed. Sure enough, once she was given the proper medication, she came back to life. Dr. Emory came to the rescue again like he had so many years before with my head injury. Needless to say, I stayed with Mom in the hospital every night for a week until she was released.

When Mom came home, she needed lots of assistance, and I was so pleased that I had time enough to be her caretaker. While recovering, she asked me to set up appointments at home with her patients. Patients loved coming to her house. It was so different than being in an office. As they waited, I made them tea and got to know many of them. It gave me firsthand knowledge of what it was like to be a therapist. For those who were comfortable with me, I was willing to give them readings from the spirit world.

After a few months, Mom returned to the office. She really found joy in being a psychologist. Helping to solve her patient's problems was her life calling.

By this time, Mom hinted often enough that she thought I should permanently work alongside her and Shirley in their offices. But I realized that mediumship wasn't enough. People were traumatized, and I wanted to possess all the tools necessary that could help them through the entire process. Actually, it was Mom's idea to get my Master's in psychology. "Kellee, all my people love you. Your work as a medium is incredible. Being a psychologist would be an amazing addition to that." It was another destiny point. I made the decision to go to graduate school, get my master's degree, and become a licensed psychologist.

It's Never Too Late

Like so many times in the past, when either looking for a job or starting a new one, I had no idea *how* I could do it, but I always managed to do it. Grad school was no exception.

I thought, *Who would take me?* It was 2009, I was 52 years old, and my Bachelor's Degree in child development was 30 years old. My grades in the 1970s were terrible because of my ADD. I never would have imagined going to grad school, but Spirit had a plan, and grad school was the next step.

After searching around, I found a graduate school that promoted what I thought was a spiritual curriculum. Although the school was an hour-and-a-half drive north of my home, it seemed to be compatible with my spiritual path. After sending in the application, I was invited to attend a day-long retreat along with 30 other potential students. Again, excitement built inside me at the idea of meeting other like-minded individuals. And although I was the oldest one there, it seemed like a perfect fit.

One of the two interviewers asked, "Kellee, what do you do for a living?" Being naive to academia, I told them the truth. "I'm a psychic medium. I do readings in my mother's office with clients who need some help with their grief." The look on their faces told me everything, and I knew that I wasn't getting into this so-called spiritual school. I drove home devastated.

Don was out of the country on tour, and when he called that evening, I told him the news. He was comforting. "If it isn't the one for you, Kellee, there's a better program out there."

The day before Mother's Day, while Holiday was visiting, I received a letter from the school. It was part of a chain email. I was the only one of the 30 who didn't get accepted. It was crushing. *How could Spirit lead me into this disaster? Hadn't I gone through enough?*

With all my spiritual maturity, I missed the fact that when one door closes, another one opens. Again, I panicked. Negative chatter took hold of my psyche. I didn't realize that Spirit had a better plan in store for me. Just remember that no matter how far along we travel on our spiritual journey, the ego's cynical and discouraging thoughts are always lurking in our minds to knock us off the path. Persistence and diligence are required if we want to continue to move forward.

Several weeks later, as I waited in the reception area to drive Mom home from the office, I noticed a young woman walk into the small office. Shirley told me she had rented the small space once a week to a young psych student named Monica.

Prompted by Spirit, I asked her, "Would you mind telling me where you went to grad school?"

She smiled and answered, "Phillips Graduate School."

I had never heard of it. "Where is it? Did you like it?"

She said, "I loved it. It's not far from here."

I went home that night and googled it. It was about a 30-minute drive from my home. Phillips was accepting applications for the fall semester, and I applied online and was quickly scheduled for an interview.

On the day of the interview, I was a nervous wreck. This time, I decided not to tell them my background. I didn't want to risk another rejection. And, to my amazement, I got into the master's program.

Being a student again was one of the best experiences of my life. This time, I was mature enough and centered enough to handle all the work. Besides, I loved my professors, and to my surprise, I was not the oldest student. There was someone even older than me, which was reassuring. Most of the clients with whom I worked at grad school thought I had been practicing for years, so my age turned out to be an indirect benefit.

I decided not to tell anyone at school that I was a medium, at least not until I had my degree. And even then, I waited until I had my psychology license. I was so glad that I ignored my feelings of rejection, believing it was a sign not to go to grad school. I would never be where I am today.

While I absolutely loved graduate school, it was the first step to becoming a licensed psychotherapist. Like all grads wanting to be licensed, I had to have a psychology supervisor oversee my 3,000 hours of therapy sessions. Shirley became my psychology supervisor. Talk about karmic payback. Graduate school may take two-and-a-half years, but the entire process of becoming a bona fide therapist took me five years.

The Exam

Several weeks before the licensing exam, I had fallen and suffered a broken left arm and right ankle. It was obvious that Spirit clearly wanted me to stay put and commit all my efforts to studying for the test. My only responsibility was to pass the licensing exam. For weeks, I diligently pounded the books.

On the week of the exam, Don had to leave on tour, and I needed a ride because I was still handicapped by the fall. Spirit intervened and arranged for my youngest half-brother, Theo, to be in town that week. Theo graciously volunteered to drive me to the exam. Spirit made sure that nothing was going to stop me from taking that test.

The night before the exam, I was filled with extreme apprehension. If I failed, it would be another nine months before I could take the test again. Anyone who has taken a licensing exam knows the heightened state of anxiety one feels. The gravity of failing such a test is unthinkable. That night, I went to bed early so I would be in the best emotional place I could be in the morning. The most amazing thing happened. Dad appeared in a lucid dream with a friend of his, asking me to help his friend's son, who was in jail. I thought, *Really, Dad?* In the dream, I said, "I have the most important exam of my life tomorrow." But Dad was insistent and told me the name of his friend. I didn't know this friend or his son. *What was I supposed to do?*

The dream was very vivid, and I couldn't shake it off. Before we left for the exam, I described the dream to Theo. "Give me a minute. I'll look it up on the internet," Theo said. "Believe it or not, Kellee, his friend, is a famous jazz musician. Dad knew him really well. I don't have any idea where his son is, but maybe we can find out."

At this point, the only thing I cared about was passing the test. Imagine my surprise when Theo found out that Dad's friend had passed away a year ago, and his son was in a Mexican jail. Still, I had no idea how Dad thought I could help his friend's son. It was certainly a mysterious request, and even though we tried to figure it out, there was no more time to waste—I had to get to the exam.

Because I became so distracted by the dream and trying to find my Dad's friend's son, my anxiety about the psych test evaporated by the time I entered the exam room. In fact, I did so well that I received a letter from the Board of Psychology inviting me to Sacramento to participate in composing questions for future exams. I was prouder of that letter than even passing the exam. I have to believe it was Dad's intervention strategy that worked.

After passing the exam, I was on my way to becoming a licensed psychotherapist. Spirit had brought me this far, and I knew in my heart it wasn't going to stop. I had nothing to fear ever again!

I began counseling clients in a setting where I was observed and critiqued. After logging 3,000 client hours, there was a two-part exam, one of which was standing before a board of examiners and answering their questions. Some say the oral exam is as difficult as the bar licensing exam. And I passed!

At times, it felt quite daunting to become a licensed therapist, but it was well worth the effort. I had a direction that made sense to me, and Spirit gave me the ability to stick with it and complete the process. Becoming a psychotherapist was a tremendous destiny point in my life.

I was one of the lucky ones because I was able to work in the small office in Mom and Shirley's suite. Since it was already cozy, I hired a decorator to design the space so it would feel spiritually inviting. It turned out to be exactly the space I needed, and everyone loved the room.

A few years after my licensing, when Mom retired, Shirley and I opened our own office together, just a few feet from that very office on Bedford Drive in Beverly Hills, where Shirley first met Mom. So, the spirit world took us full circle. Shirley worked with Mom, and then I worked with Shirley. It was obvious that the three of us were soul mates and had a soul contract to fulfill. We had made the decision that this lifetime was the one where we worked together to heal others.

As I look back at our relationship, I realize that it just makes so much sense to me. Nothing is by chance. No one in your life is here by mistake. I suggest you make the best of every opportunity the Spirit presents to you because you have made the decision to be with the people in your life before you were born. There is a plan and purpose for each one of us. Let Spirit lead the way.

Chapter 15

SPIRITUALITY AND PSYCHOLOGY

Spread love everywhere you go. Let no one ever come to you without leaving you better and happier. Be the living expression of God's kindness.

Kindness in your face, kindness in your eyes. Kindness in your smile. Kindness in your warm greeting.

- Mother Theresa

At this point, I had spent hundreds of hours in my own therapy sessions, as is required for all therapists. In therapy, I started to get relief from all the trauma I had been through. Interestingly enough, it was during these therapy sessions that I had clear insight that my life theme was "responsibility." But what I didn't realize before learning this was that I felt responsible for everyone's happiness and welfare. Huh? What a set-up! Of course, there was no possible way I could make everyone happy, and because of this, I never felt "good enough." Ultimately, I had to let go of all the anger and hurt I had hidden deep within me, which turned out to be decades of pain.

The best therapy for my situation was a process called Somatic Experience Therapy. This type of therapy is aimed at treating deep-seated trauma and especially PTSD issues. Never realizing it before this process, my PTSD was initially caused all those years ago when Holiday fell out the window. Add to it all of my abusive relationships with men in my personal life and in my business career. And let's not forget my brain injury.

In Somatic Therapy, I was guided by my therapist to focus on the underlying physical sensations the traumatic events triggered in my body. I began mind-body exercises, including breath work, deep tissue massage, meditation, visualization, grounding, dance, and sensation awareness. I was able to revisit past traumas that were literally stuck deep in the tissues and fibers of my body, release the pain and suffering, and make peace with everything that had happened to me. Finding a level of peace allowed me to open every door and make the most of every situation. It was all about understanding myself, accepting my worth, and loving myself with no strings attached despite my life theme of responsibility.

Becoming Whole

At last, I was becoming whole. I could feel my body, mind, and soul melding together. It was a new experience to be so calm and content, the way every soul needs to feel in order to fulfill their purpose here on Earth. I had wasted too much time and energy making decisions from my ego that were based on fear and anxiety. My healing was all about integrating the loving energies of my spiritual self with my Earthly life. I could no longer deny that I was a spiritual being having a physical experience.

Integrating both my psychological lens and spiritual lens made me a better psychotherapist, and I couldn't feel more at home than when I was helping patients with grief and trauma. I felt recharged and aligned with a commitment to Spirit. I'm proud to say that my mission to bridge spirituality and psychology was the path for which I was destined and one that would ease a lot of pain for many people. As I look back on the events in my life, it seems that I have stumbled on the cutting edge of a new perspective— "spiritual psychology."

Many times, clients will come to me after they have been with a conventional therapist. I can't tell you how often they have said that they couldn't share their spiritual connections with their therapist for fear of being labeled "delusional." When a client makes the decision to seek therapy, he or she needs to be in a safe environment and be able to discuss anything and everything, including spiritual thoughts, dreams, feelings, and even seeing loved ones who have passed over. Some therapists can dismiss these feelings and thoughts as imaginary, and not validating them could cause another set of problems for a client, such as isolation, depression, and self-destruction.

I mean, look at my background. If I didn't have my mother and many self-aware individuals close by, imagine how I could have ended up? Because I had to go through the trials and tribulations of my spiritual awakening, I was prepared enough to understand a client's distress as they grappled with their own spiritual identity. I was able to shine a light on a path to lead them forward.

Everyone, at some time, will have a spiritual experience. Hopefully, we will find someone with an open mind with whom we feel free to share the experience. Only by discussing such spiritual encounters can real spiritual growth take place. Without spiritual growth, a patient may have a temporary healing, but a new problem will eventually pop up because the healing did not reach the person at a deeper level.

As therapists, we must have the capacity to understand that everyone longs to be reassured that they are okay and have the self-awareness to let go of a client's personality flaws, put outer effects in perspective, and know that there is a higher order at work residing within their minds and hearts.

Likewise, mediums need to have some psychological understanding, particularly when dealing with trauma and grief. After all, most mediumship sessions are about loss, tragedy, and sorrow. Mediums must be empathetically and compassionately prepared to deal with such loss.

I always provide my clients with referrals to grief groups, Somatic Experience Therapy, or other forms of healing practices depending on the issues a client presents to me. I also use my spiritual lens to point someone in a certain direction necessary to channel their higher self.

Healing Addiction

One of the most painful traumas a person can go through is that of addiction. As a medium psychotherapist and one who has suffered severe trauma, I have first-hand insight into the pain suffered by loved ones losing someone to addiction, violence, or suicide. Native Americans view addiction as a crisis of the spirit, and existential psychiatrist Victor Frankl, a Holocaust survivor and author of *Man's Search for Meaning*, explained that addiction is caused by feelings of meaninglessness, denial, and the attempt to escape ourselves.

When someone dies of an overdose, whether through drugs or alcohol, their death can be one of the hardest to reconcile. My friend Michele Goffin, the sister of actor Jeff Conaway, was in tremendous pain from losing her brother in 2011. Jeff was well-known for his role as *Bobby* in the TV series *Taxi*. For years, Jeff suffered from drug and alcohol addiction and died of complications from pneumonia stemming from his addiction. Michelle asked for a reading to connect with Jeff in the spirit world.

Usually, the night before my readings, I often ask the person in the spirit world to come through in the dream state and give me some information. This is a good way for me to "get out of my own ego" and be clear in the details.

In my dream, Jeff showed up in the most unusual fashion. He sat outside among oak and magnolia trees surrounded by an expanse of lush green lawn, dressed all in white and accompanied by a nurse-like spirit. The three of us sat on a bench next to a white building, where I was told he was being healed of his addictions. I was not allowed into the building—that is why we met outside. Jeff had been in treatment on the other side since his passing three months before.

I learned another valuable lesson from the spirit world. The suffering that ends a soul's life in our dimension is healed when the soul crosses to the other side. If someone is dealing with addiction, like Jeff, and they pass over with the addiction, it is still very much a part of his mindset. Eventually, he will come to realize that it's just a memory of his physical existence and does not really sustain any harm to him in the spiritual lands. Eventually, there is 100% recovery. This healing is not for the physical body. The body is a mere shell and is vacated at death. Once the soul leaves the physical body, it vibrates at a much higher level—it is literally in and of light and is healed through the love of the Spirit, and the prayers loved ones say for them.

A year after the reading with Jeff Conaway's sister, James Van Praagh asked me to join him on the radio show *Loveline* hosted by Dr. Drew Pinksy. Commonly known as "Dr. Drew," Dr. Pinsky was a medical doctor who worked mainly with addiction and hosted *Loveline* from 1984 until 2016. In addition, he has hosted a variety of TV shows, including *Dr. Drew On Call* and *Celebrity Rehab.*

The night before I went on the show, again in my lucid dream state, I had another visit with Jeff. This time, he looked incredibly healthy and vibrant. He told me, "Let Dr. Drew know I'm doing fine and thank him for hanging in there and supporting me." He wanted to make sure that Dr. Drew knew how grateful he was for all the care he had given him. "Tell him that I got a lot of help when I reached here."

This particular show was going live on Halloween, and the energy portal to the other side was wide open. Before the show, I asked James, "Do you think I should tell Dr. Drew what Jeff said to me?"

James quickly responded. "Yes, you must tell him." So, I did.

Dr. Drew was quite moved by Jeff's message and was very relieved to know Jeff finally received the help he needed.

Why does a soul choose addiction? Sometimes, a soul uses addiction as a life theme in order to fully understand the experience of addiction. He or she may be training to become an addiction specialist or a spirit guide on the other side to help souls on Earth with addiction. Another possibility is the soul who passes from addiction chooses to experience addiction to stop generational addiction. A soul's passing may be a catalyst for others in their soul group to make changes and give up their addictions. Not only does the soul save lives, but it could change the course of the group's destiny.

My dad was an addict, and for my entire life, I had issues around addiction. Although I loved my father, his addiction to alcohol, heroin, and pot had deeply affected me. When he was dying of liver failure, I was concerned that seeing him would trigger unwanted feelings in me about his addiction.

In Dad's last days. Don and I flew to Taos, New Mexico, where Dad and his wife Judy lived. All of the family had gathered around Dad for his send-off. To distract from my grief, I was in the kitchen every day, cooking for everyone. At the end of three days, I said my goodbyes to Dad, and he said he was ready to "Fly out." Don and I flew back to the farm, and a few days later, Dad passed. It was August 1, 2013. After his death, I felt tremendous sadness, but I also experienced an incredible gift. I was able to forgive him.

I don't think I would have comprehended the anguish of addiction if I had not seen it up close through clients, family members, and my participation at AA meetings. And Twelve-Step

Programs when I was in grad school. Although I never had addictions, I attended many of these meetings to learn about addicts. I found the meetings to be blessed with care, kindness, and compassion. It was amazing to be in such an environment where people could share their pain and misery and yet feel safe and treated with love and respect. Attending these meetings helped me to see my father in a more compassionate light.

The Power of Dreams

Because many of my encounters with loved ones, like my comedic Dad, skeptic grandparents, and even old boyfriends, had come to me in a dream state, for many years, I kept a journal of my visits with loved ones. I encourage every reader to keep a dream journal. Not only does it help to elicit lucid dreaming, but it can also help you to remember messages from your subconscious, especially visits from family and friends. The more you write down your dreams, the more you are likely to remember them.

Freud spoke of dreams as the "royal road to the unconscious." By studying dreams, we are given access to a broader awareness of our psyche. Ann Faraday, an expert on dream analysis, recommends the use of a dream diary as an aid to memory and a way to preserve details, many of which are otherwise rapidly forgotten no matter how memorable the dream originally seemed.

It's interesting to see the inventive ways spirits appear in the dream state. One of my favorites was a visit from my jazz musician father, who showed up in the most imaginative way. I was in our childhood home giving readings. There was a knock on the front door, along with the song *Knockin' on Heaven's Door* by Bob Dylan. I opened the door, and there stood my father. He walked in, and we hugged. He didn't say a word and suddenly disappeared. He was famous for vanishing; we often called him "the great disappearing artist."

I woke up laughing because I felt so happy to see Dad. It was so like him to show up and disappear in the same instance. Seeing him no longer affected me as it once did.

On another occasion, a former boyfriend came to me in a dream and asked that I forgive him. When we were together, he was an alcoholic and very abusive. It had been 35 years since I last saw him. I was so surprised that he visited me and asked for forgiveness. It was not easy to forgive him because it brought up unhappy memories of terrible times, but in the end, forgiveness was necessary. It not only freed him, but it freed me. And from then on, in a place deep inside me, my tears turned to smiles.

Forgiveness is not condoning bad actions but rather letting go of the past and any guilt, shame, and pain stored with it. Forgiveness relieves traumas and brings peace to our minds. As Dr. Jerry Jampolsky says, "Forgiveness is, quite simply, the decision not to suffer." Never underestimate the power of forgiveness.

Coincidence or Spirit?

In August of 2014, a year after my father died, I asked my stepmother Judy to join me for a week-long class with James Van Praagh on his *Talking To Heaven* cruise to Alaska. She was both

239

excited and somewhat nervous because she had never done anything like it before. But it really didn't take much for me to coax her. "It'll be an incredible week with James, and we can explore spirituality and Alaska together. Maybe Dad might come through for us." The idea of Dad in the spirit world made Judy's decision easier as she was thrilled with the possibility of having a conversation with him.

I have always been so grateful to experience the spirit world with James. Whenever I attended one of his events, I was usually the first to arrive. This time, I wanted to make sure that Judy had the chance to contact Dad. My plan was to arrive early so we could sit up front and soak in all the positive energy.

Judy and I had a quick breakfast and excitedly walked downstairs to the event. The closer we got, the more delayed we seemed to get. People were stopping and sharing with me or asking me questions. The quicker I tried to end the conversation and move on, the more bogged down I got. As soon as one person left, another person instantly appeared and started to talk to me. This slow pace continued, and we seemed to be lagging behind everyone else. Naturally, I was getting upset because the workshop was about to begin, and all the seats up front were taken. Judy and I had to sit way in the back, and frankly, I was kind of annoyed. It was not the way I wanted to begin the journey.

We were getting comfortable when James opened the workshop with an exercise for us to do. "Pick a partner," he said, "and it cannot be someone you know." I thought, *"Oh no, I wanted to work with Judy."*

James continued, "Turn to your left or right and begin."

I glanced at Judy and shrugged my shoulders. She turned to a woman about her age sitting on her right, and I turned to a woman on my left.

The exercise had three parts. The first part was about using our intuition. The second part was about using this intuition to tune into the Spirit, and the third part was to allow the spirit world to psychically send messages. For me, it was easy. This was my wheelhouse, but I was concerned for Judy. I found myself being haunted by my old friend—responsibility. I felt responsible because the workshop was a completely new experience for Judy, and I so badly wanted her to be able to connect with the spirit world. I felt her jitters and anxiety and reassured her it would be okay no matter what happened. Then, I turned to my partner and began the exercise. I had to let go of being responsible for Judy, making it okay for her, and embracing my own experience.

After the exercise, James asked, "Does anyone want to share their experience?" To my surprise, Judy's arm flew up. It turned out that Judy and her partner had a lot in common. Both were widows who lost their husbands on the same day, August 1, 2013. Both husbands were named Lee and were professional jazz trumpeters. Finally, in the pièce de résistance, both husbands knew each other. They had played in Stan Kenton's band in the 1950's.

I can't describe how happy these two women were in knowing that their husbands had joined forces in Spirit to let them know they were watching over them. Imagine how hard they had to work to make this special meeting occur. There was no coincidence here. I truly had no idea that the spirit world had a plan for our seating arrangements. If we let go of our preconceived notions, Spirit will always guide our way.

Both Sides Now

Around the same time, Shirley's first book, *Why Can't I Change?* was published, and she was doing a weekly podcast about psychology. Every Tuesday, she would drive from the office in Beverly Hills to a studio in Hollywood. She and public relations expert Steve Rohr hosted a show called *The Dr. Shirley and Steve Show*.

One day, after a session I had with one of her patients, Shirley asked, "Kellee, would you like to be on the show?" Although I was almost finished with grad school, I still kept my medium sessions private. I still had this worry about getting found out and didn't want to spoil my chances of getting my license as a psychotherapist. Besides, I was not a public speaker and was terrified of speaking in front of an audience, even if it was a podcast and no one could see me.

I told Shirley, "No, thank you. I'm not ready to go public." But Shirley didn't give up. In the following months, she kept asking, and all the while, I kept protesting until, one day, I caved in. After talking it over with Mom, she said, "Kellee, you can do it. You'll be fine," I agreed to be a guest on her show.

Any memories I might have had of that first show with Shirley completely evaporated. The only thing I remember is the show's producer, John Williams. He was especially kind and reassuring and immediately made me feel at ease. After the show, John pulled me aside. "Kellee, you did great. Would you be able to come to another one of my shows? It's called *Spirit Speaks* about conversations with the other side." Again, my first reaction was "No." I was still uncomfortable about going public even though I thought John would be a breeze to work with. I didn't want anyone in grad school to know I was a medium.

During this time, I attended James Van Praagh's weekly development circle at his Laguna Beach home. I decided to ask him what he thought about my doing a show about conversations with spirits. He answered. "Kellee, you should do it. Spirit will help you to find your voice. You don't have to worry about people finding out. You'll be okay. And so, with James' blessing, I agreed."

By 2015, Shirley had moved on from her show with Steve and began a new video podcast and asked if I would do it with her. "Together, we can explore both psychology and spirituality." By then, I was licensed and felt Spirit push. "Yes, I'll do it." My dear Don came up with the name for the show—*Both Sides Now,* and our producer John added "TV"—*Both Sides Now TV.*

Our show lasted five years, and I loved every single minute of it. We explored both the psychological and spiritual side of every topic with great guests from psychologists specializing in trauma like Gina Ross, Dr. Stephen Terrell, and Dr. Raja Selvam to psychics and mediums Lisa Williams, Harry T, Dannion Brinkley and my dear friend James Van Praagh.

Today, Shirley and I continue to teach classes via Zoom, exploring psychology and spirituality. I am thrilled to say that at the time of this writing, James and I have our own *YouTube* show called *Both Sides Now & Beyond!* a combination of the original podcast and James' early TV show, *Beyond!* I also have my own

YouTube show called Ask Me Anything!, where I discuss Vedic astrology along with spiritual and psychological issues.

I have to say that I have been tremendously blessed because, during this entire period, I learned to let go of a lot of trauma and grief in order to heal the past and focus on my future. With healing came forgiveness and peace of mind, which allowed me to follow my true self as a spiritual medium/psychologist—a responsibility that is a spiritual priority. At last, I was able to help others find their true selves and their true callings.

Chapter 16

THE END OF AN ERA

Learn to see through confusion into peace, to see through sickness into health, to see through poverty into success and abundance, and to believe in the all-sustaining Good. Learn to trust in God and be at peace.

         -    Ernest Holmes, *This Thing Called Life*

By the end of 2015, Mom, Shirley, and I all shared the Beverly Hills office, and we were busy little beavers. The office was alive with people coming and going, and I was happy as a clam doing such joyful work. The three of us became close friends and were totally committed to helping heal our patients through psychotherapy, mediumship, or both.

Unfortunately, Mom was again diagnosed with breast cancer, and it became too much for her to continue to work at the office. As she did the first time she had cancer, she decided to see patients in her home once again. It was not an easy decision, but it was a necessary one.

Since it was only Shirley and I left in the suite, we decided that when the office lease was up, we would find smaller office space in Beverly Hills close by. It turned out to be more difficult than we thought. Commercial rentals in Beverly Hills had become extremely expensive. The term for leasing was referred to as "triple-net lease," and only lawyers and plastic surgeons could afford such high-priced rents.

We were almost defeated until Shirley spotted a small sign on an old building a few blocks away on North Bedford Drive. The office suite for lease was affordable, so we decided to rent it. We signed a 10-year lease because Shirley never wanted to go through the hassle of moving again. Although I wasn't quite comfortable with having such a long-term lease, I figured I would stay for as long as possible and rent my space if need be. The two of us spent a small fortune having it remodeled and redecorated to our liking.

A Total Solar Eclipse

In 2017, Shirley and I were humming along in our new office space while Mom stayed home, working less but still keeping busy. Looking over my astrology charts, I knew that there was a major solar eclipse on August 21 of that year. A Solar Eclipse occurs when the Moon passes between the Earth and the Sun, blocking a partial view of the Sun. A total Solar Eclipse occurs when the Moon totally blocks the Sun during its passage.

Often, eclipses can be seen in certain parts of the world. This particular Great American Solar Eclipse, as it would come to be known, would cover our entire country and would be visible in states from the Atlantic to the Pacific. That's an amazing occurrence! The last time we had such a major American eclipse was in 1918, when the US entered World War 1.

Astrologically, eclipses bring rapid changes to people's lives individually and as a society to move in the right direction, and these changes can last up to a year. If we're on the right path, it could mean achievements or favorable results. If we are on the wrong path, it could force a much-needed change in direction to get us back on track. This particular total eclipse was going to be powerful, and it was going to bring major changes to the world, especially to the United States. In the olden days, a solar eclipse was known as "the eye of an angry god." I couldn't put it any better. This solar eclipse was another omen—and it was a forewarning of enormous change.

Before any of this occurred, I wanted to go back in time to Don's sister, Marie. She had a dream of buying a farm and making it a retreat for the whole family, and in 1995, she fulfilled that dream and bought a beautiful farm in Wisconsin. Sadly, she lived only five years on the farm before she passed away.

Don took over the family farm, and every summer, we would go to the farm for some R & R. Marie was right—it was the perfect retreat—a place of peace and beauty with lots of acreage to wander around and dream. In fact, we brought Mom to the farm several times. She always said it was her favorite spot in the entire world. I think it reminded her of growing up on the farm in Indiana and all the happy memories she had there.

So, when I found out that the eclipse was traveling right over our Wisconsin farm, I made sure we were all there for this special astrological event. The eclipse would have a direct hit on us. I remember feeling such anticipation for all of the wonderful possibilities the eclipse would bring. Little did I know of the enormously unexpected and cataclysmic changes that would happen not only for me but for everyone else.

Saying Goodbye to the Old and Hello to the New

Early one Friday in December 2017, exactly four months after the great eclipse in August, while I was waiting in my Beverly Hills office for a client, I heard a loud pounding outside the office door. I went into the hall to see what was causing such a disturbance and saw a workman nailing a notice to our door. Apparently, the building had been sold, and the new owner was giving the old tenants notice that he was kicking us out.

By then, Shirley and I had been in our suite for only 18 months. When I look back to that time, we were so happy to get the office at a reasonable rent. Then I realized, *No wonder the rents were so low. The owner had intended to sell the building all along but had never told us.* I assumed that our landlord needed tenants to occupy the building in order to make a better deal for himself. Needless to say, I was speechless, and I knew Shirley would take this news quite hard. We had another eight and a half years left on our lease, and neither of us was emotionally prepared to move offices again, let alone spend more money relocating.

That very afternoon, I returned home to find the vet and Don waiting for me. Our beloved 11-year-old dog, Livvy Mae, had been very sick with cancer. Don and I had to make the difficult decision to have the vet put her to sleep. As painful as that decision was, we both knew in our hearts that we didn't want our Livvy Mae to suffer anymore. It was time. Needless to say, the whole day turned out to be a heartbreaking one.

A month later, in January 2018, Neil Diamond, Don's boss, announced he had Parkinson's disease and was retiring from his worldwide tours for good. It was an enormous shock. Don's bags were already packed for the tour in Australia. Don used to say, "Neil will never retire." Everyone agreed. Neil would never retire, but fate stepped in, and the news was beyond belief. It was very sad for all of us to know that not only Neil would never tour again but that he was suffering from such an extremely debilitating illness.

To compound our already overwhelming losses, three months later, in April 2018, my beloved mother, who was my best friend and soul mate, passed away. She had suffered from cancer for years, and as her caretaker, I was completely responsible for her in every way. Although she was very sick and getting more fragile with each passing day, talking to her about her death was too much for me to bear. I became numb to the idea that she was leaving me.

A year before she passed away, I learned the reason why she was so fearful about being left alone at night when Marc was away on business. My siblings, Danny and Carol, and I had always wondered what caused such fear and anxiety. As death drew near, with all of us around her, Mom cried loudly, "I don't want to die alone in the field." She repeated it over and over. Although we finally learned where the fear came from, it was still heartbreaking to hear her repeat these words on her deathbed.

The Field

Even though I thought Mom's fear was completely irrational, I knew there had to be a reason to send her into a complete and utter panic. There was never a time that I didn't know about this fear—it occurred all through our childhood. It meant that one of us children needed to be with her at night if Dad had a gig out of town. I joked with Mom, "That's why you had three children—to make sure that one of us would be available so you wouldn't be alone."

I had lived with the understanding that this was just the way it was. Can you imagine what this was like for us as children and then as adults well into our fifties? It meant rearranging our schedules to sleep over at Mom's house. It was really a difficult logistical challenge for all of us. My brother Danny was a film director, and part of his job was traveling all over the world for weeks and months at a time. My sister was a banker and also very busy. I was the most logical Mom-sitter, but I lived the furthest away, and with LA traffic, my dog to care for, my own busy schedule with clients, and Don traveling on world tours with Neil Diamond, it was quite a hardship for me as well.

And if God forbid, one of us wasn't available to spend the night with her because we were all out of town, then one of our spouses or friends, or one of her friends, would have to spend the night. But because Mom was such a private person, it needed to be someone who wouldn't judge her and/or criticize such an absurd personal phobia. Although she was a very well-respected psychologist and had done lots of work on herself, it didn't matter. She couldn't solve her dilemma about being alone at night.

Somehow, we all seemed to make it work. Someone was

always with Mom at night.

Oh, and the best part. She preferred for one of us to sleep in bed with her. What? Obviously, my brother drew the line at that request and slept in the guest room, and on occasion, so did I. But mostly, Mom asked that someone be in bed with her right at the time she went to sleep, which for many of us was way too early. So, no luck staying up! Unbelievable? We all dreaded those times when Marc had to go out of town on business. *Ugh!*

It would have been certainly easier to comprehend if Mom was sickly or too feeble to take care of herself. Unfortunately, her fear was too illogical for words, and she couldn't, under any circumstances, ever be left alone to sleep by herself.

When she was married to my father, Lee, she would wake up nearly every night screaming, HELP ME, DADDY! HELP ME DADDY! HELP ME! HELP ME! HELP ME! My dad used to joke that he didn't mind her screaming, but at least she could have screamed HIS name for help instead of her father's. At least he had a sense of humor about it.

I remember the time when Don was on tour to New Zealand, and Marc was out of town. Mom enlisted me to stay with her for a few nights until Marc's return. To my amazement, she asked a friend of hers to stay for a few days because her friend also had fears of sleeping alone. There I was, taking care of two grown women, both with the same fear. It was so beyond bizarre! At about 10 PM that first night, Mom was sound asleep in her room, and her friend was also sound asleep in the guest room. I was with Livvy Mae, my dog, in the office, quietly talking to Don in New Zealand.

All of a sudden, I heard a scream of terror coming from Mom's bedroom. It was so loud; it sounded like a scream in a horror movie. Even Don heard it over the phone. Mom's friend woke up and ran down the hallway, scared out of her mind. I threw down the phone and ran into Mom's room. There she was—asleep like a baby. I tapped her shoulder and asked, "Mom, are you okay?" She rolled over and groggily sat up. "Why did you wake me up? She had absolutely NO IDEA that a minute before, she had screamed bloody murder. Not a clue! And this occurred nearly every night of her life.

I felt that her fear was from a past life situation. After this latest harrowing episode, Mom finally agreed to have a session with a past life regressionist. Sweet Mary O'Day entered our life, and using her hypnosis technique, she regressed Mom to a past life when she was a 12-year-old girl living on a farm with her parents and siblings in rural South Carolina during the Civil War. There was a raid on her village, and her entire family was killed. Scared and wounded, the girl ran from her house into a field. As she lay dying, the young girl (Mom) cried, "Daddy, I don't want to die alone in the field." Her words took my breath away. I sat there listening to my poor mother, reliving a traumatic past life. The thought of her dying such a lonely and terrifying death made me weep.

Mom's past life helped us all to understand the fear she felt. It also helped Mom feel less crazy. Although she was relieved, she still couldn't be left alone, as the imprint of this incident was too difficult to release. But the rest of us felt some consolation in finally getting an answer.

At the end of her life, we reassured her that she was not alone and that Dad, her father, her mother, and her family were all waiting for her in Heaven. She said, "I know." She passed peacefully at that moment. It was as if that painful past life and her present life came together for healing. This is why I believe in my heart that healing is possible right up to that last and final breath on Earth.

Past Life Regression

Since the use of past life regression was an invaluable tool for uncovering my mother's irrational fear, I wanted to touch upon this subject as it's not discussed much in therapy sessions. After the realization of my mother's fear of dying alone in another life, I learned that some of our fears may not make sense in our present lives because they are from previous lifetimes. Understanding this gave me insight into helping clients with unresolved anxiety, and using past life regression was a good tool for uncovering irrational fears. I only know that deep-seated problems start either in childhood or another life, and I wanted to go deeper into the minds of my patients to lay bare their hidden fears. I remember my panic attack before I embarked on *Semester at Sea.* It was my first glimpse into fear as the most paralyzing emotion we can have.

Past life regression, along with age regression, is usually done through hypnosis or similar relaxation techniques. It can help to uncover issues people are either unwilling or unable to access through their conscious memories. Often, our childhood experiences like abuse and trauma are buried deep in the subconscious mind, and only using regression can bring these disturbing memories to light and accelerate the healing process.

As the term suggests, past life regression transports a person to another lifetime where anxiety and other mental disturbances are initiated. Often, both patient and therapist are equally surprised when another lifetime shows up that exposes the offending trauma. Both Mom and I were equally amazed at her past life in the South during the Civil War. After her insight, Mom became a supporter of past life regression.

So, I decided to use it whenever it seemed appropriate. It certainly helped my client, I'll call her Betty, who came to me with severe anxiety that stemmed from her mother's overbearing nature. As a child, she loved her mother but, at the same time, felt that her mother was too controlling. For that reason, she could never truly confide in her mother, and she learned to hide certain experiences and feelings. Not being able to share her doubts created a lot of stress and fear. Betty learned not to trust others and didn't depend on anyone for advice.

As Betty said, "Mom was always telling people what to do. Most people found her suggestions helpful, but I just thought of her as a busybody. And the more she told me what to do, the angrier I got. In fact, I went in the opposite direction of her advice. Because of this, I made a lot of mistakes in my life. I knew if I shared my concerns with my mother, she would just tell me how to behave and what to say. So, mostly, I kept quiet. Unfortunately, I was always second-guessing myself and lost jobs and relationships because I had no one to share my thoughts and feelings with."

I knew in my heart that my client's fears stemmed from a life before the present one. I suggested she do a past life regression with my friend and hypnotherapist, Mary O'Day. She agreed. Mary regressed Betty to a life in the feudal English countryside. She was a poor child who lived with an overbearing mother on a farm. The two of them lived together in a one-room shack next to the barn. Her mother, who happened to be her mother in her present life, was the same type of controlling person. Because the child (Betty) couldn't stand being constantly scolded and worked to the bone by her mother, she decided to run away.

"I'm probably eight or nine at the time," she recalled in her hypnotic state. "I don't know where to go. I'm lost in the forest surrounded by trees, and I step into one of those animal traps that clamp onto your leg. I can't get out of it no matter how hard I try." Betty contorts in pain as she continues her past life recall. "I'm lying under a big tall tree, and I'm suffering in agony until I go unconscious and die."

It was a tragic story, to say the least, but it helped Betty realize that her anxiety and fears began way back in another life. In order to break the cycle of anxiety, she had to forgive her mother. It definitely was a soul lesson for both of them. She realized that she couldn't run away from her feelings as she had done in the past lifetime because it obviously didn't end well. Eventually, with some psychological reframing, Betty made peace with her mother and came to see her as a good woman who was only trying to help others. After that, Betty opened her heart to trusting others and made some close, lifelong friends with whom she could share her feelings.

Past life regression is a compelling subject, and there are many books on the subject. I recommend Dr. Michael Newton's books entitled *Journey of Souls* and *Destiny of Souls.* Not only do they deal with past life regression but also with the soul's journey in between lifetimes.

The Changes Continue

After Mom's passing, I thought I couldn't take any more intense changes, but the changes did not end. My godfather, Bob Dorough, died a week later. Bobby was deeply loved by our family. He and my parents had remained dear friends for 65 years. His passing was an end to an era in my life.

But the final blow was the following week when our dear friend, Ryan Wilson, lost his life to cancer. Ryan and his daughter Kareesa took care of our farm in Wisconsin. We were all dear friends, and we were truly distressed when Ryan passed. He was one of the most unique individuals I had ever met. It was the final door closing on a year of crushing changes.

That was the moment Don said to me, "We're moving to the farm." We had just lived through a tsunami of death and sorrow, and the only respite we could imagine was living the rest of our lives on our pleasant and peaceful farm.

Holiday was already living in Texas with her husband, so I felt free to make such a dramatic change. But I was broken-hearted to say goodbye to Shirley, James, and my dear family and friends in California. Inwardly, I knew it was the right move for us. The time had come once again to let go of the old and begin anew. It took a year to tie up all the loose ends in Los Angeles, and in June 2019, we moved to our beautiful farm in Wisconsin. Kareesa began working as my assistant; she has been an incredible blessing. In the corner of my eye, I could see her dad giving me a thumbs-up.

Nine months after we moved to the farm, COVID-19 hit the world in 2020. Spirit had taken care of us by moving us out of Los Angeles and gifting us with a new life on the farm. Who could have ever imagined that Marie's dream of living on a farm so many years ago would be our place of refuge during the worst time on the planet?

All the changes in such a short amount of time would have been disorienting and debilitating to the Kellee of the past. However, I willingly accepted the changes Spirit had planned, even the one that was the toughest—Mom's death. Words cannot express the pain in me. I felt as if I was alone on an island with no land in sight. It was too surreal.

Trying to Make Contact

About an hour after Mom died, I received a call from James. I hadn't had the time or the wherewithal to call him, so I didn't have a chance to tell him of her passing. He said, "Kellee, I'm calling from the airplane. Your mother came to me. She said, "Tell Kellee I'm NOT dead. I'm ALIVE and no longer in pain." Mom always said if she couldn't get through to me, she would go through James and let him know she was okay on the other side. She kept her promise.

Before Mom's illness, she and I would often talk about connecting with each other when she passed. I told her, "Don't worry, we will be so in tune, it'll be easy." Little did I know how I came to eat my own words.

Every day, family, clients, friends, and former patients of Mom's asked if I had "seen her yet." I always answered, "Not yet." *Why couldn't I see her? This should be simple for me; I do it all the time.* I was so naive. I did not or could not imagine a world without her or that my grief would be so devastating. Even seeing her in my dreams would be too much for me to handle. It was my agonizing grief that was preventing spirit contact.

So many people assume that mediums can speak to their loved ones on the other side all the time. But that isn't how it works, at least for me and other mediums I know. Just like I tell clients who struggle to communicate with a lost loved one, the pain of grief can be so great that it can cloud up the energy flow needed to connect with the other side. Intellectually, I knew Mom was around me, but I was too emotionally distraught with heartache and hurt to feel her presence.

Night after night, I asked Mom to please visit me. It took five months after she passed to get through in my dreams. In the dream, Mom, Don, and I were having lunch just like we used to do. Mom looked absolutely beautiful—no longer sickly or weak from cancer. We talked and laughed and had a good time together.

Then I realized in the dream that Mom had passed, and suddenly, it was almost too much to bear. I started to cry, telling her how sad I was without her. She was so tender and calm when she said, "Kellee, I can't do anything about it. This is something I can't fix." I knew that her death could not be changed, but still, I was too upset that I woke right up. I couldn't stop crying, nor could I go back to sleep. Knowing she was not coming back was beyond heartbreaking.

Days later, I was fortunate to be able to share my dream with Judy, my stepmother, who had always been receptive to the spirit world. She was sympathetic to my misery and wanted to make me feel better, so she shared her dream about seeing my father.

In her dream, Judy sat in a crowded theater watching a play. After the play was over and everyone left, the lights went out. She stayed all alone in the dark when suddenly my dad appeared next to her. At first, she was excited to see him. Then she realized he was dead and never coming back. She became too upset in the dream, especially when he disappeared. She said, "I woke up flooded with tears. I thought I would be so happy to see him because he had been gone five years. So you see, Kellee, there will always be sadness because we miss them no matter how many years go by. Time will help to ease your pain, and remember, our loved ones will always be a part of us."

Judy was right. Eventually, as time went by, I felt better. But I never anticipated the kind of emotional pain I felt in the dream. In fact, I thought that being with Mom would make me ecstatic. I realized that if it was so painful for me, it was probably as painful for others to connect with loved ones, too. That's why I tell my clients to be patient and "give yourself time." Spirit will communicate with us when we're relaxed, and our energy is not blocked by the heaviness of sorrow. And even when the pain ends, the memories of love linger indefinitely. And, of course, I know that this experience with my mother has made my mediumship even stronger.

After my dream, I thought Mom would not come back for a while, but she came to me in a dream a few nights later. This time,

259

I was happy to see her because I had made an effort to accept the fact that she was gone. But it took about two years to go through all the stages of grief and to come to terms with my mother not being on Earth anymore.

Grieving For Loved Ones

It does take time to process the loss of our loved ones. Some can do it more easily than others, but grief is definitely an individual journey. After Mom died, I entered the second stage of grief—anger. I was angry because there was no time for me to process her passing, as I had the responsibility not only to my patients but to hers as well. Additionally, because Mom didn't make plans for her death, it meant I had to take care of all her private and business affairs as well as the family. As sick as she was with cancer, she never prepared for death, mentally, emotionally, or financially. She couldn't face the loss of her wonderful life.

On many occasions, I had tried to have that conversation with her, but she just couldn't go there. So many people go through similar experiences with loved ones facing death. For some, the end is too much to accept, and they are unable to make any preparations. For others, they don't want to burden their family, so they take care of all the arrangements beforehand.

I mention this because it's important for each of us to prepare for our own time of passing so that the ones we leave behind are not put into difficult situations. Death often brings out the worst in people. Some people blame others, others battle over money and furnishings or particular objects, while others stay away altogether. I have seen it happen too many times in the hundreds of sessions I have had with families.

Mom was my best and truest friend. I really miss her laugh. She thought everything about the human condition was funny. And she was right—it is funny. But the magnificent part of our relationship was as colleagues. I still miss having a glass of wine with her after a long day of work and consulting about a client. Mom had an uncanny ability to sort problems out and design a correct course of action. She had innate wisdom about the confusion a client was going through. In the end, no matter the issue, she would say to me, "It'll be okay."

Months after Mom's death, I would pick up the phone to call her and tell her about a patient or a reading and then realize she wasn't there. I went through every single stage of grief: *denial, anger, bargaining, depression, and acceptance*—some stages lasted longer than expected, and some were very brief. Elizabeth Kubler-Ross discusses the stages of grief in her book, On Death and Dying, as a part of the framework that helps people learn to live without what they have lost.

Then, one day, quite unexpectedly, the fog lifted, and I was my old Kellee self again. To be honest, I still pick up the phone to call Mom, but now I'm calling her in my dreams. I know she's my angel and guide and will always be my support system.

Mom and I talked so much about writing this book together. She was by my side throughout all the incredibly different spiritual situations I had experienced and would constantly evaluate my psychological distress. My spiritual awakening greatly challenged her rational reasoning system. She was a left-brain psychologist,

261

following normal therapeutic procedures and practices. Yet, she was completely open to my psychic/spiritual work, which enormously influenced the way she practiced her therapy, particularly in regard to people's spiritual belief systems. She found comfort and joy in knowing that there was life on the other side and that her family and friends would all meet again. Today, I feel her presence around me, and it helps me sort through every test life brings.

To say that this was the end of an era is an understatement. So, what have I learned? I knew the eclipse would bring changes, but it brought so much grief to me personally and to the world in general. Grief, like trauma, doesn't go away. It stays deep within our minds and bodies. But we can learn to function with it. The cycle of grief was one of the most amazing experiences I have ever had—it exposed me to a deeper sense of empathy for loss and our attachment to loved ones and our time on Earth. It has helped tremendously in the healing work I do with my clients and others, for which I am very grateful.

Chapter 17

───⌐⌐───

THE PAIN OF LOSS

Grieving is real. It's an unavoidable part of the human condition, and we don't need to suppress it in order to survive it.

- Maria Shriver, *I've Been Thinking*

For a year, I knew Mom was dying. I had anticipatory grief, knowing she would be gone, and there was nothing I could do to change the outcome. Many people face this type of preliminary grief, especially if a loved one suffers from a long terminal illness. A person may grieve during the entire time a person is sick. That was me. There were times when I literally could not breathe.

After my mother's death, I was a complete basket case. No matter how much I had learned from the other side, I was still unprepared for her loss. When she died, I went into a kind of embryonic state—I couldn't move; I couldn't tell whether it was night or day or what day it was. I felt stuck, and all my spiritual knowledge flew right out the window. My life stopped because her death was so final. None of us are immune to the agonizing feelings the death of a loved one brings, not even me. Her death pretty much confirmed to me that everyone grieves differently, and there's no right or wrong way to mourn.

As a medium, I've been privileged to be in the sacred space with so many who have transitioned from this life and those who have suffered loss. In this chapter, I want to touch on the many types of loss that a person may experience. My friend James once said, "Our work as mediums is a compilation of all of our life experiences, and we are here to utilize these experiences to assist grieving souls who are in need of healing and enlightenment.

Unexpected Loss

Because there are many experiences of grief, it's hard to say if one is more significant than another, but based on my experience, I'm going to begin with the gripping, traumatic grief of sudden, unexpected loss. I also put this death into the category of complicated loss and grief. An unexpected loss includes the complexity of dealing with the event that caused the death. Usually, a person may think that things could have turned out differently—if only I did this or if I said that ... (fill in the blank).

Sudden loss is a death resulting from an unexpected and unforeseen event, like a car accident, murder, suicide, natural catastrophe, mass shooting, plane accident, stroke, or heart attack. I also put death from COVID into this category. I have worked with several people who have suffered a loss due to the recent pandemic, and the trauma of not being able to be near or say goodbye to a loved one in the hospital was too much to endure. I want everyone to please believe me when I say your loved ones are never alone. Loved ones on the other side, spirit guides, and even beloved pets prepare for a person's homecoming no matter how or when they pass.

I don't believe anything is random or capricious. Every movement is divinely timed. Souls choose most of the important aspects of their lives, and this includes how and when to die. I am often asked: "Why would a soul choose a difficult or tragic ending?" The answer is complicated, and from our three-dimensional human understanding, it can seem unloving and uncaring. But from a spiritual level, the meaning can be more profound than humans are capable of grasping. An untimely death may be due to karma, or the death could help the family left behind to make better choices or the death could be necessary for the growth of the soul who passes. The choice of death is ALWAYS made before a soul incarnates.

When I do a reading about someone who dies suddenly, two questions often come up. The first question is about future events. "Am I psychically able to foresee or predict a tragic event and prevent it from happening?" I can only say that the intelligence of the spirit world will only show me what I'm allowed to see. No medium or psychic has the ability to prevent or create experiences that are destined to occur.

The second question I am often asked after the sudden passing of a loved one is, "Was there something I could have done to prevent it?" My answer is, "No, I don't believe so." There are lessons to be learned in all areas of life, and death is a lesson for those who have passed and those still on Earth. There are many events that we simply have no control over and that are beyond our limited human scope of understanding.

I've counseled parents who have lost their children to school shootings. As painful as this is, I always say the same thing—"Your beloved children are angels and want to shine a spotlight on gun control." The souls of any children who die are brave warrior angels who chose a limited time on Earth to make a noticeable difference. They bring light into the darkness; they always have a mission and purpose.

I've had many a parent share with me that the night before, they had a bad feeling about sending their child to school. There is a reason for that. As a planned event from the other side, the parent would intuitively feel something. But it doesn't mean they could have prevented it. Again, the soul ALWAYS has a choice before it incarnates. The soul chooses a particular life and death for spiritual growth. I promise you will see your loved ones again, and it will be a glorious reunion.

When a sudden loss occurs, a person usually has persistent feelings of guilt. Perhaps there was an argument beforehand, or a person was too busy to express love or to say goodbye before their loved one left for work, or there was a last-minute change in plans, and it was the final time the person saw a loved one alive. Perhaps there were many things left unsaid. A number of emotional issues come to the surface to be looked at for the person left behind. There is the sudden event itself and also the shock of receiving a life-changing phone call.

It has been my experience that souls who pass suddenly are not in pain when they pass. There is a sort of "blankness" they go through so they don't feel pain. Yet they are very aware of the pain their death has caused their loved ones still alive, and they always seek their forgiveness. They usually wish their loved ones know that they are alive and well and don't want them to live the rest of their life journey in pain. They always assure their loved ones that they will meet again when it is time to return home.

The loss of life itself is great enough, but additional stress comes from police involvement, court appearances, lawyers, money issues, and additional losses such as a home or job. Just when I think I've seen it all, I am truly amazed at how much I have witnessed people's sufferings and the resilience they have to survive life's most tragic events. Often, I am moved beyond tears. Absolutely none of it is easy, and it takes time to process the grief. Frequently, I recommend psychotherapy and Somatic Experience Therapy. I have found this combination extremely helpful for sudden or tragic death, especially PTSD.

Loss of a Child

Without a doubt, this is the most painful and crushing loss anyone can experience. The death of a child attacks all belief systems. We all feel that it isn't natural for a parent to survive their child. "How could this happen? Why did this happen? How could God do this to me?" Questions arise all the time, especially if there is an accident. "Why did my child die and your child live?"

The pain is always about the loss of sharing in the child's future: graduations, weddings, grandchildren, and the dreams they had that will never come to be. All of this plays out with the loss of children. The pain is so visceral it feels as if the heart is literally breaking.

I have had profoundly moving sessions with parents who have lost children. Usually, parents are so devastated that they're not entirely in their bodies during our sessions. One couple came to see me after their beloved 13-year-old daughter was tragically hit and killed while walking across the street in the middle of the day. She was struck down by an angry driver who had just lost his job and was taking out his rage on everyone in sight. Not only did the family have to deal with the grief of losing their beloved good-natured daughter, but they also had to be in and out of court for nearly a year during court hearings and the trial of the man who committed the crime. This was complicated grief on all levels.

Sometimes, this kind of tragedy breaks up a family, as parents blame one another for the tragedy as if one of them could have stopped it. I remember how my marriage to Craig quickly went downhill after Holiday's accident. He blamed me for not taking responsibility for her, and I walked around the house like a zombie. The two of us were so devastated and broken we could hardly look at one another. Ultimately, it was the end of our marriage.

But the opposite can occur—parents struggle with the loss of their child, but their bonds can become stronger, and they can often grow closer. Because of all the school shootings in this country, it seems especially important at this time that parents get help, not only from family and friends but also from trained therapists and whatever healing therapies work for them.

I recommended a wonderful book describing why children pass and what their souls are doing from the other side of life called *Growing Up In Heaven* by James Van Praagh. It is one of the best books written about grief and the loss of a child.

Loss of a Parent

This may be a big loss for many. If we had a good relationship with one or both parents, full of love and support, it would be a sad loss. For some with a close bond, like my mother and I, it can be very difficult to let go and move on. But losing a parent is usually expected as our parents get old and frail.

However, a child losing a parent can leave a lasting imprint for the rest of the child's life. The death of a parent can shake the foundations of a child's belief in the world as a safe place. In a detailed study of pediatric grief following parental loss, Pitt Department of Psychiatry researchers found increased rates of depression and functional impairment within the first two years after the parent's death. Along with depression, symptoms such as anxiety, PTSD, skipped schooling, less academic success, lower self-esteem, and more sexually risky behaviors are common.

Some of the hardest sessions I've experienced have been with young people who have lost a parent at an early age. They're always curious and want to know if their deceased parent sees them or is aware of the life they have on Earth. I assure them: "Yes, they do know, and, yes, they watch over you all the time!" Often, the parent comes through and tells the child how proud they are of them and how they are assisting them from the other side of life. Their love continues on—only from a different space. So, very often, a deceased parent becomes one of the child's spirit guides.

But what happens when we have a particularly difficult relationship with a mother or father? How do we grieve that one? Is there guilt? Do we have any feelings at all? It's been my experience that often if the parents have issues, like personality disorders or addiction, they will work through those issues on the other side. Parents with addictions can cause enormous, complicated grief. It's a love-hate battle for the children. I had such feelings for my Dad. I loved him with all my heart, but there were times when he was too much to handle, especially when I was a teen. I know that my Dad finally got the help he needed in the spirit world, as many addicts do. Often, he would appear in my dreams, and the next morning, I would always wake up smiling. It's also very common when a parent becomes "self-realized" on the other side that he or she asks for forgiveness of the child harmed by their behavior.

What about sexual or physical abuse by a parent? This is another form of complicated grief. Again, complicated grief can include intense pain and suffering for the relationship that never healed because the abuser never communicated any apology for their wrongdoing before they passed away.

There is a wonderful Gestalt Psychotherapy technique called *The Empty Chair*. It is a simple and powerful exercise that anyone can do alone in their home. I encourage clients who struggle with difficult or horrific parents to use this technique so they can let go and move on. This technique can be done without a therapist, although a therapist can help as a neutral observer. Using the "empty chair," a client role-plays with the person with whom they have had a traumatic experience. The technique is designed so that a person can work through any internal conflict with themselves or others. The technique also helps one to see the situation from a different perspective and gain insight into his or her feelings and behaviors. It is also perfect for dealing with someone who has passed away. When I use this technique in a mediumship session, the soul is literally present in the chair. Below is the technique.

The Empty Chair

Place two chairs facing each other. You sit in one chair and face the empty chair. In the empty chair, picture the person with whom you are experiencing conflict. Then, speak to the chair. Explain your feelings, thoughts, and how you see the situation. You will probably get very angry and may even rage at the person. It's important that you don't hold back. No matter what you say, the soul in the opposite chair can take it.

As you express your feelings, after a while, you may begin to feel some release and/or lightness in your body. Emotions held back for years have come to the surface and have been set free. This could be the first time you have been allowed to confront your abuser. Understand that the soul who has passed now resides in a "mentally enhanced" world, so they hear every thought and word you speak.

After you've shared your emotions, and only if you feel like you want to go further, move to the empty chair. This time, you respond to what was said from your abuser's perspective. You're taking on the other person's role. In your mind, listen to what they have to say. As you feel more relaxed, you can begin moving back

271

and forth several times between chairs, exchanging dialogue.

This is a powerful exercise. A person begins the process of releasing thoughts and emotions that may have been pent up for years. At the same, they may gain some understanding of why the abuser did what he or she did, but not so that any of their bad behavior is excused. Abusers usually learn their abuse from someone else who abused them.

In addition, please know that souls have a life review on the other side and experience all the joy happiness, as well as all the pain and suffering they have inflicted on others. It may feel like people are getting away with things here on Earth, but they never do. Nothing is missed on the other side. Karma, or the law of cause and effect, is a real thing. No one is excused from the law of karma. NO ONE.

Loss of a Spouse or Significant Other

Loss of a spouse is very challenging and particularly devastating, especially if the couple had been together for many years and considered themselves soul mates. It's not uncommon that the remaining spouse passes away shortly after from a broken heart. In fact, it's pretty typical.

However, sometimes there is guilt for not being there when a spouse passes, or a spouse feels he or she didn't express "I love you" enough, or they think that they didn't take better care of their spouse. None of that matters to the soul that has passed. First of all, please believe that your significant other wants you to know how much they love you. There is only love and understanding; they never want you to feel anything but love.

I have seen countless orbs around the spouses left behind. An orb is a transparent ball of light energy that is connected to spirits. Orbs can be spotted in photos, videos, and even on security cameras. We are all energy, and energy doesn't die. It merely changes form and transcends. These balls of light can be different shapes and colors, capturing the essence of what a person is like in the physical plane. Look at your photos. You may see orbs around people in the pictures. Your loved ones are always close. I've even seen orbs that look as if spirits are kissing their beloveds.

Sometimes, a soul on the other side will help to find a new partner for their loved one on Earth. I always find this funny because, frankly, who knows the one left behind better than the one in Spirit?

Spouses often asked me, "What if I fall in love again? What happens to my first love? Will my first husband come and get me when it's my time, or will it be my second or third spouse?" Humans complicate everything. Look at the possibility of having more than one great love in your life. Our hearts and souls are large, and we can hold the space in our hearts for lots of love.

What if a couple didn't get along in life? Do they meet again on the other side? Once, James told me of a client whose father came to her in the reading. Then, suddenly, her mother showed up. The client asked, "Are they together?" James thought that was a strange question, but when he observed them, he could see they were not together. James laughed. "Actually, they're on two different planes of existence, so, no, they're not together." His client smiled. "They fought like cats and dogs all through their marriage, so I didn't think they would want to be together on the other side. If you would have told me they were, I wouldn't have believed you."

To me, these two bickering souls probably moved on to different paths. Souls that marry in one lifetime usually have been together in other lives, but there is always karma and lessons to be learned. So this tells me that their karma and those lessons have been completed, and those souls have progressed to other levels away from each other.

Loss of a Sibling

I work with this loss often, and it is a loss that is not discussed enough. Some people have a better relationship with a sibling when he or she is on the other side than when the person is alive. Sometimes, losing a brother or sister can feel like losing a part of yourself. Think about it. We incarnate into the same dynamic circumstances as these siblings. We share a unique history with them, like common memories growing up together, significant experiences, and maybe secrets that only siblings share with one another.

Our siblings know us better than anyone. We may fight a lot or hang out a lot. Sometimes, they are our rescuers' mentors or tormentors. They push our buttons because they know what triggers us the most.

Losing a sibling can lead to feelings of insecurity. The constant in our lives is gone. Sometimes, it may feel as if a weight has been lifted. Losing a sibling can turn into complicated grief, depending on our relationship with them. Knowing that our siblings will review what they have done on the other side can also be a relief if they caused us and the family a lot of trouble. It's also possible that our siblings become guides for us—this may bring us consolation.

Loss of a Grandparent

The loss of a grandparent may be the first big loss for many people. This may be the first funeral or memorial service that someone attends. Sometimes, a grandparent may be the most important person in someone's life, as they offer support during times of crisis in a family system.

A grandparent is very different from a parent, and for many children, grandparents are heroes, especially if there's a family crisis, a parent dies, or parents get divorced. Children have an entirely different experience with grandparents than they have with their parents. Usually, a grandparent has more patience and time than a parent and can be a great teacher to a child.

If a grandparent dies, let your child talk about their cherished memories, and if possible, give them something special that belonged to the grandparent. I still have my beloved grandmother's big yellow mixing bowl and large spoon that she used to make all of her delicious cakes and prized matzo ball soup. I treasure these mementos and always think of her when I use them.

Because losing a grandparent is often the first big loss, there is a tendency for a child especially to become more preoccupied with death and dying. Usually, it is the first time someone has experienced grief. The loss of a grandparent brings with it the possibility of a spiritual awakening and a call to higher consciousness. Their death can help us to see a bigger picture of life.

An adult with a busy life and a family may feel guilty for not spending enough time with a grandparent. This is also true of older aunts and uncles. It's normal. However, loved ones on the other side completely understand and do not want anyone to feel guilty. Egos cause guilt; Spirit creates love.

Loss of a Friend

We love and cherish our friends, and our friendships often run deeper than family ties. Friends bring us such emotionally intimate support. There's nothing better than a trusted friend who makes you laugh or cry. The loss of a supportive friend can cause a deep chasm of grief. Losing a close friend is likely to trigger a series of emotions, such as shock and disbelief, along with guilt or regret for some of the things you may have said or done. The inability to talk about feelings is quite likely in the early days of loss.

Again, because of so many school shootings in this country, it's possible that your child is grieving the loss of a friend. It's important to explain how that loss affects them—like they won't be able to play together anymore. There won't be sleepovers, birthday parties, school activities, or sports with each other. Encourage them to ask questions about their friend and be as honest as possible with your answers.

Be on the lookout for any behavioral changes such as bedwetting, refusing to go to school, not doing their homework, wanting to be with their lost friend, etc. If your child is having a difficult time, seeing a therapist in school or privately can be enormously helpful.

Loss of a Pet

Our pets are members of our family and sometimes mean everything to us. The grief and intense sorrow over losing a pet can last for many years, and some people never recover from it. Some people may not understand or empathize with your loss; sometimes, they may make it worse by judging your feelings for losing an animal. However, the connection we have with a pet is emotionally significant, and our feelings can run deep.

I am very sensitive to this loss. As a medium, I work with animal loss and will often send a client to work with an animal psychic. I still cry when I think of my own precious dogs and cats who have died. I do want to mention that when I'm doing a reading, my dog Charlotte will open the door to my office and sit in the chair behind me. That's when I know that there's a message from a beloved pet on the other side for my client.

All animals are part of the Spirit, and they have souls. Pets can act as our guides on the other side. I suggest that if you want more information from your pet, see a pet psychic/medium. When it is our turn to cross over to the other side, our beloved animals will be waiting for us at the Rainbow Bridge, ready to greet us back home.

Be Vulnerable

Because we will all experience loss, I always suggest expressing your love while still on Earth. We are here to cultivate compassion, empathy, and kindness. Be vulnerable, and let go of guilt, sadness, and pain. You have to deal with your feelings; otherwise, they will lodge in your body and may cause serious complications like emotional issues or physical illness.

As souls, we incarnate to expand our awareness. If life on Earth were easy, what would there be to learn? Contrary to popular opinion, there is more to living than accumulating things or having adventures. The majority of our life lessons are related to the relationships we have on Earth, so losing these relationships can be tough and heartbreaking.

Whether you believe it or not, our real home is on the other side. Earth is a temporary existence, and we are here for a finite amount of time. We work very hard on the other side to put together a road map for each incarnation. We meet with our guides, soul group, and even ascended masters (souls with great wisdom) to decide the best way to learn certain lessons that will expand our consciousness. It's all about learning and growing, and the best way to do this is when we connect with others and form lasting relationships.

PART 4

THE UNPREDICTABLE

Chapter 18

LIFE ON THE FARM

In the stillness of your presence, you can feel your own formless and timeless reality as the unmanifested life that animates physical form. You can then feel the same life deep within every other human and every other creature. You look beyond the veil of form and separation. This is the realization of oneness. This is love.

- Eckhart Tolle, The Power of Now

After Don's sister Marie passed, Don took over her beautiful farm. The first time I visited the farm was in the summer of 2006. I was looking forward to meeting Don's family because I had heard so much about all of them and couldn't wait to get together. It was Don's family's Semiannual Corn Fest on his niece Peggy's farm, and besides all the festivities, there would be lots of corn. I couldn't wait!

When we arrived at the farm, I marveled at the beauty of the landscape and the tranquility it inspired. After we put away our belongings, off we went to the family reunion. Peggy was the first one to greet us. Family and friends from all over the country had gathered to celebrate, and I loved being introduced to everyone and spending time in such a restful setting while learning who's who in the family.

As Don became deeply immersed in a conversation with a cousin he hadn't seen in a long time, I grabbed a piece of farm-fresh roasted corn and began to explore the vastness of rural life. I thought to myself, I must have lived on a farm in other lifetimes because I felt right at home walking along the dirt roads, seeing the animals grazing and crops growing in the field. Even the aroma of the hay awakened something in me that felt so familiar.

Meeting A Starseed

As I walked up one of the rolling hills eating my corn, I spotted a young man walking down the hill towards me. He had a huge smile and the brightest blue eyes I had ever seen. I couldn't help but smile when I saw him because there was something magical about him.

He introduced himself, "Hi, my name is Jacob." His boyish charm was disarming, and I immediately felt that he was someone whom I had known.

Shaking his hand, I looked into his eyes, and I could feel that his energy was different. Suddenly, I uttered, "You're not from here."

"No, I'm not. I'm glad you noticed. Most people don't."

Just in case he misunderstood me, I said, "You know I don't mean around here, like Wisconsin."

He said, "Yes. I understand completely. I'm not from here."

"Where are you from?" By then, I was so curious.

He just pointed to the sky and announced, "Andromeda."

Wow! That caught me off guard. "What are you doing here?" I was eager to know all about someone not from Earth.

Jacob explained, "I'm a traveler. I've been to other planets, and I've come to Earth to observe and explore what life is like here. It's very different from all the places I've been to. People on your planet are usually nice and big-hearted, but they also have so many limitations. It's difficult to relate to them because their emotions get in the way. Unfortunately, relationships are the hardest for me. But I love the ability to explore Earth and all its customs and fixations. By the way, I'm a musician—I play guitar."

Of course, he's a musician.

"Does your Earth mom know about you?"

He answered, "Yes. My mother knows and seems to understand to the best of her ability." Jacob continued, "She knew when I was a baby that I was very different from my sister." Jacob explained that his mother was a therapist and seemed to be more open-minded about life, and he adored her for that and all the love she showered on him as he was growing up.

Jacob went on. "My father and I don't have much of a connection. He's a doctor. I appear to be a puzzle to him. But it's okay—we still get along."

At that moment, Don wandered over to us. "I was wondering where you went off to," Don said to me. Then he turned to Jacob. "Hi, I'm Don. I haven't seen you before."

Jacob smiled, "I'm Sue's son." Sue was actually one of Don's first cousins, but Don had never met his second cousin Jacob.

"I guess I've been traveling so much that it's hard for me to keep up with everyone, although Sue did tell me about you. We'll have to get together later and catch up. By the way, do you live here?" Don asked.

"No, I'm from Virginia," he answered. I looked at Jacob and winked.

"Well, great to meet you." And off Don went to get some corn.

Jacob and I continued our conversation. "It's good to meet someone who recognizes who I am. Sometimes, it gets lonely. Most people on this planet don't understand much beyond their own little world. They're not very evolved. Sometimes, I think they're sleep-walking through life. But that's just my observation."

Jacob was quite blunt about what he thought about earthlings. Our conversation was quite illuminating. Although this meeting took place before I became a licensed therapist, I knew Jacob's appearance was a sign of spirit. I realized that other beings like him would play an important part in the future of my practice. I knew that beings like him would show up, and I would be able to help them relate to their human existence and the companions they would meet along the way.

When I got back to our farm, I was anxious to look up *Andromeda* on Google. I learned that it's a galaxy next to the Milky Way, about 2.5 million light-years from Earth. Holy smokes—that's a long way to travel! How could I ever forget Jacob and my first encounter with an intergalactic being?

Intergalactic Beings

When I finally became a therapist, slowly but surely, I began to see other souls like Jacob. Even though they are not from here and are very different in many ways, they are still a part of the spiritual universe, and the Spirit has sent them here for a purpose.

Starseeds, or Intergalactic Beings, from other galaxies, are born into normal families. Some may even walk-in without being born. They are unique, gifted, and highly evolved beings who are definitely in the minority of Earth's population. They make up about 2-3% of the 5-7% of highly evolved beings presently living on Earth. Like us, Starseeds are spiritual beings, and they are learning lessons for their souls' advancement, similar to us on Earth. Every soul has something to learn.

The number of intergalactic beings traveling to our planet increases during times of unrest, dysfunction, and chaos on Earth, and many intergalactic beings travel back and forth between galaxies. At this particular time, they're here to raise the Earth's vibration and, by doing so, hasten the evolution of the planet to a higher level. I know it sounds quite strange. Just writing this makes me think of the movie *Men in Black* and all those kooky intergalactic characters, and I have to laugh. But having experienced Jacob and others like him, I can say for sure that these beings really exist on Earth, and they look just like us.

Author Ruth Montgomery wrote many books about intergalactic beings. In *Aliens Among Us*, she explains that "most of the space travelers now visiting Earth are from places in the spectrum of galaxies beyond the Milky Way. They are from far older civilizations than the earth's. They are now rushing in as seldom before to awaken earthlings..." Even our own government is finally revealing their secret findings about UFO sightings to the public. And it's amazing to see so many shows on *The History Channel* about "aliens" on Earth.

Starseeds are often seen as loners and can appear aloof or eccentric. Many can't pinpoint why they don't fit in or don't belong here. Coping with life on Earth can be a struggle for these "alien" souls, as ours is a planet of trauma, sorrow, destruction, and pain. The idea of pain is a very difficult concept for them. I find it a great responsibility to work with the population of planetary visitors because not only does it validate who they are, but by helping them, I am broadening the awareness of love and light in all souls. And funny enough, meeting Jacob confirmed to me that these galactic beings are being sent by Spirit for the purpose of helping us. But the spirit world didn't give me much time to rest, as another amazing experience was about to greet me.

My Hero

Since I was born and raised in Los Angeles, I never had any idea that one day, I would actually live on a farm. As usual, Spirit had a plan I would never have envisioned for myself. Our small town in Wisconsin was definitely a far cry from the sprawl of Los Angeles. It brought back all those memories of my mother's farm in Indiana, a place where everyone knew each other and looked out for one another. After living my entire life in LA, I couldn't imagine what it would be like living in a rural area. For sure, patience was required. Life indeed moved at a slower pace; no one was in a rush to do this or get that. It was a totally different mindset than the one I was used to, but one which I eventually grew to love.

When we made the momentous decision to move to the Wisconsin farm in 2019, one of the first people to help us was Willy. He was an elderly man who lived in our small town. He and his team helped with the entire transport from Southern California to the farm. Don and I will always be grateful to Willy for his kindness and attentiveness. Willy brought his granddaughter Caitlin to help us move in. She was about 16 and looked like an all-American girl—athletic, strong, and beautiful. She was a very hard worker, not spoiled, and had no hidden agenda. She was kindhearted like her grandfather, Willy.

As they brought in boxes, I began to unpack my new home office. It was a compilation of the Beverly Hills office, my home office, and my mother's office. I had many of Mom's cherished items, two of which were incredibly special–her beloved Eames chairs. Mom purchased them in the early 70s when she was establishing her practice. There were four of them altogether, and after my parents divorced, Dad took the other two.

I was astonished to see Caitlin carry the heavy Eames chair into my office. She carefully put it down and went to retrieve the matching ottoman. I remarked, "Caitlin, you're being very gentle with the chairs, and I appreciate it."

She replied, "Grandpa told me they were very expensive chairs and to be extra careful."

"Would you like to have a seat?" I asked.

"Really?"

"Absolutely. Sit back, put your feet up and relax. Some famous people sat in them. They're my therapy chairs," I leaned in and said in jest, "Now tell me your problems."

Surprisingly, Caitlin started to tell me her worrisome story, which made me feel unprepared. Instantly, I found myself in therapist mode. Technically, it was my first case in my new office.

"I feel anxious all the time," she said. "I can't sleep, and I feel very guilty."

I asked her, "Do you know why you feel guilty? Did something happen?"

"Yes," she answered.

She continued, "It happened two years ago. My other grandfather, whose name is Ted, was supposed to pick me up from school. At the last minute, I called him and told him not to pick me up because I was going to play volleyball instead."

Caitlin explained that her grandfather, Ted, was already on his way. He had just picked up her cousin Kim. Tragically, Ted's car was struck by a drunk driver. Ted was killed instantly, and her 12-year-old cousin Kim was badly injured.

Caitlin was on the verge of tears as she told her story. "It was my fault. If he picked me up like he usually does, he would have avoided the accident. My grandfather Ted would still be alive if I didn't go and play volleyball."

I could tell Caitlin had been suffering for the past two years, and I'm sure the rest of the family had to cope with their pain as well.

I looked over her shoulder and saw her grandfather, Ted, behind her. I knew I had to say something.

Caitlin had no idea that I was a medium as well as a psychotherapist. I wasn't sure she would understand, but I made a promise to Spirit years ago that if there was a situation that needed my intervention, I would make it obvious. This was one of those situations.

"Caitlin, I'm so sorry you had to go through such a painful experience. It's awful to lose your grandfather and nearly your cousin to that drunk driver."

Caitlin's eyes grew wide as I spoke.

"Do you know what a medium is?" She nodded her head. "Not quite sure, but I've seen someone on TV."

I explained, "I'm a medium and a psychotherapist. "I want to talk to you on a very personal level if that's okay with you."

She said, "Yes. If it would help me."

I felt her pain, grief, and suffering, and they were too much for her to hold onto anymore.

"Your grandfather Ted is telling me he was carrying cheese in the car with him. He always gave you a ride home after he picked up the cheese. Is that right?"

"Yes," she said, smiling. "He did pick up cheese to sell at the market every week."

"He is saying that you ate breakfast together every day."

She nodded at the memory.

I continued. "As he was driving home, he noticed a car coming towards him, weaving in and out of the lane. He looked in his rear-view mirror and saw the car behind him was filled with children. He is saying that he knew the drunk driver would have killed the family behind him, so he swerved into the other lane so the car would hit him and save the family and your cousin."

Caitlin cried out loud, "Oh, Grandpa."

"Please know your grandfather was a hero. He died saving a family. He is also telling me the same drunk driver had been in trouble before. This time, he will be going to prison for a very long time."

Caitlin began to cry.

I wanted to finish quickly so I could comfort her. "He said it was his destiny, and you had absolutely nothing to do with the accident. You were not supposed to be in the car. You were meant to be at volleyball practice."

Caitlin continued sobbing.

When she could speak, Caitlin explained that the same drunk driver had killed a pedestrian the year before. "He was in jail for a while, but then they let him out."

She said, "I feel better now. I love my grandfather. He was a hero. It sounds like something he would do. The family in the other car said many times it was a miracle they were not killed."

Caitlin said, "The trial is coming up. Would you come with me to the trial? My family would like it."

I answered, "I'll let you know."

Because I had just moved to the town and had already planned a trip, I wasn't sure if I could attend the trial. Also, I wasn't sure if I wanted people to know I was a medium. I didn't know how they would react to that piece of news.

Caitlin felt such relief she asked, "Do you think you could see my dad? He's having a hard time about the accident. I think you might help him."

Forgiving the Unforgivable

I agreed to see Mike, Caitlin's father. I wasn't too sure if he would agree to see me, but the following week, to my surprise, he showed up with Caitlin. I had no idea how she got him to say yes. He was a big, burly truck driver type, a *Hell's Angels* sort, and I'm quite sure seeing a medium was never going to be on his bucket list.

He and Caitlin sat on my peacock-blue couch. Above it hung a huge watercolor by an artist who specialized in tropical fish. I had a fish obsession, and apparently, so did Mike's dad, as I was about to find out.

I could tell Mike was jittery. It's quite common for anyone coming to me for the first time to feel nervous. They have no clue about what I do and what would happen. I explained a little about myself and how I worked. I tried to make Mike feel as comfortable as possible. I told him, "I know this is the last place you probably ever thought you would be, but I think I can help. You can relax."

I told Mike that I would record the session. Usually, people are so dazed and confused by what is being presented to them by the spirit world that they forget everything I say.

As I spoke to Mike, I could feel his father, Ted, in the room. I heard Ted say, "Tell Mike about the tropical fish."

"Mike, your dad tells me he loved tropical fish," I said. "The two of you would scout out the best fish and go from town to town looking for fish. It was a hobby you two shared. You thought he was nuts, but he just loved those fish."

Mike nearly fell off the couch.

Then, I described Ted's personality. "His proudest moment

291

was becoming a school superintendent."

Mike stared at me and nodded.

I continued, "He's saying that you're his only son and that the two of you were close. You're a great husband and good father to your girls, and he's especially proud of how you're taking care of your mother."

Ted went on and talked about special fishing trips and get-togethers with friends—events only Mike would know.

Mike listened closely, trying to absorb everything.

Finally, I said, "Your dad wants you to forgive the drunk driver. He's saying, "Do it for yourself. Please don't carry that anger anymore because it will eat you alive.""

I can't tell you how many times I've heard this plea from the other side. Spirit beings are always telling their loved ones to forgive and move on. Forgiveness is a powerful lesson for the soul. It's not always about the person who wronged us; it's more about learning to love ourselves enough to forgive ourselves and others. When we forgive ourselves, we come to a place of peace in our hearts.

I explained to Mike, "Your dad says the drunk driver will get the maximum sentence, but he knows that jail time is not going to matter to you."

Mike agreed. "He's right, it doesn't matter. I can't let this go. I can't forgive this guy. He killed my father and destroyed my family."

Mike described the moment he received the phone call from the police. "I had to walk into the kitchen and tell my mother that her husband was dead. My parents were married for 50 years and had never been apart. My mother was totally destroyed. She's not been out of the house since."

Mike's story left me breathless and speechless. My heart pounded; I could feel his pain and helplessness. Eventually, I knew his pain would turn to rage.

"Mike, your loss is devastating," I said. "I cannot imagine how horrific that moment must have been for you."

The entire time I sat with Mike, I asked Spirit to please help me to bring some form of peace to him. Spirit gave me an answer. "Let me share a story with you so that you can understand how karma works."

I sketched out the following story to Mike. "A couple of years ago, Dannion Brinkley—an author who wrote a book called Saved by the Light—was a guest on my podcast, *Both Sides Now*. He had a Near Death Experience." I wasn't sure if Mike understood an NDE, but I wanted to continue the story before he lost interest.

"Dan was struck by lightning and woke up in the morgue 28 minutes later. He was considered dead because he had no pulse. Dan explained that during the time he was supposedly dead, he went into a bright light and crossed into the spirit side. There, he met with a high council of advanced spirit beings. He had to look at his life and feel every pain he had ever caused anyone. Dan served in the Vietnam War and killed people, many innocent people. He was told by the council that he had to feel the death of the ones he had killed, including all the pain the families who were left behind had endured. When he woke up in the morgue, he saw life here very differently, and his near-death caused him to rethink everything about why we're on this Earth. He has written many other books and goes around the world teaching people about the

293

spirit world and why we must answer for everything we do and say."

After telling Mike about Dannion, Mike asked, "Do you mean the drunk driver who killed my father will have to experience the moment I had to tell my mother? And how she collapsed in my arms? And then tell my wife and kids?"

I simply said, "Yes. He'll feel all of that grief and pain. He'll have to feel the pain of everyone who has been hurt by his actions."

He took a long, deep breath, probably for the first time in two years, and thanked me. "Knowing that brings me some peace. Will you please come to the court trial? It'd bring my family comfort to know you're in the courtroom."

"It would be my honor," I replied.

Two weeks later, the trial began, and I sat in the back of a very crowded courtroom. I looked at the back of the drunk driver on trial; he had a very dark aura. I could tell he was a lost soul whose addiction was passed on from his father. Each member of Mike's family stood up to speak their feelings directly to the drunk driver. It was a very emotional experience.

I could sense Ted's spirit in the courtroom and knew he was proud of his family, especially his son Mike. The judge gave the drunk driver the maximum sentence of 20 years to life. When it was all over, Mike hugged me, and the peace I felt in him was priceless. He looked straight into my eyes and said, "Thank you. I can begin to live again."

What Goes Around Comes Around

I've mentioned "karma" a few times already in the book. Karma is a controversial subject in the west, but not in the East, where it is part of the philosophy of all the major religions. The law of karma, or the law of cause and effect, is one in which I, too, believe. It doesn't only apply to past lives but to the life we live now. Since everything is energy, our thoughts and actions are also energy. Thoughts are things. And matter and form respond to our thoughts. Be aware of what you think and what you say because it will come back to you. The same goes for your actions. We've all heard, "What goes around comes around." That's the idea of cause and effect. It is said in the Bible, "Do not be deceived: God cannot be mocked. For whatsoever a man soweth, that shall he also reap." (Galatians 7, King James Version)

And I might add, be careful what you wish for because you may get it, but it may not be what you thought it would be, or it may be more of a chore to handle than you want.

When I finished writing this chapter, I took a break and looked at my Facebook page. I saw the day, October 20, the third anniversary of Grandpa Ted's death. My heart goes out to Mike and his family and all families who have lost loved ones because of drunk drivers. I can only hope that each person can find peace knowing that death is not the end but a door to life on the other side. I've been very fortunate to be able to work with clients like Caitlin and Mike on such profoundly personal soul matters. I honor each and every one of them, and I want them to know that I learn more from them than they learn from me.

After we settled into life on a farm, Don and I agreed that it was the wisest move we had ever made. We love our farm life. It's so different from the life we had in LA. It's an idyllic world and very laid back. Although it's really cold in the winter, it's very invigorating. It's just a beautiful spot where we can take one day at a time. When we lived in LA, everything seemed to move faster, even though the traffic moved slower. And our schedules were always filled, so it seemed we were always at work. It's nice to be able to kick back, relax, and breathe in the country air. And don't forget the corn!

Chapter 19

THE PANDEMIC

I no longer mourned for the deceased because I knew they'd transcended to another realm, and I knew that they were happy! It's not possible to be sad there. At the same time, I also knew that even their death was perfect, and everything would unfold in the way it was meant to in the greater tapestry.

- Anita Moorjani, *Dying To Be Me*

By July 2019, James and I had become great friends, and it was always easy for us to be spontaneous with one another. That is why we both decided to share our interesting insights and conversations with others by creating our podcast, *Both Sides Now And Beyond*. It seemed like a natural fit. Besides spiritual, medium, and psychological guidance, I had my astrology advice to share on the program. Because I have studied both western and Vedic astrology for many years, our viewers always seemed to love it when we would discuss current astrological events on the podcast. I remember that year vividly because James and I had many deep conversations about what we both saw for the future of the world—astrologically and psychically. Remember, this was 2019. How can any of us forget?

Since my field of expertise is in Vedic astrology, which is also known as Indian or Hindu astrology, I checked out our charts and found some phenomenal occurrences. When I looked at the year 2020, my discussion with James turned serious. Astrologically, I had never before seen the types of alignments that were looming on the horizon. There were eclipses, several planets in Capricorn, and retrogrades. All these alignments meant a huge change in 2020, not only for us individually but for everyone on the planet, and not only for one year but for the entire decade that followed. Every sign was pointing to be a double whammy.

Psychically, I saw a huge shift in consciousness. I saw that life as we knew it would never be the same again. I thought it might be a result of another terrorism attack like 9-11. "Pandemic" was something that didn't come to mind. I don't believe anyone has ever been given all the pieces of the puzzle by Spirit. It would be too much to handle.

Astrologically, I knew that March 2020 was significant, and there would be a complete change of life for every single soul on the planet. It was going to be huge, but I didn't know exactly what it would be.

In February 2020, James and I were in Chicago having dinner with David Viggiano, an old friend of James. David was a wonderful, kind soul who had worked with James for several years. He was a straight shooter, a public relations guy, very clever, and not easily fooled.

James said, "Go ahead, honey, tell David what you see going forward."

I began. "I believe 2020, and possibly the entire decade will bring enormous change that none of us have ever experienced before. These changes will be difficult to understand. There will be another terrorist event or something so significant that all of our lives will be challenged. Whatever it is, it will be quite profound."

David gave me a quizzical look. I don't think he really put a whole lot of credence into what I said. I'm sure he thought I was a little nuts. A month later, when the Corona Virus stunned the world, he called me. "I couldn't believe what you said last month. I thought your prediction was a little, so shall we say it out there? Who would have thought that something like this pandemic could happen? I'm not looking forward to the rest of the year. It's going to be one big mess."

No one would have believed how all our lives would change because of the virus. Moving forward in this decade, there will be more trying times. The war in Ukraine is certainly something no one had expected. Then, in 2021, we had the January 6th uprising at the U.S. Capitol, which is still having repercussions for all of us as we head into the next election cycle. Can it get any worse? I can only say, YES, it can, but I don't know exactly in what way.

It is also my understanding that everyone presently living on Earth signed up to be here to experience this time of upheaval and ultimate transformation. We all bought the "E-ticket for the soul," much like we once had to have to ride the Matterhorn rollercoaster at Disneyland. Only this ride is not going to be much fun.

299

Purpose of the Pandemic

So why did this virus happen? I get this question a lot. From a spiritual standpoint, it was a planned or fated event. Its purpose was crafted to literally stop us in our tracks. We were all going in a million different directions at lightning speed. I believe the Spirit said STOP NOW. It's time to go inward. Time to reexamine your life. Spend time in nature. Watch the birds. Smell the flowers. Appreciate and reevaluate your values and where you're headed. Make the necessary changes to live a more *mindful* life. Ultimately, the pandemic's message was to help us find meaning in our existence.

For me, I found a deeper purpose in my work. I felt Spirit wanted me to be a guiding light for people as they went through their deepest fears of survival, isolation, and death. We all felt unsettled about our loved ones, children, homes, jobs, and what to do if we got sick? "How long will it last?" Or, "Will my family be okay?" were questions we all had. But I had faith that humanity would survive and move forward.

At the onset of Covid, like most people, I was uncertain about a lot of different things. Thoughts swirled around in my head. *Were masks enough? Should I be around other people? Should I get tested? What if I get sick? Should I go to the ER?* There wasn't a moment that went by that I didn't think of my mother and wondered what sort of advice she would give. She was always my "go-to" for everything. But even she had never faced a pandemic. Eventually, I came to the conclusion that she would have been ASKING ME what to do. And that is when I felt a "grown-up shift" in myself. I became the one with the answers. I became HER "go-to" gal.

James and I talked every day about the future and how both of us could help the world. That was when we decided to kick it up a notch. James began doing a daily show on YouTube called *Soul Care* to provide a place of spiritual retreat for people. It was a show where people could sit in their homes and learn meditation and grounding, communicate with loved ones in dreams, deal with emotions during the pandemic, and connect to Spirit for support and peace. A couple of months after that show began, the two of us went full force into our show, *Both Sides Now & Beyond,* to help people understand change, spiritualism, psychology, and, of course, astrology. People have taken great comfort in these shows during the lockdowns, and I'm happy to say they still are to this present day.

Let's not forget that millions of people have died around the world from the pandemic. There must be a spiritual reason why so many souls chose to leave the Earth. I know we all have something to learn from this crisis. Perhaps we have to cherish the ones in our lives and forgive those who are thorns on our sides. Maybe we have to come to terms with the destruction we've caused to the Earth and choose a new course. I think the pandemic is Spirit's wake-up call that we all must change and find out who we truly are. As Eckhart Tolle says, "Very unconscious people experience their own ego through the reflection in others. When you realize that what you react to in others is also in you, you begin to become aware of your own ego."

Only when we recognize that we are making decisions and judging others from the ego self can we learn to let go, take a different direction, and make choices from our Higher Spiritual

Self?

Loss of Clients and Friends

Like everyone else, I was not immune to the devastating loss of loved ones and clients from Covid. Using Zoom, session after session, I was on the front line dealing with everyone's emotions, especially fear and loss, and it seemed brutally relentless. It was a harsh reality that the whole world had to deal with. I know people in other countries had it much harder than us here in the states. In Europe, everyone was on lockdown. People weren't allowed out of their homes except to buy necessities. There were mandatory curfews. It was as if the whole world came to a grinding halt. I would never have imagined that what I saw in the astrological charts the year before meant the end of the world as we knew it.

By the end of March 2020, some of my clients had already tested positive for Covid. They varied in age, ranging from young professional parents with a small child to a 68-year-old man caring for his 92-year-old mother. Each client had their own story to tell of illness and survival. And then, I began to hear of loved ones dying.

I personally lost my close friend Paul to Covid. I hadn't heard of Paul's passing from anyone, so I was unaware that he had died until one day in November 2021. While I was working in my office, I felt a presence in the room and glanced up. There was Paul floating over my desk. It was a brief encounter, but I knew right away that he had passed. I was so shaken up; I couldn't believe it. Once I stopped shaking, I looked him up on the internet, and sure enough, he had passed away from COVID-19 a month before.

Paul and I had known each other for 45 years. He was someone who profoundly changed my life. We met in Germany when we were both 16 years old. My father accepted an offer from the German government to work as a musician. Paul was our next-door neighbor. His father was an American doctor in the army. The two of us discovered that we had so much in common and quickly fell in love. He was the first boyfriend to tell me I could do anything. He believed in me and encouraged me to follow my dreams. I believed that he could do anything, too. We were emotionally supportive of one another and remained close for a couple of years. Eventually, life had a way of separating us. When my parents divorced, I stayed in Los Angeles to be with my mother, and Paul ultimately ended up in law school on the East Coast.

When Paul appeared to me in Spirit, all the events of the time we were together flooded my memory, and his loss deeply affected me. I took some time off from my heavy work schedule to grieve. If this could happen to him, it surely could happen to anyone, and that idea alarmed me even more.

When the vaccine was developed, like many people, I was hesitant to get it. But after Paul's death, I immediately made an appointment to get vaccinated. I was thankful that Spirit interceded to assist scientists and doctors in formulating a vaccine and made it available so quickly. I can't imagine how many lives have been saved because of it.

Who knows how long the pandemic would have lasted without the vaccine. My feeling is that there would be many more people leaving the planet, but at the same time, I don't believe everyone signed up to leave. Spirit made sure that those who were here were supposed to be here. Those who left accomplished their mission, although saying that to anyone would be hurtful. Please know that your loved ones meant to leave; it was part of their souls' destiny. They are involved in your everyday life and look out for your welfare from the spirit side. Many of them are now your Spirit guides, angels, and teachers.

Just as Paul came to me, many loved ones will come to us to let us know they're on the other side. Even though we can't see them, we can sense their presence, either by an aroma, a picture, or something familiar that we know about them. Sometimes, we can be doing something, and our loved one comes to mind. We could be driving our cars and passing a building or a sign, and we are immediately reminded of them. Or a song comes on the radio that causes us to remember. I tell my clients that signs like these usually mean our loved one is there at that moment. But mostly, loved ones visit us in our dreams. In the dream state, we are completely relaxed and can spend time traveling to various levels of consciousness. Dreams allow us to be more open and receptive to a spirit's presence. Loved ones are always trying to make themselves known to us. Watch for the signs because they are around us daily.

Love Affair in the Time of Covid

This next story is a cautionary tale told with the permission of my client. She felt it was important to share it and hoped it could help others in a similar situation.

Victoria was one of my first clients when I was in graduate school. I was pleased that she wanted to continue therapy with me after I began in private practice. I have probably learned more from Victoria than any other client.

Initially, Victoria came to me for depression. She was in her mid-forties, married 20 years to George, who was 10 years her senior, and childless. She had just finished nursing school and was about to embark on a nursing career when both her parents had passed away within the year. Their passing caused Victoria to go into a tailspin.

However, her grief was not the main reason for therapy. Victoria confided about an affair she was having. She was upset because her boyfriend John would not leave his wife. I have to be honest—I didn't see that one coming. She had been having an affair for a couple of years. Often, John would come over to help her husband do odd jobs around the house. It was difficult to believe that: 1. she was having an affair, and 2. that the person she was having an affair with was a friend of her spouse and was frequently at her home helping him with odd jobs. I know it happens, but it was a first for me.

It was obvious that Victoria had a lot of issues, not only because of the affair but because she was unhappy in her marriage and unhappy in her life. She had bouts of suicidal ideation and mania, and they got worse after her parents' deaths. Unfortunately, Victoria was on an emotional rollercoaster and had tremendous guilt, but she couldn't stop her affair. When Covid hit, she became a basket case because everything in her life took a turn for the worse.

I had never met either John or George, but I grew to know them over the years during my sessions with Victoria. One day, she came into my office and was livid. "John is taking his wife and kids on a cruise. How can he leave me at home? I have to take care of George." By this time, George was at the beginning stages of dementia.

She went on, "John promised that when he comes back, he'll take me on the same cruise." What could I say? I had told her often enough that she had to end the affair, but my words fell on deaf ears. As soon as she mentioned John was going on a cruise, I had a bad feeling. I urged her, "Please tell John not to go. I have a horrible feeling that he'll catch Covid on the cruise. She naively said, "Oh Kellee, Covid is nothing. It's like the flu. He'll be fine."

I pleaded with her, but she wouldn't listen. She was so caught up in the affair she couldn't see straight. And as a nurse, she knew better. Sadly, affairs change people; they get caught up in emotions and make bad choices and decisions.

At the onset of the pandemic, cruise ships continued their schedules but soon enough became petri dishes for the virus. After the cruise ended, John and his family had to go through a Covid screening on board the ship. It took 24 hours until everyone was tested and allowed to disembark. As soon as he was back home, John headed straight to Victoria's house. He spent time helping around the house. Then he and Victoria went out to dinner, leaving George with Victoria's sister.

The next day, John called Victoria to tell her he didn't feel well. Two days later, John was admitted into the hospital with Covid and was put into an induced coma. Because no one was allowed to visit anyone in the hospital during COVID-19, neither John's wife and family nor Victoria could see him. The worst part for Victoria was not knowing John's condition, and she was beside herself with worry. To add to her distress, her husband George contracted COVID-19, and unfortunately, because he was already compromised with dementia, he did not survive. He passed away after a few weeks. At this point, Victoria was riddled with guilt, especially since she didn't know whether John would live or die.

Miraculously, John did recover; he was one of the first Covid patients who had been in a coma for three months and survived. Eventually, he and Victoria met for a drink. When she saw him, she was horrified—he had lost 50 pounds, appeared totally emaciated and was very weak. How in the world could she tell John about George's death? When Victoria came to her session, she was bereft with grief. "I just couldn't tell him that George died."

She waited until John got his strength back before she broke the news about George. When that day arrived, John was overcome with remorse and guilt. The thought that George caught Covid from him knocked him to his knees. She showed John her memorial to George in the backyard—a bench engraved with his name, flowers, and his ashes spread underneath his favorite tree. Two weeks later, Victoria was diagnosed with breast cancer.

Do I think her cancer was karma? Only Spirit knows the answer, but Victoria began looking within and questioning her life choices and the consequences of her actions. Each day, she lives with enormous regret and grief. Fortunately, Victoria recovered from breast cancer and has made many changes in her life. She has dedicated her life to helping others and finally has stopped seeing John.

Once in physical bodies, we humans make our lives very complicated, and our choices and actions become even more chaotic during extraordinary times. My daughter Holiday, who is also a psychologist, always tells her patients that no matter what's going on, "make good choices."

Between the pandemic and the recent political landscape, we are all being tested by Spirit. Who are we really? What choices are we making? Are we behaving with kindness or hostility? When we reach the other side, we will all see our lives in review. I suggest we make it as "clean a life" as we possibly can. If there's an opportunity to make a better choice, make it.

Let me say that the pandemic was a major hardship for everyone. As I said in Chapter 17, most people who have lost loved ones during the pandemic went through the trauma of not being able to be close to their loved ones in the hospital and say their last loving words and goodbyes. To those who lived, it was their worst nightmare—always wondering if the "other shoe would fall." The lucky ones who survived the pandemic often have "survivor guilt"—"Why did my wife die and I made it through?" I want to reiterate that your loved one who passed does not want you to feel guilty. It was their time and not yours. You still have lessons to learn on Earth.

Also, not being near loved ones as they pass is the spirit world giving us a gift. See it as a blessing, not a curse. Your loved one didn't want you to see their suffering. Again, your loved one in Spirit doesn't want you to feel guilty or angry. These are emotions of the ego. Your loved ones in Spirit have transcended into a spiritual atmosphere where the ego is no longer in control. They don't want you to feel anything but love and to carry the memories of love in your heart. Don't think of them as "dead," as that is disrespectful. They are very much alive. They are with you as guides and teachers from the other side. I can't say it enough: you will all be reunited again.

Acceptance, Surrender, and Faith

The pandemic was not the most painful lesson I faced in this lifetime. It was accepting that my old life was over, and I had to begin again. I was 42 years old, and everything was going for me when bam! Something unforeseen happened. As petrifying as it was for me at that time in my life, ironically, I never thought that it was unfair, nor did I complain. *Why me?* Inwardly, I knew, *of course, why me?*

My experience prepared me to help people deal with their unforeseen loss, abandonment, isolation, and extreme change caused by the pandemic. Life can truly turn on a dime. When I was suffering, I was fortunate to have my mother by my side to support and console me. But in addition to Mom, I had spirit guides and angels to give me direction. I can't stress this enough—WE ARE NEVER ALONE.

Sometimes, we have to start all over again to live our best lives and to get on the right path for our souls' growth. Looking back at that time in my life, going through a spiritual awakening, I was in a lot of emotional and mental pain. I had no idea where my life was headed, but I knew I had to let go of my past. It was my "dark night of the soul."

I had to surrender any hope that my old life would return. I couldn't continue to look backward because I was keeping myself from moving ahead. I had to be compassionate towards myself. I had to understand at my core that all the changes were fated by Spirit. I had to have faith that there was a plan in front of me and that I would be guided. I had to force myself to look within. I had to believe that all my incredible spiritual experiences would lead me to where I needed to be. I had to learn to let go, and for me, like most people, letting go is not easy. *Let Go and Let God* became my new mantra. Let it be your mantra, too.

Chapter 20

SELF-REALIZATION

Seeking after wholeness is the Spiritual Warrior's quest. And yet, what you are striving to become in actuality is what you already are. You must become conscious of your essence and bring it into form, express it in a creative way.

- *The Book of Runes*

By now, you would think I had faced all the major spiritual challenges I would ever have in my lifetime. Yet, as I often say, as each day emerges, there are new opportunities to learn and understand in order to grow. There was one I never saw coming.

As I said in the previous chapters, my mother had breast cancer twice. The first breast cancer was during a deep emotional love affair that ended in sorrow. Was her cancer the result of that heartbreak? At the time, I didn't have a clue about the mind-body connection and didn't think thoughts and emotions could cause physical ailments, but eventually, it dawned on me that her emotional pain did contribute to her diagnosis.

Over time, as I became spiritually aware, I realized that everything we think and do creates. Our thoughts, emotions, bodies, and lessons are unified into one being, and everything we experience is exactly necessary for spiritual growth. I also believe that Mom's cancer was a choice she made on the other side as a way to bring her to her own spiritual awakening.

Giving Too Much

I didn't understand back then that an illness was a lesson in forgiveness, but as Louise Hay says in her book *You Can Heal Your Life*, "All disease comes from a state of unforgiveness. Whenever we are ill, we need to look around to see who it is that we need to forgive." It could be other people, or it could be ourselves. Most of the time, we need to forgive ourselves.

Louise also states in her book *Heal Your Body: The Mental Causes For Physical Illness and the Metaphysical Way to Overcome Them* that cancer is: "Deep hurt. Long-standing resentment. Deep secret or grief eating away at the self." She goes on to say, "Breasts Problems: Over mothering. Overprotection. Overbearing Attitudes." Wow! I can see where these mental causes are applicable to both my mother and myself.

It's obvious that we came into this lifetime together to learn a spiritual lesson—to let go of old hurts and overly responsible attitudes. These difficult lessons were a way for us to open our minds and hearts to a higher vibration of love and to get closer to our true selves and inner wisdom. It took us a while, perhaps most of our lives, but I believe that all cancer has the potential to bring everyone closer to God.

When Mom had cancer a second time, I felt that it had to do with the never-ending responsibility that she took to heart and held onto it like it was some great treasure. Her professional responsibility defined her life. It was impossible to take her out of the role of doctor/psychologist. In this sense, she was intractable. Asking her to take time for herself was something that she considered absurd. No—not in this lifetime.

Mom was a force to be reckoned with, and poor Marc was up to his eyeballs trying to reckon with Mom. Although he was a hard-working lawyer, when he had the time, he loved to take vacations and relax. Often, he would plan incredible trips for them, but Mom would buck at the idea of "vacation" as if it were poison. And even on a forced vacation, she would end up working. She continued to take calls from patients at any time of the day or night.

Because mom's behavior sometimes bordered on rigid, with an overbearing and over-protecting attitude towards her patients, my responsibility to her was as her one and only trusted confidant. Of course, I had to be just as responsible as she was. Our relationship was one of real enmeshment.

Enmeshment is a term introduced by Salvador Minuchin that is used to describe an overly close and intertwined relationship. "It could be between family members or in a romantic relationship. In family enmeshment, boundaries between family members blur with individuals sharing similar thoughts, feelings, and behaviors." That fits our relationship to a tee.

In a sense, my great responsibility role grew not only because I was an empath but also because I was learning from Mom and *her* life. I was *on call* and *on high alert* pretty much every day of

313

my life. If Mom ran herself ragged, I was the only one who could manage her, which meant my life was devoted to her and her neuroses.

Her overprotective attitude began when I was quite young, maybe three or even younger. At the time, my dad was an addict. Mom felt that if she had more education, she could make more money to take care of the family, especially if something bad happened to him. She could never rely on him, so she leaned on me for total allegiance and support. Basically, I was her "partner," if you will, supporting her by being responsible for my siblings and the household while she worked and went to school.

Once she earned her Ph.D., Mom's responsibility for her patients became all-consuming. She stepped into prominent power, and as a mother hen in charge of her chicks, she gave them everything she could and never stopped. At the same time, her mental and emotional resources were being drained dry. That's when breast cancer reared its ugly head the second time. It was another reminder of the message from the Indian psychic— this time, I applied it to Mom. If you give of yourself to everyone, in the end, you have nothing left.

My Cancer Scare

The enmeshment with my mother was so great that I couldn't tell the difference between what she felt and what I felt, and my great responsibility roared on. Since responsibility has been my life theme, I guess you can say that I picked the right mother and partner to be with this lifetime—for sure!

Keeping all this in mind, I was 35 years old when I felt a lump in between my breasts. Holiday was eight years old by then, and I was going through one heck of an abusive relationship. Knowing that breast cancer can be hereditary, I quickly made an appointment with my gynecologist. He ordered a biopsy, and I had an appointment that same afternoon with another doctor to get the biopsy done. Unfortunately, the doctor doing the biopsy stuck the needle into my breastbone several times but couldn't get any fluid. "Come back next week, and I'll try again." I thought to myself, *You're kidding. No way will I be coming back to you.* It was a very painful process, and the thought of doing it again set off an inner alarm.

When I got home, I called my mother and told her the grisly details. Being a breast cancer survivor, she panicked. She knew all too well that if I did have breast cancer, this flop of a biopsy procedure would have spread cancer cells throughout my body. Immediately, she called Dr. John Stehlin, her breast cancer doctor in Houston. It was Dr. Stehlin who saved her life 15 years before and was one of the first physicians to treat breast cancer with lumpectomy rather than radical mastectomy.

Dr. Stehlin urged my mother to get me on a plane to Houston. With a genetic history of breast cancer, I'm sure he feared the worst-case scenario. So, Mom and I were on a flight to Houston that night. We checked into a hotel, and the next day, we saw Dr. Stehlin. The following morning, I was in surgery. It all happened so fast.

I remember Dr. Stehlin saying to me, "There's a 70% chance you'll wake up with no breasts, but I will do everything I can to save them." His words were the scariest thing I had ever heard, but I had to trust him to do the right thing. Remember, at this particular stage in my life, I was still clinging to the physical world and had not yet learned the spiritual aspect of life. I was unaware that this could be Spirit trying to convey a *wake-up* message.

To say I went into surgery with great trepidation is an understatement. Being a responsible nurturer like my mother, I seemed to be mirroring her in every aspect, and I had the dreaded sense that I was headed down the same road as her. Our emotional attachment to one another was overwhelming, and like I said, I didn't know where she ended, so I began. Even though I was 35, I certainly didn't know who I was as Kellee. I guess you might say I wanted to be the perfect duplicate of my mother because, in my mind, she was perfect. Whatever roles we played in other lifetimes, this life must have been a continuation of a very similar pattern. Both of us were healers, but in this life, my guess is that we had to learn to HEAL OURSELVES! Not so easy!

I was in surgery for three hours, and Dr Stehlin had to scrape off a tumor the size of an orange on my breastbone. It left a huge scar, but thankfully, I still had both breasts. The good news is that the tumor was BENIGN. I thought, *Thank God, I will live.* I WAS CANCER FREE! I felt so relieved that I wouldn't die before my Holiday grew up.

Although that lump on my breastbone was not seen in a mammogram, I continue to self-check and continue to get a mammogram every year, and I encourage every woman to do the same.

Responsibility Calling Again

Fifteen years after my cancer scare, I made the decision, along with advice from my doctors, to have breast-reduction surgery. My breasts were always attention grabbers, and I had my share of attention, unwanted or not! I can't tell you how many times some man tried to grab at my breasts. On the other hand, given my life theme of responsibility, I think my breasts have served me well in the role of a "comforting mother" to souls in need. But I had suffered from neck, back, and shoulder pain from carrying and supporting large breasts my adult life, and I felt it was time to do something about it. I was turning 50, and this surgery was going to be a gift to me.

I found a wonderful doctor in Beverly Hills, chose the date, and was looking forward to what it would be like to live without neck strain and back pain. To say the least, I was excited about having a new body. However, a few days before my surgery, Mom had begun to have trouble walking. She was in constant pain, and it was urgent that she have hip surgery to remove and replace the old hardware in her hip from the previous hip surgery she had in 1981. Again, everything happened quickly. Needless to say, her health came before mine, so I didn't have breast reduction surgery.

My responsibility theme again kicked into high gear. After canceling my own surgery, I took care of Mom, managing to finish grad school with a Master's degree in psychology.

In the following years, I completed the 3000 hours of client sessions and was ready for my licensing exam, which is done once a year. There was a nine-month-long wait to take the exam.

Because I had the time, I decided once again to have breast-reduction surgery. So, for my 55th birthday, I found another surgeon and, again, set the date. However, fate stepped in a second time. There's a saying, "If it's not one thing, it's your mother!" I have a needlepoint pillow with this catchphrase on it, and I absolutely cherish it.

This time, my mother was diagnosed with breast cancer for the second time, 33 years after her first diagnosis. I immediately canceled my surgery and put all of my energy into taking care of Mom. My responsibility to Mom took precedence, and I found myself running as fast as I could from one doctor to another with my mother. Mom tried everything, from nutrition to holistic medicine, from psychic healers to meditation. She was going to beat this cancer, especially if I had anything to do with it.

By this time, Mom had seen me go through a lot of experiences that were part of my spiritual awakening. It took both of us a long time to finally recognize that we were spiritual beings and not just physical bodies. When she got breast cancer the second time, it was her turn to learn from me, but it was very hard for her to give up being the "doctor in charge."

Lessons In Acceptance

The next thing that happened was strange yet insightful. Mom and Marc owned a second home in Palm Desert, CA, and on the weekends, they would go there to relax and get far away from anything to do with cancer. When they were out of town, I was free for a few days to relax and unwind without focusing all my attention on Mom. By now, you can see I was always hyper-vigilant about

Mom and her health.

One Thanksgiving, while Mom and Marc were spending the long weekend in the desert, Mom fell and hurt her hip and couldn't walk. She began having trouble breathing and getting faint, but she refused to go to the hospital. Don and I were up north on the farm in Wisconsin, visiting Don's mother, who was 97.

Holiday called me. "Mom. Nana is dying in the hospital. What do we do? She refuses to take her medication."

As usual, I started to panic. Another emergency and I wasn't there to take charge. And then, Spirit intervened, and it came to me. "Tell her that her guides told me she must take her medicine. It's not her time to die now." Well, that did the trick. By this time, Mom believed in Spirit guides, and she didn't hesitate to follow their counsel. She was totally invested in spirituality, mine and her own, and she trusted my ability to communicate with the spirit side. It was amazing to see the change in her.

Mom lived with cancer for another five years, during which time I somehow managed to pass my licensing exam and begin my own practice. I was doing both psychotherapy and mediumship sessions and taking care of Mom. It was a very heavy load, and I did everything I could to save her from breast cancer, but it was not in my control. She passed away in 2018 when I was 60 years old.

After Don and I moved to Wisconsin in 2019 and had time to settle in at the farm, I decided once again to schedule breast-reduction surgery. After all, wasn't the third time the charm? Don's niece referred me to an incredible cosmetic surgeon, and I met with Dr. K in Madison. My surgery was scheduled for April 29,

2020. This time, I thought it was a slam dunk; however, I was wrong again. The pandemic changed everything, and all elective surgeries were canceled.

I can't tell you how deflated I felt. I had to hide my upset feelings about this third cancellation and put all my energy, attention, and responsibility into my clients during the pandemic. I never worked harder in my life. I saw eight to ten people on Zoom every day. Many had Covid during their sessions with me and were asking for hope and healing. I felt pulled in many directions, and dare I say, at the end of each day, I was emotionally drained.

Additionally, I communicated with most of the therapists I knew, sharing stories and exchanging advice. This included my beloved daughter, Dr. Holiday Bean. She and her husband, Dr. Anthony Bean, run The Telos Project, a non-profit public benefit corporation for mental health in Texas. Their staff encompasses several psychologists and psychotherapists, and all were on the front lines of mental health during the pandemic. I knew Holiday needed my strength, support, and comfort so she could, in turn, lift up and guide her staff.

Besides working all day long, I did two video shows a week— one with James Van Praagh and my own show, *Ask Me Anything*, where I answered people's questions about astrology, psychology, spirituality, death, dying, and grief. Somehow, I also managed to squeeze in classes on Zoom with Dr. Shirley Impellizzeri about trauma recovery using my psychological and spiritual lenses.

All through this time, my beloved Don was my rock. After a long day, I would just fall into his arms and sob. Without him, I think I would have been hanging by a thread or flapping in the wind. His support kept me going.

For me, the years 2020 and 2021 were all about responsibility. I worked around the clock. I was deeply concerned for the souls in the world, and my unceasing responsibility to help others was in overdrive. By October 2021, although things were still hectic, I thought it was time to reconsider having breast reconstruction surgery for the fourth time. I contacted Dr. K and was told the soonest I could get an appointment for a consultation was January 17, 2022. And so, the process of having surgery began all over again. Dr. K was wonderful from the start. He explained that because elective surgeries had been postponed during 2020 and part of 2021, his calendar was backlogged. The soonest he could schedule my surgery was August 17, 2022, so we set the date.

You'd think by now I'd given up. But the symbolism of "breast reduction" didn't escape my mind. Maybe unconsciously, I was trying to lessen my workload by reducing my over-nurturing behavior and creating more balance in my life.

I Thought All the Numbers Added Up

Numerologically speaking, August 17, 2022, was an auspicious day. I added all the numbers: August (8) + 17 (8) + 2022 (6) = 22. In numerology, 22 is a master spiritual number, meaning "the builder." I interpreted it as being "rebuilt." I knew it was a powerful day, but it turned out to be more than that. 22 is also a karmic number, and its high vibration requires balance. It was a double-edged sword—the ideas of "being rebuilt" and simultaneously "finding balance." Double-digit numbers can also be warning numbers. If 22 is reduced to 4, it means hard work, stubbornness, and intensity.

I remember being somewhat uncomfortable in the days leading up to the surgery, and I tried to dismiss my anxiety as normal. *Who doesn't get nervous before an operation?* Anyway, that's what I told myself. But my instinct was beginning to feel like doom, or to a greater extent, dread, and doom. I was feeling more unsure every day and didn't feel exactly 100% comfortable going forward with the surgery. *Was Spirit trying to send me a message?* But being stubborn, I was determined to get this surgery. After all, I had waited so long, in fact, for decades. Somewhere in my mind, this surgery actually felt destined. I surmised that if there was something to learn, I had to learn it, even if it wasn't going to be easy.

Surgery was scheduled for 8 AM, and the drive from home to the Surgical Center in Madison took 90 minutes. Don waited in the reception area as I was escorted to a room where I would be prepped for surgery. The procedure required an overnight stay.

Dr. K talked to me right before surgery. I'm sure he was surprised when suddenly I blurted out, "I don't want to die!" He looked directly into my eyes and said, "Kellee, you're not going to die." He was incredibly calm and reassuring. From our first visit, I knew that he was compassionate and empathetic, and I felt like I knew him from another lifetime. His confidence gave me a sense of relief. The next thing I knew, a nurse rolled me into the operating room. I had a date with Destiny, and it was about to unfold.

Three hours later, Dr. K greeted Don in the waiting room and informed him that the surgery went very well. "She'll be in recovery for a few hours. After that, they will move her to a room for the night." Don came to see me, and although I was a bit groggy, I was not in pain. I was certainly glad it was over. The nurses were really wonderful and took great care of me. Don stayed with me until all my vital signs were stable. By nightfall, he kissed me goodbye and returned to the farm.

A Night Visitor

Several hours after Don left, I was alone in my room, falling in and out of sleep. At midnight, I woke up with a start. I sensed a visitor in the room, and it wasn't a nurse.

I opened my eyes and saw a young boy, about 12 years old, floating above my bed. He had long blonde curly hair and big blue eyes. He was staring at me, and I stared back. "What's your name? I asked.

"Matthew," he replied.

"How did you pass?"

"From Covid. This was my room."

At that very moment, the head nurse walked in and turned on the overhead light. The bright light startled me more than I saw this young boy. She brought me orange-flavored Jell-O and my favorite beverage, ginger ale.

I had to ask, "Was this Surgery Center used during Covid?"

"Yes. It was the children's ward."

I froze. I told her, "I just saw a little boy named Matthew right before you came into the room."

She looked at me and said in a matter-of-fact way, "Yes, many people have seen Matthew. He was my patient in this very room."

323

She described him. "Long blonde curly hair and blue eyes. A really sweet boy." She started to get misty-eyed thinking about the little boy.

The next day, before Don and I left for home, I met with Dr. K. again. He explained, "There may be side effects that could arise after surgery, like fever, infection, swelling, and discharge from the wound. "If you have anything that looks out of the ordinary, call me immediately." Then he asked, "How was last night? Did you get any sleep?"

I told him what I saw. He said, "What do you mean there was a 12-year-old boy in your room at midnight?"

I had to explain about myself and my ability to see spirits. Dr. K took it pretty well, although he seemed very skeptical. I think he chalked up my imaginary friend to all the drugs in my system. Little did he know he would have more interesting conversations with me at a later date.

Unusual and Unexpected

I was so happy the surgery was over, and I was back home. I looked forward to feeling stronger every day. My closest friends, James, Shirley, Charlene, Laury, and Mary Ann, all called. Even my stepparents and siblings called to see how I was. Everyone was relieved that I was back home and in recovery.

Unfortunately, my dear friend and mentor, the brilliant Mavis Pittilla, passed away three days after I returned home. Mavis was born in the United Kingdom and dedicated herself to Spirit and spiritualism. She traveled the world over as a pioneer in physical mediumship, lecturer, and healer. She was a master teacher to other mediums, including myself. Although all her friends knew she had been sick with cancer for a while, like many of her students, I was thrown for a loop and deeply saddened by Mavis' passing.

As I stayed in bed to recuperate from surgery, I felt a kind of exhaustion I had never felt before. I couldn't tell whether it was my sadness and grief about Mavis or if something was wrong with my body. As crazy as it may sound, I didn't really understand Dr. K when he described "things to look for" and couldn't tell the difference between "normal" and "unusual or unexpected" side effects. Even though I wasn't getting any better, I was so out of touch with my own body that I waited ten days until I was scheduled to see Dr. K. for a follow-up appointment.

Unfortunately, that was my first mistake. I should have seen him the moment I began to feel bad. The second mistake was seeing Dr. K's PA (Physician's Assistant). I know there are many bright and capable PAs, but that was not the case with this particular person. She looked at my wounds, said something about blood not connecting in the veins, and that I should come back in a week. She should have alerted Dr. K immediately about what she saw.

Back at home, whatever was going on got worse, and I knew something was terribly wrong. Two days later, Dr. K called, "Kellee, come to the office right away." When I arrived, he took one look at my wounds and said, "You're going to need another surgery. There's dead tissue by the wound, and I have to remove it." He explained further, "This is an unusual complication. The veins didn't connect where they were supposed to connect, and

325

your tissue wasn't getting blood, causing it to die off." If I had waited another week, who knows how bad it would have gotten—possibly turning to gangrene. All I could think of was, *Oh, God... another surgery.* I prayed to Archangel Michael for help. *Please don't let me die.*

Don and I started for the hospital at dawn on August 30 for the second surgery. A backup of eighteen-wheelers in front of us made it difficult to see the road ahead. As Don changed lanes, a squirrel ran across the road, and our car hit it. I could tell it was dead under the tire. I felt so distressed about killing the squirrel, and immediately, my mind went to the dark side. *Could this be one of those animal omens? What was the message of a dead squirrel? Will I survive this surgery?*

Instead of the outpatient Surgical Center where my first surgery occurred, this surgery took place in the hospital. When I was being prepared for surgery, Dr. K came into my room, and again, the words just flew out of my mouth. "I don't want to die!"

Dr. K assured me, "Kellee, you're not going to die. You'll be fine. You'll be home soon. Sometimes, this can happen to a patient. Don't worry. I'll take care of it."

After the second surgery, Dr. K met with Don. "The surgery went well. I removed all the dead tissue, but I want to keep an eye on her." This time, I stayed in the hospital for two days. After that, Dr. K felt I was doing well enough to send me home to rest. Again, he said, "If there is anything, and I mean anything, that doesn't seem normal, you need to contact me right away." He gave me his private cell number. "Call me any time, day or night."

This Time I Listened

I was pretty exhausted and scared after the second surgery. Even though Dr. K was confident, there was this lingering feeling that my problems weren't over. Besides, I felt emotionally drained, having to start the healing process all over again. Sleeping on my back was extremely uncomfortable. Luckily, I didn't have any physical pain, so I didn't need pain medication, only Tylenol or Advil. Mostly, I needed sleep.

My poor assistant, Kareesa, was overwhelmed. Originally, I thought I would be out of commission for three weeks, but this was turning into a much bigger ordeal than I expected. Kareesa was incredibly busy rescheduling all my clients and fielding calls from family and friends. I had scheduled a three-part class on *Atlantis and Lemuria* on *YouTube TV, but* that also had to be canceled. I know a lot of people were disappointed.

The next few days, I slept or rested in a recliner. I didn't have the energy to do anything else. A few days went by, and I began to notice that my breasts felt really sore. Again, I didn't put two and two together and just thought it had to do with my two surgeries. But my left breast was hot to the touch, and worse, the wounds underneath the breasts didn't look good.

A whole week went by, and I was still feeling sick and exhausted. It was September 8th, Don's birthday, and I had planned to do something special for him since he had been so supportive and wonderful to me. He never complained and tirelessly took care of me with such love and devotion. Despite not feeling well, I had enough energy to get off the recliner and make him dinner. He really didn't want me to cook, but I wanted to take care of him. I was the responsible partner—even if I was in the worst shape of my life. I managed to make him one of his all-time favorites—chicken parmesan.

After dinner, I nearly collapsed. Don got me into bed, and the next morning called Dr. K. That afternoon, we were in Dr. K.'s office once again. My anxiousness was at an all-time high because I knew something was really wrong. He took one look at me and said, "Kellee, you have a decision to make. You have a pretty bad infection. I can send you home with antibiotics and see if you're feeling better in a few days, or I can admit you into the hospital right now and put you on an IV drip of antibiotics."

"What would you say if I was your wife or daughter?" The look in his eyes gave me my answer, and I agreed to go back to the hospital. This time, I knew it was the right thing to do. I know it sounds far-fetched, but to me, Spirit gave me an outright warning—the dead squirrel—and this time, I paid attention. I heeded Spirit's intervention to put myself first and to take care of myself.

Two hours later, Dr. K met me in the hospital room where I had just had a PICC line inserted into my left arm. It would remain there for several days, so I needed to get comfortable with it. Dr K. said, "Let's see if there's any change in the infection in the next 24 hours. Otherwise, it's back to surgery to clean out the infection in both breasts."

When he said surgery, I emotionally checked out. This whole process was becoming unbearable. Two surgeries were difficult to wrap my head around. But a third surgery? Needless to say, it was a rough night in the hospital with another surgery hanging over my head. I was on the verge of another panic attack. To say I was worried is an understatement. I prayed to the Spirit to take care of me because it was obvious that I wasn't doing a very good job on my own.

Speaking My Truth

On Saturday, September 10th, Dr. K walked into my room with the results of the blood tests. He explained, "You have a serious bacterial infection, and I need to operate." My heart sank, and I could feel a lump in my throat. I held back tears. Clearly, I had no choice. I had to have another surgery, which was scheduled for early the next morning, Sunday, September 11. Historically, it was not a good day, and I felt like I was staring down the barrel of a gun. *I hoped the date was not another omen!*

I tried to spiritually and karmically make sense of this entire experience. *What was this really about?* Being a Virgo, everything seemed chaotic, and I needed some order. My mind was working overtime trying to figure out what the heck was happening. I needed guidance to see the bigger picture.

One of my favorite quotes by Eckhart Tolle came to mind: "Life will give you whatever experience is most helpful for the evolution of your consciousness. How do you know this is the experience you need? Because this is the experience you are having at this moment." I felt this was exactly the predicament I was in, and I had to speak up. It was time that Dr. K and I had a meaningful and deeply spiritual conversation.

When Dr. K came back into my room that morning, I told him how I believed all the surgery problems had to do with balancing karma. I explained what I meant by karma and how I felt my spirit guides were directing the whole surgery situation. I also told him that he and I had made a karmic contract together on the other side before we came into this incarnation—he as the doctor and me as the patient. I told him that I believed we knew each other from other lifetimes.

Dr. K was a wonderful listener, and to my surprise, he was fascinated by what I had to say. I'm quite sure his patients didn't discuss karma or Spirit guides before surgery. He asked questions like, "What do you mean by being spiritual? Who's on the other side? What is a sacred contract?"

We talked for about an hour, which helped to reassure me that I would pull through. On the practical side, I was concerned. "Do you think my body can handle a third surgery?" Dr. K was confident. "Your heart and lungs are clear and strong." And for the third time, I asked. "Am I going to die?" And for the third time, he emphatically said, "No, you're not going to die!" "I promise you, Kellee, you will get through this and will heal really well." He smiled. "I'll see you bright and early tomorrow morning."

Don arrived with a wonderful lunch and remained with me until about 9 PM. I felt so much love for Don. He was a trooper, driving 90 minutes each way every day back and forth to the hospital. He would be back in the hospital by 7:30 the next morning. Let me just say—everyone needs someone like Don. His support and love got me through this nightmare. He is the greatest.

Surrounded by Love

An hour after Don left, for the first time since this entire process began three weeks before, I began to feel scared that I might not make it. Facing a third surgery was discouraging, to say the least. I truly wanted to live. I couldn't help but think how furious I would be if I died before finishing my work on this planet and I had to repeat a lot of things over again. No way!

It was 11 PM, and the lights were still on. I couldn't sleep, feeling too afraid and too sad. I had to calm down if I wanted the spirit world to get through with a message. My fear and anxiety were only blocking Spirit's presence. So, in a meditative state, I began to pray to my spirit guides, Archangel Michael, God, and Mom. "I need your help. I'm afraid and overwhelmed. Please be with me." Then I began to cry.

There was only one door to my room to the left of my bed. On the right was a recliner and a large window. Suddenly, I heard footsteps walking towards me from the right side of my bed.

I turned to look. *What's happening?* Then I knew.

I called out, "Mom!" In an instant, I could feel my mother's loving arms embrace me. I had no doubt she wanted me to know that she was with me. Because I was so incredibly comforted by her love, I quickly fell asleep and slept through the night.

A nurse entered my room precisely at 5:30 AM and turned on the bright overhead light. She began to check my vitals. At about 6:30 AM, Dr. K arrived to check on me. As Dr. K stood in front of my bed explaining the procedure, I saw a bright green aura splash across his body, emanating about a foot around him. It was a sign from my guides. They wanted me to see that Dr. K was a healer

331

and that I would be fine. The color was a bright "kelly" green. How could I mistake their meaning? My spirit guides have a shrewd sense of humor.

Team Spirit

By now, I knew the drill. After surgery, I would be rolled into my room, and Dr. K would visit with the results. However, this time, it was not Dr. K who came to see me. It was a different, very tall doctor.

When he entered the room, I asked, "Who are you?"

"I'm Dr. M, an infectious disease specialist."

My mind went blank when he said his name because all I heard was "infectious disease."

I panicked. "Do I have Covid?"

Dr. M answered. "No. You don't have Covid, but you do have a serious bacterial infection."

"Am I going to die?"

He said in a matter-of-fact tone, "No. But you will be on an IV drip of antibiotics around the clock until we discover the bacteria you have. Once we know what kind of bacteria, we'll switch your drip to the right antibiotics for the bacteria."

"Is it Staph? Is it Sepsis?" I was panicking.

"We don't know at this time. Once it's analyzed, we'll know. It'll take 48 hours.

"Oh God." I felt like I was going to be sick.

As Dr. M left, he said, "I'll see you in two days with the results from the lab.

This was incredibly scary news, to say the least, and I felt myself leaving my body in fear again.

An hour later, Don entered my room with dinner, and I wanted to jump out of bed and hug him. His presence was exactly what I needed to feel safe. After I told him the latest news, he was stunned but remained calm and positive. "Kellee, the antibiotics will clear up the bacterial infection. You'll be okay." He also brought me lots of good probiotics and healthy, nutritious food to counterbalance all the antibiotics and strengthen my immune system.

Exactly two days later, Dr. M returned with the results from the lab.

I looked at him and asked, "What do I have?"

Dr. M said, "There are three strains of bacteria."

I thought to myself. *Is this a joke? For sure, I'm a goner.*

In pure panic mode, I asked, "Doctor, does this mean I'm going to die?"

"No. It just means that the new antibiotics will knock out all three strains. These drugs are very effective in treating the bacteria."

After Dr. M left, a nurse hooked up the IV bag with the new drugs. Don wasn't able to visit, and because I was alone, I felt very vulnerable. *What is Spirit trying to tell me? What did I do to myself to have so many types of bacteria?*

As I felt more and more desperate, a gloom fell over me. My emotions were all over the place, and I was losing hope. Again, I needed to get calm, but it was hard work. At that moment, I looked at my door and saw a nun standing in the doorway.

I was in a Catholic Hospital, and the first thing that came to my Jewish/Southern Baptist mind was the thought, *They're sending in a nun. Next, it'll be a priest. For sure, I'm going to die.*

I said to the woman, "Are you a nun?"

"Yes, I'm Sister Pam. I heard you've been here a few days and wanted to check in to see how you're doing."

I just started to sob. All the fear and emotions that I had bottled up had exploded inside, and I couldn't control myself.

Sister Pam said, "It's all right dear—tears are the soul expressing itself without words."

Her comment was so profound and consoling—it was what my soul needed to hear. Immediately, I thought, *My spirit guides sent Sister Pam.*

After a 30-minute intimate conversation together, Sister Pam left. By then, I was in a deeply quiet place. The second she walked out the door, my phone rang. It was James. Talk about timing!

He didn't say "Hello," he just bellowed. "Kellee, listen to me. You're not going to die. Well, we'll all die at some point, but you're not going to die NOW!"

And his words pulled me out of the depths of agony, and my mind filled with light. The end of this whole ordeal was within reach. Thank you, James.

I stayed in the hospital for a total of ten days. When I finally turned a corner and my bacterial infections were under control, I was sent home with powerful oral antibiotics.

Setting My Intention

It took about three months to fully recover. The next time I saw Dr. K to check that my wounds were healing, we had another spiritual conversation. I explained that after everything that I had experienced, I knew I had to change my current situation.

He asked, "What would that look like?"

"In the three months off, I spent time in nature, writing, resting, restoring, and renewing myself. I want my life to continue. I'm going to do what my soul had planned long ago before my ego-driven responsibility theme got so out of control. I'm going to cut way back on my practice and work three days a week, and for the rest of my time, I'll do the things I enjoy—resting, writing, walking in nature, cooking, and spending time with Don and our dogs.

This entire experience made me see I was way off course. I was spread too thin, trying to be the responsible person for everyone. That couldn't be my destiny. Taking care of others at the expense of my own physical and emotional health prevented me from teaching, writing, and reaching a larger audience. My weekly shows do that, and I want to continue them, but the individual sessions eventually would have to come to an end.

And it wasn't death that I was afraid of. I know that when I pass, I will be on the other side with my loved ones. As Dr. Raymond Moody says in his book, *The Light Beyond,* "Dealing with NDEs has changed the way I feel about *life after death*. In fact, I never use that phrase anymore. Instead, I think there is only life. When the physical body no longer functions, the spirit leaves and goes on living."

My fear of dying was about not completing the work I came here to do. I made a contract with Spirit to help uplift the planet, and that's my main responsibility. I am very excited that I will complete my spiritual mission. Our producer and sage, Rene

Ringnalda, once said, "One must set their intentions." I set my intentions, and I'm not going back to the way things were.

When I lay in the hospital, all I could think of was my trip to India in 1979 and the psychic who read my thumb, telling me that I had a choice this lifetime. I could use my psychic power to heal, or I could work myself to death as I had done in a previous life. Over the years, that memory would pop into my mind, but mostly, I ignored its meaning. But as I grew older and worked around the clock, pushing myself to the limit, I started to pay attention. There's only so much time we have on Earth, and I knew I had a choice. Even though it took many years, three surgeries, and three serious infections, I finally got the message.

Wake up, Kellee! Take care of yourself. Love yourself enough so that you can take care of others. Anyone with *responsibility* as a life theme *must set boundaries.* As we're instructed when flying in a plane, put on your own oxygen mask first before you assist another with theirs.

Life is about risks. I had no idea that complications would occur after surgery. During a fifteen-year period, my breast reduction surgery was canceled three times. *Was Spirit telling me not to have surgery, and I wasn't listening?* I've thought about this many times. I came to the conclusion that it was canceled all those times because I wasn't emotionally ready to handle the experience.

If I had the surgery when I was younger and a different person, not yet spiritually equipped to deal with the complications, the outcome might have been tragic. Because I had inwardly grown and acquired divine wisdom, I was able to handle this extremely karmic set of circumstances. I still believe it was a good decision to have breast-reduction surgery because I was led to a greater spiritual awareness.

After all these years, I finally realized the person I was meant to be, thanks to the help of so many guides, those still living, and all those in Spirit.

EPILOGUE

Know thyself.

      -   The Temple of Apollo at Delphi

This, above all, is to thine oneself to be true.

      -   William Shakespeare, *Hamlet*

Some of your greatest advances you have judged as failures, and some of your deepest retreats you have evaluated as successes.

      -   A Course In Miracles

I wrote this book to encourage people in all stages of their lives, no matter the depth of despair, to persevere and move forward. I want to inspire all souls who feel stuck and need hope that if I can do it, you can do it. You can move through anything. You can make a change. And if you can't do it alone, find some help. Remember, spirit helpers are always nearby. Call on them.

I call our experiences on Earth "soul adventures," but most of the time, they feel like "soul misadventures." Every person will experience his or her soul in a different way and will have the opportunity or several opportunities (if we miss an opportunity) to experience life's big lessons: betrayal, disappointment, sadness, loneliness, self-sabotage, abandonment, loss, trauma, and grief. We can also experience great love, joy, hope, patience, compassion, and a deep spiritual awakening. As souls, we choose the gamut that life has to offer.

Ever since I can remember, I felt a panic in my heart. I think about that now and know that it stems from growing up with an addicted father and watching my mother throw herself into her work so she didn't have to deal with her emotional fears about my dad. Addiction is a destructive force, and anyone with an addiction in the house can tell you that family life is a house of turmoil. My dad was a great inspiration to me but also a disaster when high. It's apparent to me now that I was always looking for Dad in my relationships with men. Unfortunately, I found him too many times in abusive, alcoholic partners. I certainly had a lot of karma to clear up from the past.

Following in Mom's footsteps, I spent a lot of time trying to shut down my feelings, but as an empath, it was hard. I was completely sensitive to everyone's emotions and felt totally responsible for everyone's well-being. When I began seeing spirits, I didn't know what to think and how to feel. Most of the time, I was confused. When I lost all the things I thought were important, I felt like a failure. But my failures were actually wake-up calls from Spirit to go in another direction. What I thought were successes were actually keeping me from my soul's responsibility as a therapist, spiritual medium, and healer.

As a caregiver my entire life, I have always been on high alert and seemed to run from crisis to crisis like other caregivers—

firemen, doctors, nurses, EMTs, and psychotherapists. Unfortunately, the one thing we have in common is that we don't take enough care of our own needs. Many of us find it difficult to set boundaries; I certainly had my share of not setting boundaries. In all honesty, I would have been furious at myself if I had given everything to everyone and had nothing left for me. Everyone needs to have boundaries.

My "awakening" process took me away from what I thought I was supposed to be doing and brought me to where I was supposed to be. There are no straight roads. Roads jig and jag— some are off the beaten path, some are side streets that lead to dead ends, while others are lanes that lead to boulevards. I also believe that each one of us has a *knowing* or a higher sense that directs us on a certain path. Sometimes, it might feel like fate, but it's more like synchronicity. It's as if we're at a fork in the road, and we have two choices. Either one will get us to our destiny or purpose; however, one may take longer than the other. Ultimately, all roads get us to where we're supposed to be, but, and I can't stress this enough, WE HAVE TO PAY ATTENTION.

Spirit is constantly trying to get our attention. It sends us signs—*pay attention!* I often think of these signs as breadcrumbs. Like the fairytale of Hansel and Gretel, where Hansel drops breadcrumbs to find the way home, Spirit wants us to find our way home by dropping what I call "spiritual breadcrumbs." Wonderful spiritual medium Mavis Pittilla called them "Droplets of God."

There is a silver thread that connects us with the infinite, and when we enter life on the physical plane, it is most certainly forgotten. Many of us have had variations of the "dark night of the soul." It's a crash-and-burn moment and often the catalyst for change. Relationships end. We are betrayed. Plans fall through. The doors won't open. Conflict occurs. People get sick. There is a great loss. I know from experience that the challenges we face turn out to be our greatest gifts. They are our opportunities to grow and share similar experiences with other souls.

From a spiritual standpoint, we are here to learn from every experience, which is neither positive nor negative. Each experience is for our soul's growth. But we must reach our soul, and that is a deep spiritual and psychological inner process that takes time, plus a strong desire to wake up. I find, more often than not, that life is about recovery from difficult and demanding situations, all of which make us stronger.

The other thing I discovered is that we incarnate with a primary theme. Mine was responsibility. Other themes include leadership, peacemaker, humanitarian, innovator, rescuer, teacher, healer, etc. Your primary theme starts in childhood. It's like a thread that weaves in and out of your life experiences. It's a very consistent theme, and you will come to know it by the situations you find yourself in that repeat over and over again.

Then, there is a secondary theme. This is usually the biggest obstacle you will have to overcome on your journey. Addiction, fear, victimhood, negativity, anger, hurt, jealousy, and betrayal are some major obstacles. And no matter how highly advanced we may think we are, we are always in a constant state of spiritual growth, learning from our primary and secondary themes.

When I have a session with a client, I quickly access the soul to see if the person has taken on a complex and intense incarnation. I call this "being born in the middle of the ocean." The life path the soul has chosen often includes early childhood trauma that leads a person on many paths in search of healing (like me). Ultimately, the soul learns to accept what it has endured with compassion, empathy, and love. The trauma and pain of life lessons do not define who you are. How you live in spite of such suffering is important. That's what defines you.

Relationships are our best teachers, and the more difficult ones are our greatest. Most people want to shy away from bad relationships, but I ask you to look at them as the ones that will help you to grow. I've had my share of very harmful and hurtful relationships, and out of them came a fresh new beginning that was necessary for my advancement. At the same time, I've been really fortunate on this journey to have such wise counsel and dear friends in my soul group. I count my mom, Don, and James as those who have helped me survive the unbearable. I couldn't have done it without their love, support, and guidance.

If you want to awaken to your soul's calling, you must have faith in your soul, along with a strong dose of courage. "Faith is the substance of things hoped for, the evidence of things not seen." (Hebrews 11:1). Spirit is constantly testing us. The world is always in conflict. How do you perceive what's going on in the world and your life? Are you expecting the worst to come, or do you have faith in a change for the better?

Having faith is the recognition or belief that there is something greater than the self, something more to being human than sensory experiences. The greater whole of which we are all a part of is cosmic and divine in nature. With faith comes trust. Trust is letting go of control and letting Spirit lead the way.

Spirit will always connect, but we have to quiet our thoughts through meditation and prayer if we want to hear that still small voice within. Only the ego is loud and demanding. As White Eagle says, "The secret of strength lies in the quiet mind." Because I was shown so many mystical and supernatural experiences, I knew Spirit was pointing the way—*here is your true mission*. Never underestimate Spirit's still small voice inside you.

And for goodness sake, keep it light. There's a lot in this world to smile about. Laughter lifts everyone. That's the one thing I love about working with James. He's always cheering me up with his beautiful smile and sense of humor. The two of us are continually having fun and laughing.

Finally, believe in yourself. Do your best to be kind to others. Have compassion and empathy. Love yourself and love one another. You are safe. No one is ever lost. Your soul will grow immeasurably, which is why you took this trip in the first place. Wisdom is everything. Change is God's greatest gift. Don't give up. Listen! Your soul is calling. You can't escape your destiny. You come from the Spirit, and you will return home to the Spirit in Heaven, your eternal home.

ACKNOWLEDGEMENTS

Life is full of wonder, surprises, and complications. I have certainly had my share of challenges that have deeply tested my faith. I want to thank all of the people in my life who stood by me and supported me with compassion, empathy, and kindness.

My mother, Dr. LaWanda Katzman-Staenberg. My husband, Don Markese, my best friends, James Van Praagh, Dr. Shirley Impellizzeri, Charlene Testa, LN, Sandy Guerra, and my beloved daughter, Dr. Holiday Bean. My siblings, Carol, Danny, and Theo Katzman, have taught me more than I could have ever imagined. My father, Lee Katzman, was the most creative person I had ever known, and my stepfather, Marc Staenberg, encouraged me all the way. My stepmother, Judy Tipton Katzman, and your love for family is so deep. My son-in-law, Dr. Anthony Bean, is an inspiration to me. Peggy Miller, forever grateful you saved me during the pandemic. Rosann Markese, the kindest person I know, MAC, you kept your promise to my mom to watch over me and continue to be my soft pillow. BP, your help changed my life, Kareesa Wilson. Seriously, I could not have done any of this without you. Maryann Bishop, you were there from the beginning and always filled me with love. Stacy Phillips, you always believed in me. Rene Ringnalda, our producer, thank you for your wisdom and kindness. Finally, my two grandchildren, August and Lulu, what gifts you are to me. Gigi loves and adores you. I could not have made this journey without all of you and your love, patience, guidance, and encouragement. Truly, from the bottom of my heart, thank you.

To all of my therapy and mediumship clients, I am eternally grateful for allowing me into your heart and soul. I've learned so much from every single one of you. It's because of all of you that I am able to accomplish my life's purpose.

A special salute of gratitude and thanks goes to my two special spirit guides. Wow, thank you for taking this journey with me. I know at times, you must have been shaking your heads. I can't imagine how tough it was to see me in some of these predicaments. What a karmic agreement we must have! Lastly, I would like to thank Linda Carwin Tomchin, who took the various threads of my life and weaved them into this incredible tapestry that I am about to share with you.

Finally, please note that some names in the book have been changed to protect privacy.

AFTERWORD

To me, being spiritual means to be more compassionate, caring, and kind. It means reaching out to people with a loving heart without expecting anything in return.

-   Brian L. Weiss, M.D., *Same Soul, Many Bodies*

A question I am often asked: Which do I prefer—mediumship or psychotherapy? The truth is I use both lenses at the same time. Depending on the session, more emphasis may be placed on mediumship and my ability to deliver messages from a loved one. Or the opposite, more emphasis may be on psychotherapy and my listening to what the client is going through and knowing that there is a direction I can steer the person towards. In every session, believe me, I am using both skill sets. Along my life path, I also learned Vedic astrology, numerology, and Destiny Cards, all of which I use when necessary. I love my work and use whatever is possible to assist my clients in realizing they are souls navigating through human experiences.

Psychotherapy is talk therapy in a supportive environment where the client and therapist collaborate openly and without judgment on emotional and psychological issues. Many of the issues revolve around self-worth, self-acceptance, self-love, and forgiveness. Through psychotherapy, we can learn to address our problems, find solutions, face our challenges, and change our perceptions and attitudes. Each of us has free will, so we can choose to learn and move on or stay stuck in despair, anxiety, depression, anger, and pain.

Mediumship, on the other hand, deals with transcendent issues based on a soul's covenant with the Spirit. Each one of us has a soul contract. The contract is made with a specific intention for the particular incarnation. The people in our lives are part of the soul contract and are an important and unavoidable part of our growth. There are no accidents. Everything in our lives is a planned event. As a spiritual medium, my soul contract is to raise my consciousness in order to reach as many souls as I can.

What is a Medium?

Simply put, a medium is someone who is able to communicate with souls on the other side. There is no such thing as death. There is only a transition from the physical being to the spiritual being. While on Earth, our soul is having a physical experience or a physical expression of the soul. The soul never dies. In fact, it thrives on the other side.

Once the physical being has completed his or her mission, the soul makes its transition and returns to its true home. A medium is sensitive and intuitive enough to see, hear, and feel information from souls on the other side.

I'm often asked, "Are people born mediums, or do they learn to become a medium?"

In my experience, there are several ways a person becomes a medium. I have experienced three specific ways. First, I inherited the gift of mediumship from my grandfather. Often, mediumship is shared within a soul group. Second, I had blunt force trauma to the head, which altered the pineal gland in my brain (the psychic third eye). Awakening the pineal gland gives a person insight beyond the physical world. The third way was through spontaneous clairvoyance, in which I saw relatives, angels, and Spirit guides reach out to me from the astral dimensions. And I can add a fourth way. I studied and practiced with other mediums in a development circle to improve and refine my abilities.

How Do Mediums Interact with the Dead?

Think of a medium as a radio frequency. The medium is able to "tune in" to a certain station. After years of deep meditation and sitting in spiritual developmental circles, mediums learn how to raise their vibration or frequency while a spirit on the other side lowers its vibration. A "meeting place" is created where a medium and a spirit are able to connect.

To do this, mediums have to clear their minds, usually through meditation and contemplation, so that a soul is able to project images or words into their thoughts. Mediums interpret these words and images when they read with loved ones. That is why it's important to choose a medium that is spiritually evolved enough to interpret the messages without their ego presuming information or judging what is being said.

Souls, on the other hand, usually seek a particular medium

with which they can communicate. Often, this occurs a few days or weeks before a session begins. Sometimes, a spirit may actually attend a medium's demonstration to study how the medium connects with the spirit world. They learn a medium's specialties, sensitivities, and even their sense of humor. They can spend time around a medium to learn how to work with a medium.

Some mediums specialize in different areas. There are mediums that specialize in criminal investigations, missing persons, and past life situations, and there are even artists who can draw loved ones.

I am a spiritual medium. I discuss the life of the soul who has passed using a spiritual perspective. I come from a loving, non-judgmental understanding of how brave souls are to incarnate. I am life-affirming and positive. Because I am also a psychotherapist, I often attract souls who have suffered from mental illness and some sort of mental or emotional breakdown. These can include anxiety, depression, bipolar disorder, schizophrenia, or personality disorders. I am able to psychologically and spiritually help a family understand their loved ones' emotional states before they pass.

Another question I am asked is: *What happens to a person who commits suicide?* This passing is often difficult for the living to understand. These particular souls almost always want me to explain that they are not in hell or purgatory. They are not being "punished" for taking their lives. The idea of punishment stems from religious beliefs, and while I don't in any way try to diminish such beliefs, I know from my contact with the Spirit that there is no fiery hell. The only hell I found was in the negative thoughts of my clients. As I have said in the book, a soul will have a life review and will feel any pain their passing may have caused their loved ones.

A soul may choose suicide as part of its soul contract. Another view may be to make loved ones aware that souls never die. Sometimes, certain souls commit to accomplishing too much in one lifetime, so they may add an exit clause in their soul contracts to leave early and end their unbearable pain and suffering. There is never any blame for a person's suicide because, as I said, we choose our "death" just as we choose our "life" on the physical plane.

Is there a Difference Between Psychics, Clairvoyants, and Mediums?

All mediums are psychic, but not all psychics are mediums. Because mediums are able to raise their vibration to a high-frequency level, they can connect to the other side. Psychics, on the other hand, have the ability to interpret the past and present and even foresee the future but cannot receive messages from spirits. A medium is able to do everything a psychic does and communicate with souls that have passed.

Mediums communicate in different ways—visually, audibly, physically, and through feeling. Usually, one or more of these abilities are stronger than the others, and a medium uses the strongest ability to receive messages.

Clairvoyance is clearly seen. Does a medium see with physical eyes? On occasion, I can see through my eyes, but most often, mediums see through the third eye, the spiritual eye, or the

6th chakra located between the eyebrows. Pictures and images from spirits are projected into the spiritual eye of the medium. These images may include memories, objects, dates, names, etc., only a loved one knows.

Clairaudience is clear hearing. Mediums can hear the soul's message. This can include names, sounds, familiar expressions, and even songs. This happens to be my strongest trait.

Clairsentience is a clear feeling. Some mediums get "the chills" when the soul is near. They sense the soul's communication through the feelings in their body. The medium can sense the way a person died and the emotional state of the soul when it passed.

Physical mediums are rare. These mediums can draw ethereal energy or ectoplasm from the higher dimensions and manipulate it into physical forms like a soul's body, face, or even an actual voice.

Other mediums use automatic writing or drawing to communicate a message. Still, others go into a trance and use a "control," a soul on the other side that communicates with other souls to present their messages.

All mediums are in different states of knowledge and depth. Some mediums are beginning their particular spiritual journey, while others have been developing their mediumship for lifetimes. I'm in the latter category.

What Should I Expect When Sitting with a Medium?

The client or "sitter" should expect an empathetic, balanced, psychologically- sound medium. The medium needs to understand grief and loss. The medium should give good evidence of the loved one on the other side. Often, this includes names, dates, physical traits, personalities, occupations, and information about a soul that only a client would know.

Often, the loved one only wants the client/sitter to know they are very much alive and flourishing and no longer in pain. Sometimes, the client/sitter feels like they didn't do enough for the loved one, and they have a lot of guilt. Souls forgive any transgressions a sitter is holding and, in turn, ask the sitter's forgiveness for the same. Mediums usually receive words of encouragement to pass on to the client. If a medium gives you a lot of negative information, I suggest you find another medium.

After the session, clients should feel relieved and relaxed and, most importantly, free from guilt. It's not uncommon for a client to cry and release pent-up emotions. Often, I hear, "I can breathe again." Or "The weight has been lifted." I had a situation recently where I was given a message by the soul that "it was okay" for the client to remarry. In fact, the soul wanted to help facilitate the new relationship.

Every reading, like every soul, is different. As a medium, I am filled with gratitude to bring loved ones together again. I wish you all much love on your journey.

RESOURCES

The Diagnostic and Statistical Manual of Mental Disorders, Fifth Edition, the American Psychiatric Association (APA)

Talking To Heaven, James Van Praagh, Signet, a division of Penguin Group, New York, NY

Growing Up In Heaven, James Van Praagh, Harper One, a division of HarperCollins, New York, NY

Wisdom From Your Spirit Guides, James Van Praagh, Hay House, Inc., Carlsbad, CA

Meditations with James Van Praagh, A Fireside Book, Simon & Schuster, New York, NY

Why Can't I Change: How to Conquer Your Self-Destructive Patterns, Shirley Impellizzeri, Ph.D., Sunrise River Press, North Branch, MN

The Quiet Mind, White Eagle, the White Eagle Publishing Trust, Liss, Hampshire, England

The Divine Romance, Paramahansa Yogananda, Self-Realization Fellowship, Los Angeles, CA

Journey of Souls, Michael Newton, Ph.D., Llewellyn Publications, Woodbury, MN

Life After Life, Raymond A. Moody, Jr. M.D., Harper One, a division of HarperCollins, New York, NY

The Dream Game, Ann Faraday, Harper & Row, New York, NY

Vedic Astrology—Easy and Simple by Anatoly Malakov, Amazon.com

Somatic Experience Therapy: www.traumahealing.org

Suicide and Crisis Lifeline: www.988lifeline.org

Alcoholics Anonymous: www.aa.org

QiGong: www.ancientwaveqigong.com